i could Always be a Waitress

B.J. RADCLIFFE

3

"These words should be printed in lipstick on every
mirror in every girls' restroom in every high school:
'you are one man away from becoming a bag lady'."
—*Ellen Goodman, Passages, 1963*

This is what my life looks like: my husband is driving
too fast. A policeman pulls our car over to a stop,
comes to the passenger side where I am sitting,
and says to me, "I'm giving you the ticket
because *you* let him drive too fast."
—*Joan Baldwin, housewife, 1966*

"Skeeters? Sure. We had black *clouds* of skeeters.
Huge as birds. And lightning bugs, until the spray trucks
came. Gators 15 feet long, cottonmouths—
and we swam where they swam
and we drank sulfur water ever' day.
Shoot—*this* ain't my daddy's Banana Bay, with all these cars
and tourists. I'd rather take the skeeters."
India Bayh, age 100, last surviving
member of original settlers' family,
Banana Bay 1977

I am 74. I am a grandmother. I am about to divorce my second husband.

I may have 20 more years to live and I refuse to live it by being someone's housekeeper. What I want is for another woman to come along, see my husband's M.D. letters and decide this spells out the Man of her Dreams. I will gladly hand her my vacuum cleaner.

I do not want her asking me about him beforehand. She would be chased off by my words.

Divorcing is a little like committing a crime—the first time it hurts like hell and the second time it's more or less routine.

Not for Quentin Forster II, M.D., of course. I find that after crying, nagging, lecturing, staying unemotional, sounding like one of the Valkyries, being counseled, sleeping alone, giving up negotiating sex, being sweet, being sour, coming closer, moving farther away, writing notes asking for a little fun time in between football games, trying to engage when the other party won't—after none of these have worked—it's time for a lawyer.

Also, as a lifelong Episcopalian I have had to work through the unfortunate idea that having accumulated two ex-husbands puts me soundly on the Slippery Slope To Hell.

Anyway, the statisticians who make up the actuarial tables assure me I may live until I am 83.9 years old: but I have never smoked and I can't even have one drink without my face flushing, and I consider myself a good driver, so unless some speeding attention-deficit teenager on soft drinks with a cell phone stuck to his/her ear hits me in the middle of U.S. #1, I figure I am good for another 20 years.

What brought this all on is that I found my journals from the '70's. I did not recognize the woman who wrote, "Take kids to pediatrician," "Eggs, cheese, milk," and " movie with Robert ". However, those coded words brought back blasts of memories and I wondered if I had ever known the non-assertive woman who wrote them.

Also, I may have just committed a murder involving one of my key lime pies and I am sitting here shivering in shock and writing fast, trying to get this all into my computer (yes, yes, even my pie recipe) while waiting for the police to find my bloody red and lime-green footprints, realize they are singularly mine out of a population of 80,000 or so and show up at the door of my rented 55+ house in Oak Glen to arrest me, thus giving my retired neighbors plenty to talk about as they stand clustered in the middle of the street, staring at the cop car in a good-natured way ("Excitement! We have excitement!").

I'll tell you one thing: I am not ever making this particular pie again.

Joan Gibson Baldwin Forster, I hardly knew ye.

COUNTRY SINGER CONFESSES SHE HAS FALL-BACK PLANS

..."before she became big, she says
matter-of-factly, she worked as a waitress
and a barmaid and in a shoe factory.
'I keep my beauty licenses
up to date in Florida.
I don't think I'll ever have to use them.
But if the need ever arises,
I know I can go to the beauty shop.' "

from a phone interview with Tammy Winkle,
as quoted to Max Kelly, reporter for
the Banana Bay (Florida) Tribune, January 17, 1977

Joan Baldwin (Mrs. Robert Baldwin, noted in the Banana Bay Tribune, May 3, 1976, as chairman of St. Barnabus' annual rummage sale) pulled her husband Robert's shiny black 1963 MGB up to the Banana Bay Airport ticket booth. She cranked open the window and thrust her head out at the same moment the attendant's outstretched hand offering a ticket hit her neatly in the throat.

"Hey, I'm sorry, ma'am!"

"Uh--it's all right, really."

"Didya drop something?" He stared at the ground with her.

"No—I was just making sure I hadn't scraped the sidewalls against the concrete curb."

"Uh huh." A horn sounded behind her.

"And I *didn't,* either!" She managed a bright smile and took the ticket. The attendant was already looking toward the next car in line.

Leaving the window down, Joan circled the parking lot. Sweating, she waited until she was away from the toll booth operator's sight before she coughed several times to make sure her throat was all right. The hot August Florida sun soaked into the back of her blouse, so that when she leaned forward there was an unpleasant feeling of skin peeling away from the black leather upholstery.

She fought her panic. Now what had Robert said when he'd briefed her about parking in a safe place for his beloved car? Oh, why did her Ford have to be in the shop today, of all days!

Joan rubbed her wet palms on her pink polyester slacks, recently purchased from the "Wear It Again, Sam-antha" Consignment Shop and frowned, remembering Robert's instructions:

"Do NOT park near another car. Do NOT park near a car with teenagers. They don't care if they scrape expensive paint jobs. Do NOT park in an open area, either—you never know who will park next to you. And definitely *not* next to a Cadillac. Cadillacs are owned by old men with little old wives who can't see over the steering wheel and who can't pull the door open and then can't *hold* it open and who bang it into another car. And NOT by a car with trash on the floor—those people have kids and they let them get away with *murder.* My car is on its way to being vintage and I'd better see it looking good as new when I come home."

Joan found a parking space between a new Chrysler and a sporty small foreign car. Okay. That should be safe enough. Both black cars, so if they scraped Robert's paint it would be the same color.

She eased herself out of the MGB, took a gasping breath of air that tasted as though all the oxygen had been burned from it, and hoisted her tan vinyl purse over her shoulder. She checked a second and then a third time to make sure she had taken Robert's keys from the ignition—he had the only other set and he was now descending from Atlanta 25,000 feet up. She winced, picturing herself calling, "Throw me the keys, Robert! I locked yours inside!"

She checked a fourth time, sweating. She locked the door and tested it. Yes, locked.

All right. And here was the parking ticket, red, turning her wet hand a light shade of pink. And here were the keys in the other hand. No marks on the sidewalls. God's in His Heaven.

She snapped the keys and the ticket into an outside compartment of her purse and, walking obediently between a path of two painted yellow lines reading ALL CARS STOP FOR PEDESTRIANS, which she didn't believe for a minute, entered the Banana Bay terminal. She rubbed her dyed hand with a piece of tissue and carefully disposed of it in a container beside the door.

The cold air hit her like a boxer's punch to the stomach. She felt her intestines cramp. "Stop it," she told herself. "Calm down. This is no time for a rush trip to the ladies' room!"

She checked the ARRIVALS board and then sat where she could watch Gate 4. Banana Bay had an oversize terminal and airport for its population, due to its proximity to the Cape—hence the four gates.

She sank into one of the wet-looking plastic chairs attached to the others in her row. She looked up at the ceiling (acoustic tiles with lots of dizzying holes in them) and mentally reviewed her to-do list:

Babysitter Melissa from next door at home with Excelsior, who should nap until Joan is back with Robert;

Pete at the river fishing, staying near other fishermen for safety;

Melissa to PLEASE get Susan's number just in case daughter Susan (who had not phoned in two years) phones;

Roast thawing in the refrigerator—roast thawing—roast thawing—Joan could not remember if she had taken it out of the freezer. No! She hadn't! What would they eat tonight? Robert had been away for four days and would expect a home-cooked dinner—she and the boys had been happy with cereal, scrambled eggs and toast while he had been out of town;

There must be something else. Library books returned? Dry cleaning?

Remember to bring book to read while waiting at airport. She pictured the book at home by the front door. Oh, well.

Joan looked around the waiting room. The sounds grated against her eardrums-- voices of travelers, each louder than the next; metallic announcements about the next flights.

The carpeting was new, she noticed. The swirling pattern made her eyes water. Probably chosen by a group of drunken students from the community college. The inky chemical odor hung in the air. She sensed (rather than stared at --too dangerous for her stomach) that the bright orange plastic seat she had fallen into was clashing with her pink print blouse and pink slacks. She swallowed hard, thinking about the colors.

Trying *not* to think about the colors.

But across the aisle the electric blue plastic seats and the grapey purple seats were no better. There were absolutely *too* many colors here. Was the selection committee composed of manic employees from fast food restaurants?

Had she been moving her lips? Joan peeked around the waiting area. Nobody met her eye. All right, okay. Just relax. Think of something soothing. It's only colors. Think of a soothing color. Like the pink you're wearing. Quiet, calming pink. The pink of holding rooms in police stations for violent prisoners. The nice pink icing on a birthday cake. Calm your respiration. Breathe in and out. Think about how your heart is slowing down now, slower, slower. Calm and peaceful. Calm and peaceful.

But now a huge bottle, Pepto-Bismol pink, captured Joan's thoughts. She wiped her hands—damp again! --was this a sign of *menopause?*-- unsuccessfully against her purse and the plastic seat. Her glance rested on two welcome words: LADIES ROOM.

Joan stood up, squinting to shut out the nauseating decorating scheme. Was anybody watching her? Would she pass out right here beside this awful orange seat, so they would call an ambulance and she would view her name on the television set in her hospital room while Robert waved medical bills in her face, demanding, "Where are my car keys?", and the headline in the newspaper would read "LOCAL MENTAL HEALTH COUNSELOR GOES BANANAS IN BANANA BAY!"

Would they come to her office and tear up her diploma, declaring, "Joan Baldwin, you are a fraud!"

She forced herself, gripping her purse, to move toward sanctuary. People were waving, calling to each other, hugging each other, chasing after little children. She was only a face in a crowd, invisible, a soon-to-be middle-aged woman, pretty enough, with a forgettable face and body. People didn't stare at her, but at least they didn't shudder. So what they saw was a mid-height, mid-weight, mid-blonde with hair permed, every now and then when she couldn't stand it the way it was, (naturally straight and thin), at LoRayne's Beauty Parlour. Clothes brought home from the consignment store.

Robert hated that she went to "Wear It Again, Sam-antha". She kept an old Jordan Marsh shopping bag in her car so she could hide her second-hand bargains in it, in case Robert was in the house.

A four-year-old boy in a black felt beanie with Mickey Mouse ears suddenly blocked her path. He scowled, pointed a fake gun at her brown eyes and shouted, "Bang bang! You're dead!"

A tourist, pint size. Where was the kid's mother? If Joan had felt less panicky she would have cocked her finger at him and played along, the way she used to when Pete was young.

"I said bang bang! *Bang bang! You stink*!"

Joan stared. "Michael!" sang out a voice, and the boy, eyes narrowed, turned. "Are you being *nice*?"

Joan zigzagged past Michael, wishing she dared grab the ears and stamp on them, saying in a W.C. Fields voice, "Go away, kid, ya bodda me," and, legs rubbery, pushed open the heavy door to the ladies room. Inside was another door, at right angles, like an airlock. She pushed this one open, too. How did women in wheelchairs negotiate this impossible turn?

No coins needed for the stalls anymore, thanks to a lady state legislator who had argued it wasn't women's fault if they couldn't stand up in the open like men. That was a relief.

She smiled at her joke. Attagirl. If you can laugh you're not dying. She slid shut the bolt on the inside of the stall farthest from the entrance door and sat down heavily, letting her head fall forward between her knees. She listened. Good. Alone. She wiped the sweat from her forehead with a piece of toilet paper and put her other hand to her pounding heart.

Okay. Now concentrate on the breathing first. Say, "No one has ever died from a panic attack. You know this. You have studied this problem. It has a name. It is called agoraphobia. You know what causes it."

"--no, I don't" sobbed a smaller voice inside Joan's head. "--and I'm scared."

Don't be. There is nothing to be scared about. You merely have too many stimuli rushing about and overloading your brain. It does not matter that you are 40 years old. There's always the chance that you have lived other lives and you are now doing penance for having locked someone up during the Inquisition. You feel as though you are going to die--

--well, *that* doesn't make me feel any better.

--and if you stay with this sensation, let it happen, you know it *will* pass. So. Calm down. Hold your breath. Count to six. Let out your breath. Hold your breath! Say any magic word you like.

Uh—Robert Baldwin.

--if that's the best you can do. All right: Ro-bert Bald-win, Ro-bert Bald-win. Now let out your breath. Count to six. Keep saying your magic word.

I may keel over.

Shut up. You will not. Get-ting calm-er, get-ting calm-er--

Joan opened her eyes. Before her, scratched into the bright blue metal door she read KIM GOES DOWN I DO NOT !!! KISS MY GRITS and other more specific anatomical injunctions.

Teach them how to spell and this is what happens. Joan wondered briefly if she should add her business phone number to the others on the door. No. Only weird people would call, and they wouldn't pay their bills.

No--only weird people sat on the toilet seat and *read* these stupid door messages. She didn't want to think *why* people had to sit here long enough to etch them. This could give a person hemorrhoids--

Okay, on the bright side, all she had to do was stand up, walk outside, get the car and drive back across the causeway. Across the causeway, back to their home in Banana Bay Beach, into the house, then down the hall to the bedroom, and then under a stinging hot shower—water therapy-- until the panic went away.

An image of Robert's disapproving face floated before her. He didn't believe people should ever be ill. *He* never was.

Her panic mounted. Then how would *he* get home? He would have to take a taxi. He would show up at the house thin-lipped, unsmiling. Eyes accusing—you were supposed to pick me up at the airport. You're my wife. *That* is what wives do. Why else would I leave my car and my keys with you?

She scrunched her eyes shut tight. Now she was in the air traffic control tower watching a blip on the screen—Robert's plane. Blip and then--BING! the blip disappeared

Oh, that was *easy*. Neat. Quiet. Here one minute, gone the next. Good-by, Robert.

Her heart tattooed a punishing tango of beats. Good grief--how could she even think of doing that to Robert?

And others, innocent people, were on that plane. Joan put the blip back on the screen.

Maybe this particular panic attack was from something she'd eaten. Joan reviewed breakfast: orange juice, coffee, one scrambled egg, one piece of toast. Eaten outside in the early morning while Excelsior and Pete still slept and the ground was dewy. While the neighbors' sprinklers shooshed around and the rotten-egg smell of the underground sulfur water pumped to the St. Augustine grass soothed her—the nose-wrinkling smell of Florida in August. Joan knew of some old-timers who drank only that water and swore it made them healthier. That's what old—what was her name?--India Bayh, who still had a few of her own teeth at a century old, maintained.

Marmalade on the toast. Well, of course. *That* would do it, bring on this sweating and wishing she was dead.

A hypoglycemic moment.

Someone was shaking her metal door.

Joan looked down through the bottom of the stall door at a pair of sneakers, large, the sides cut out to accommodate some painful-looking corns. Above those, chocolate-colored legs gave away the race of the wearer.

"Hey. Anybody in here?" The door was shaken again.

"Coming right out." Joan raised her head, adjusted her slacks, flushed the unused toilet and unlocked the door.

The owner of the sneakers was busy spraying a mirror and wiping it with a paper towel. Joan saw a woman about her same age with a pair of brown cheeks plump as a chipmunk's and a gold tooth that flashed as the woman smiled.

She tried not to stare at the ample tee-shirted chest.

"Ma'am, I didn't mean to hurry you. I jest came in here to clean. I didn't hear any noise and I thought I'd better check. See, sometimes we get kids in here smokin' pot--"

The chest was looking more and more inviting. Joan felt a strong compulsion to cry, "Oh, *help* me," and lay her head on those breasts. Headline:"WOMAN GOES BERSERK AT AIRPORT"--

"Missus, you okay?" The gold tooth disappeared.

"Yes, thank you. I think the heat got to me--"

"Ain't *that* the truth. Gonna get worse before it gets better, too." The gold appeared again.

"I suppose." Joan slid the purse strap onto her shoulder and pushed open the doors before the woman could say, "Nice outfit. Now I seen that exact same pink outfit there on Miz Smith when I did her bathroom."

Well, at least that was one positive aspect of agoraphobia. Replace one stress with another and the first would fade away for a while. And never, ever tell anyone you were feeling panicky. Always look strong. Her mother and Robert would both approve, not that they spoke to each other.

A quick check of the board showed Robert's plane still on time. Still Gate 4. Why had she crashed his plane? What a crazy thought!

By now more people had gathered and were standing in sticky cheerful clumps of families and friends.

Lonely? Come to the airport. You're sure to meet someone you know. Joan waved to a woman she'd taken a local college course with; then she eased over to the newsstand so she wouldn't have to talk. She pretended to read the book covers. She picked up a can of Florida Air with a SENDING YOU SOMETHING FROM FLORIDA message on it. She examined a plastic alligator and then a tiny crate filled with tiny plastic oranges.

Oh, if she'd been born a male! She would now be a male therapist and she'd— *he'd* know just what to do with his clients who had agoraphobia.. He would prepare himself by stroking his beard. He would say, "Hm-m-m," in a low voice. Everyone knew that people prefer low voices. James Mason. Orson Welles. Sean Connery.

She/he would tamp his pipe, pretending to be engrossed in it, taking a long time to light up, appearing contemplative while hiding behind his smoke screen searching for answers.

But no. Here she was female. And she couldn't stroke her hair, say. Too seductive looking. She couldn't get away with clasping her hands behind her neck and leaning back in her chair—again, that appeared too sexy. She couldn't pretend to find a run in her stocking while she she took time to think—that was too disorganized and sloppy.

Bad combination—sloppy and sexy.

She wondered if Sigmund Freud, with his beard and pipe, first specified that a therapist had to be a man:

"ZO, FRAU BALDWIN—YOU VANT TO BE A *MEN*. YOU VISH TO VEAR ZE PENTS IN ZE FEMILY."

No, Doctor Freud, I vant—uh, *want*-- to be a *woman*—a woman who is desired and desirable, instead of having to be an invisible 40-year-old mother and grandmother--

"AH. YOU LEFT OUT 'VIFE'. VOS DOT ON PURPOSE?"

Doctor Freud, for the life of me, I don't even know why I *wanted t*he plane to crash.

She swept with the crowd funneling to Gate 4. Joan wished she'd used the mirror in the ladies' room to check her lipstick.

"Announcing the arrival of Eastern Airlines Flight Number 403 from Atlanta."

Screams of joy, the bawling of babies, the cries of delight and recognition: the conversations with the incoming passengers sounded all the same--"Boy, is it hot!"-- "Hot enough for you?"-- "What heat!"-- "Hey, we saved you some heat!"-- "--like an oven!"-- "Bring us any cold air?" "You kidding? Atlanta in August? Wow! This is like a steam bath!"-- "--steam bath!"-- "--steam bath!"

Joan spotted Robert. There he strode, all six feet of him, unaffected by the camaraderie, in a wrinkle-free suit. How did he *do* it? She pulled her blouse away from her still-damp back and consoled herself that in high school he hadn't worn deodorant until she insisted, because none of her friends would double-date with them until he did. So-- because of *her* he smelled good. Now *there* was an achievement worthy of Nobel.

"ZO, FRAU BALDWIN. YOU VANT TO MAKE YOUR HUSBAND ROBERT INTO A SISSY MEN VIT PERFUME."

No, Doctor Freud! I just want him to be able to sit on a plane next to people without having them blame *me* for not making him wear deodorant!

Robert's face was as bland as smooth vanilla custard as he surveyed the noisy crowd for Joan's face. When their eyes made contact the custard expression did not change.

She did not jump up and down. Robert did not approve. Once when he'd been gone on one of his many business trips, Joan and Pete had silk-screened tee shirts at home and worn them to the airport, a small one covering Excelsior, another one over Pete's arm for his father. When Robert had spotted the family all dressed alike and sporting the words "BANANA BAY" (several people had even asked where they could buy one) he had walked past them without a flicker of recognition, and had refused to speak to any of them until they had "settled down". Joan had folded Robert's tee shirt across the chair in their bedroom. It stayed there for days until she put it in a drawer. It was still there.

Robert did not kiss her hello. She'd known since their high school dating days that he considered public displays to be juvenile.

She had believed him.

"Robert! How are you? How was your flight?"

"My baggage is this way. I'll tell you after I've had a drink."

She trotted, a panting short-legged puppy, past all the hugging, kissing people, trying to keep up with his long strides--"Can't you even walk *beside* me?" he said, turning and addressing her somewhere over her head. He skillfully weeded his suitcase from the rest, poking his long right arm in among the chattering passengers to extract his expensive leather suitcase from the baggage carousel.

See, Doctor Freud, besides being male, it would have been nice to have been taller, too. Look what tall people can do. You know what happens when I put on a mid-length dress with my five feet three inches—I look as though I'm walking in a trench.

"Where is the car?" Robert asked.

"In the parking lot." He glanced sharply at her-- this was neither the time nor place for *jokes*.

"Good-by, Bob!" A man yelled to Robert. Robert's face pulled into a half-smile and he nodded across the luggage.

"We sat together on the plane," he said to Joan, forestalling her questions.

"But--he called you *Bob*, not Robert! Nobody ever calls you Bob, or Bobby--!"

"Ye-es. Try to persuade someone otherwise after he's had a couple of martinis--" Robert led the way to the MGB as purposefully as if he had parked it himself. He walked around it with deliberate care, his right hand feeling for any touched-up dings and scratches.

"Where's my key?"

He watched, a slight frown between his clear blue eyes, as she fumbled in her purse. "Don't you ever clean that thing out? And where did you ever *buy* such a tacky--?"

"Jordan Marsh," she said quickly. "Here they are. You want me to drive?"

"*I* will drive."

Robert unlocked the trunk, positioned his suitcase inside its pristine interior, lowered the lid and then unlocked the driver's door.

"This a new scratch?"

"Gee, I don't think so. I mean, I've been so careful--"

"The *boys* been in my car?" His voice, composed, demanded an answer.

"I never let anyone in your car while you're out of town."

"Um-hm-m." He sat down, adjusted the seat and mirrors with maddening precision. His hands caressed the steering wheel. She moved, sweating under the August sun, to the passenger door. Robert reached across and unlocked it.

What would happen if she refused to get in until he hugged and kissed her hello? What would he *do?* Would he call attendants in white uniforms, who would agree with him that she was crazy because next to him (he was so calm) she *was?*

Flushed, Joan got in and sat down.

"This leather is hot. No shade you could find, I suppose."

"Nope. There's only one shade tree in Florida and it was taken."

She remembered a "Pogo" cartoon: it had been raining in the swamp for days. Albert the Alligator took over the swamp's presidency. Then it stopped raining and he claimed credit for it. Some of the animals complained about his bragging and Albert, disgruntled, told them, "Why not? Happened durin' my admin-ee-stration, didn't it?"

I alone am responsible for the heat , thought Joan. It's happening during my admin-ee-stration:

"MRS. BALDWIN. WOULD YOU PLEASE TELL THE COURT JUST *HOW* YOUR HUSBAND BLAMED YOU?"

Well—he, uh—he looked at me funny.

"AH. HE LOOKED-AT-YOU-FUNNY."

Well, when you say it you make it sound different, Sir, but I can assure you--

"AH HAH. HE NEVER *BEAT* YOU? WELL?"

No, Sir, if by "beat" you mean--

"ABUSIVE TO HIS CHILDREN, THEN?"

No--

"AND YET YOU CONTEND HE *BLAMED* YOU, MRS. BALDWIN? DO YOU REALIZE YOU COULD BE IN CONTEMPT OF COURT HERE? DO YOU REALIZE YOU ARE PERJURING MR. BALDWIN'S GOOD NAME?"

"...I said, who has the boys?"

"Oh." Joan blinked. " Melissa. Excelsior, anyway." She sighed at the thought of their grandson in his crib, napping. "Pete's out fishing in the Indian River."

There was no response. "We haven't heard from Susan yet." There was a short expulsion of breath from Robert. "That's why I got Melissa. From next door. To babysit Excelsior."

Again, no response. "Pete and I cleaned the pool this morning. Even the filter," she added proudly.

Robert expertly eased the MG into second gear and passed a Chevrolet. "More old people here than ever before," he grumbled. He shifted into third gear. His car responded smoothly.

It must be that old people were her fault, too. "WELCOME TO FLORIDA" state the billboards. "MOVE DOWN HERE AND GET IN ROBERT'S WAY SO HE CAN BLAME HIS WIFE!"

Joan rested her left hand on the curved and carpeted drive shaft compartment between the bucket seats. Odd how this had the same configuration as Robert's muscular thigh. Maybe she should tell him, "I love to drive your car and put my right hand out to stroke this drive shaft-- " --no. She'd have to explain too much and the next time her car was in the shop he wouldn't let her borrow his.

She sighed and squinted, pretending she was a visitor seeing this area for the first time: the homely pelicans at the side of the road, unimpressed by all the traffic; the funny gray herons (or were they cranes?-- she still wasn't sure) waiting for the fishermen to catch something they could share, man and tall bird standing as buddies beside each other; then the wonderful feel of liftoff, driving across the new high-rise causeway which had replaced the old wooden drawbridge, so that at the top the Atlantic Ocean shone to the east before them through the Australian pines and the palms, past the expensive homes lining the Indian River—wouldn't the Ais Indians marvel at all this if they came back? Now all that remained of the long-vanished tribe were covered-over mounds of their debris—shards of pottery and heaps of old oyster shells—their trash piles.

Now the ancient Indian mounds were reduced to brilliant green zoysia-covered berms beside the driveways of the rich. *Jungle*—Florida was jungle, never forget it, just lying in wait beside the road, humming the hum of multitudinous bugs, patiently waiting to stretch carnivorous lush tentacles across the asphalt and tent it over so that, unattended, the entire state would revert to primitive gardenia-scented sensuous silence even before the last human inhabitant had moved out in defeat.

Joan pictured the area of Banana Bay and Banana Bay Beach covered with vines and trees and only the slapping sounds of mullet hitting the water to break the somnolence of --oh the *smell* of-- tropical reproduction and the care-less attitude of the plants in this wild Garden of Eden that laughed at, that didn't need man to survive--

Somewhere just south of here had been a pineapple plantation to rival Hawaii's until a killing frost dashed the planters' dreams, back in the late 1800s. A little boat once had carried happy picnickers from the mainland to the beach, left them not far from here at the riverside dock which once held a primitive train track running from river (actually a saltwater lagoon) to ocean, deposited them by the same boat bringing ice and mail to the few who lived in this rattler- and alligator-infested spit of sand, for a day of innocent fun.

Squinting at the ocean shining in the reflected afternoon sun, Joan thought of the first pioneers in this area, only a hundred years ago or so, who would take themselves in skiffs from the west side of the Indian River to the ocean after a huge storm, looking for any evidence that a ship had gone down off the coast as they hunted for signs of barrels and crates bobbing in the surf, barrels perhaps filled with flour or other useful supplies, trying not to think of the lives lost on that same ship that brought them sustenance, all of the early citizens surviving hardship after hardship so that she could now sit in air-conditioned comfort next to her husband--oh, what a place to live! What a time to be alive! What a--

"Oh, look! Look!" Joan cried, so that Robert's hand rocked the steering wheel slightly and he scowled. "There's Pete fishing! Pete! PETE!" she called to the slim young tanned boy at the river's edge who waved in return. "Oh, he doesn't have a *hat* on! And I *told* him--!" She rolled down her window.

"Well, we are not stopping. He has his bicycle and he can get himself home. I'm not getting that river stink in my car." Robert passed Pete without slowing down.

"We'll see you at home!" Joan called back. Pete had already returned to his fishing. She breathed another sigh, this time of relief. Since Pete had his bike with him, that meant it wouldn't be on the garage floor in Robert's way.

☆ ☆ ☆

Into the double garage with its Fiberglas opaque door. Out of the car and into the concrete and stucco house through the laundry room. Past the kitchen with its shiny aqua appliances and terrazzo floor, upon which, if you dropped a jar of mustard, you stepped back fast so as not to get hit by flying glass, and then had to stop everything and clean before it could permanently stain the floor yellow; and into the master bedroom with its dark paneling, jalousied windows, sliding glass doors and orange flowered draperies and bedspread. Joan had liked the color combination at first, but now spent time just staring at it, wondering if it might not be a little *too* modern. Maybe new throw pillows--

She also disliked being on the other side of the house from the boys. What if they had a bad dream or something and she couldn't hear them crying?

"Pool looks a little green." Robert had dumped his suitcase onto their king sized bed that looked out onto the back yard. "I thought you said you cleaned it."

"I *did*! And tested it this morning." Joan said. "I just paid Melissa. She's gone. Excelsior's still sleeping."

"Did you test it the way I showed you?"

"Yes. It's fine, really. You can test it again if you--"

"I plan to after I take a shower." His face was still bland. He still had not kissed her. He went into their bathroom and shut the door.

Joan took his clothing from the suitcase. The folded unused underwear and socks went into the dresser. The rumpled clothing went into the hamper. Sometimes Robert folded his *used* underwear and she couldn't tell the difference. That was when she gave up and threw all of it into the wash.

The stacks of brochures from the engineering seminar he had attended went to his desk in his den that used to be Susan's room. The toilet articles went to his side of the bathroom counter. The matchbooks he collected from restaurants he visited went into a little stack for Pete. She read their names with growing envy.

"Robert," she opened the bathroom door cautiously and called to the silhouette behind the clouded shower door," how about we go out for dinner tonight? Melissa says she can come back."

She counted to ten. She knew one of his rules was that he not be noticed when he was behind a door. One time she'd spoken to him, the bathroom door ajar just that *little bit* while he was sitting down, and he had ignored her for several hours after that.

Robert's Rules of Order, he called them. All of life would be smoother if people just followed *rules*.

"No," he said, shutting off the water. "I've been eating in restaurants all week. I want to eat here at home. I don't want much, anyway. They served us stuff on the plane. Don't you have any food in the house?"

Her heart fell. That long a speech meant no eating out for the entire week end.

"Some steaks, I mean," he continued, " if you didn't feed them all to *Pete* while I was gone." He stepped out of the shower, a towel around his lean middle. "I wanted to take a dive into the pool, but not in water full of algae." She started to remonstrate, then changed her mind. She and Pete had swum there this morning.

"I'll ask Pete to check it again when he gets home." She placed Robert's toilet articles on the bathroom counter. "He looked like he was having such a good time—"

All at once Robert's long-fingered hand with his heavy M.I.T. class ring pushed Joan's head into his moist hairy chest, and a few tears of relief escaped her to mingle with the shower water.

"Oh, Robert, I missed you."

He kissed her then. "Lock the door," he said.

Radar.

The kids had had radar from an early age. Joan would check on them and they'd be engrossed in a TV show at their end of the house, but as soon as the master bedroom door clicked shut and locked, they were hammering on it: "What's the capital of New Mexico, Mom?"

"Can I have a cookie?"

"I get two cookies if he gets one."

"No fair, Mom!" "Mom!" "MO-*THER*!"

Joan locked the bedroom door. Robert looked at Joan. She mentally calculated how long Pete could stay at the river before the heat got to him How long Excelsior might nap. When that child woke up he had a shriek like a noon whistle. She'd have to get to him before he got on Robert's nerves.

Robert dropped his towel to the floor. She could see he was ready. "Did you miss it?" he said.

Why "it"? Why did he never say "miss me"? Just "it"? *It* pointed straight at her, veins raised, the circumcised tip aiming at her like a pink mushroom cap. It seemed to be smiling.

She tried not to look at the damp towel. Could they get through with sex before the towel mildewed the bedroom carpet? Everything in Florida went musty in minutes. Did Robert drop towels all over his motel rooms, uncaring that a maid would have to pick them up?

Oh, yes, she could see that he was ready. What would he do if she followed through with a playful spontaneous compulsion to reach out there between his legs, grab him in a friendly handshake, and say, "Welcome home, you. And you too, Robert." Would he laugh? Would he hug her and tickle her and *laugh*? No, better not. If anything on him needlessly relaxed it would be her fault.

Look how carefully he folded the bedspread back. She ground her teeth: he was so *neat* about some things. Maybe she could get to the wet towel while he was folding--

No. He settled her back on the sheets she'd found on sale at Penney's. His blue eyes were so close now.

An image of cutaway sneakers and a brown pillow-sized bosom intruded. She shut her own eyes to block out any interference. Was that the back door and Pete coming home, a fishing hook in his hand and needing to be driven to the emergency room and her car was in the shop and Robert would be mad at any blood in his car and he couldn't get out of the car at the hospital anyway, because people would see how large and extended he was and know what they'd been doing and Excelsior was, she was *sure* he was sobbing huge choking sobs right this moment in his crib, poor motherless baby, missing Susan, their daughter, Susan who had given him that terrible name and nobody knew where Susan was, and what if she was calling right now, *right now* to say, "I'm sorry, I'm sorry, I'm sorry, I want to come home"--

"Good?" he asked. She knew it really wasn't a question.

"Um-*hmm*," Joan answered. She'd have a better chance, she told herself, when she wasn't so distracted.

Robert, spent, rolled over, eyes closed, and began to snore. He would need another shower, Joan thought as she moved carefully away from her sleeping husband without making a sound, picked up his towel and hung it over the top of the shower door to dry. Sex always made him sweat.

She lay down again beside him. He thrust out an arm and laid it across her breast, then began his quiet snore again.

Would there be time to thaw the roast? Should she make a trip to the store after he woke up? She could leave him a note, but he wouldn't like that--Robert never liked waking up to an empty house. And what would she do about Excelsior? Pete could watch him, but when Pete came home he'd want to dive bomb into the pool first thing. She'd have to wait and look for him so he'd be quiet and not wake his father. But she was naked and she needed to put something on before Pete came home—oh, why couldn't she just relax and enjoy sex and not *worry* so much about everything?

And, Doctor Freud— I still want to be a woman. But I sure wish I had two brains the way men do —one in the head and one in the penis, so I could turn off the one in my head and concentrate on my own pleasure; so that (myself a big fat pink thermometer turned concave) I could tell when I'm ready and when I'm done—what a handy gadget to have!

Is that the garage door? Is Excelsior starting to cry? If Susan comes home and I'm not here, does she have a key to the house?

And oh the cry of the housewife, the housewife who has a husband and the loan of his car and a good son and a beautiful grandson, even if I never wanted to be a grandmother this young in my life, the housewife with the kitchen and the self-defrosting turquoise refrigerator and the double ovens-- and oh, Lord, help me-- *what* can I serve Robert for dinner?

☆　☆　☆

Joan Baldwin Forster: 2011

Banana Bay Beach is not a bay, nor can it boast a banana crop. It does have a very nice beach. This one-mile square area on a spit of sand stretching from north of the Cape down through the swamp and sawgrass to the billionaires' mansions in the next county south was once (billions of years ago itself) a sandbar out in the Atlantic Ocean. Now dry land, it was founded, along with the mainland area Banana Bay, by Benjamin and Anna Bayh and their relatives after the Civil War.

I have watched every rocket shot, most of them from our back yard, since we moved here in 1963 from Connecticut. Before we left I had given away my books of Green Stamps, sure that we were heading into total backwoods, and was surprised to find not one, but *three* Episcopal churches in Banana Bay and the towns just north and south of it.

So the inhabitants were civilized here. There was also a Green Stamp redemption center. So much for the set of pots and pans I'd been yearning for. I'd have to start over.

I got a job almost instantly as organist in one of the two smaller churches. I am a pianist and I also taught myself to play organ and I find it so amusing that all the important parts of my life are that way: self-taught. Anyway, church organists are always at a premium. Not that the pay is so great.

When Robert would be going out of town on yet again one of his seminar trips (we moved here because of his job) , I would say, "I wish I could go with you."

I would usually be holding a wet mop or a child's head over the toilet. Oh, if only just once he'd said, "I wish you could go, too." but his response was always, "Your reward is in heaven."

"How come *yours* isn't? I want my reward *now*," I would think. But I never said it aloud. Not good to anger both husband and God at the same time. And in these Equal Rights for Women days I had to be extra careful.

Anyway, the Bayhs. They were not the first ones here. The town on the mainland west of the Indian River lagoon was originally settled by two freed black slaves who opened the first post office and school. Then when the Caucasian Bayhs from Canada moved in and others followed, the town was too self-consciously close to the Civil War to want to claim its black heritage; so the town of Banana Bay was named for the white founders instead of for George and Jeremiah Washington. This was before Ben Bayh rowed his skiff across the then-clear Indian River water to the beach and proclaimed the land as far as he could see, "FOR BEN AND ANNA BAYH", although Banana Bay would not see any growth until the Florida land boom in the 1920s. Ben wanted to name the town after his Canadian hometown, but the settlement's drunken sing-songers had their way: "Ben an' Anna Bayh, Banana Bay/ Where skeeters bite you night and day."

India Bayh, the town's firstborn, loved to tell the story of her mother's piano coming to their house on a barge, through Sanford and then down the river to town. The first evening Anna put her hands to the untuned keys to play, a trio of fascinated Ais Indians crept up to the window. Anna screamed and the story has it that one of the Indians entered the house and placed Anna's fingers back on the keys for some more Stephen Foster.

India said her mother screamed because the piano was so far out of pitch and she was so far from civilization. India was a year old at the time, but she swore she remembered.

When the nation's bicentennial (and Banana Bay's centennial) festivities came to town in 1976, India was 99 years old. She attributed her long life to daily dips in the local sulfur water and to never having been married. The mayor and councilmen, after having spent all their extra money on bunting and fireworks, decided to honor old India at the same time – with a ninety-ninth birthday party and enormous cake!

And who knew she would survive to be a feisty 100 and demand (and get) *another* birthday celebration the next year before choking to death on a wad of coconut cake baked by our new Episcopal priest's wife Margaret?

✭ ✭ ✭

Anyway, I have decided that I will take down all my boxes from the attic. I will dispose of everything useless so that when I finally die there will be no detritus for relatives to deal with.

Not that I intend to die soon, although I tripped last year, my sandal making a misstep off my own office steps as I left work one evening (and I blame Derreck), so that my foot twisted around and I fell heavily onto my right elbow, which shattered to such an extent that now titanium screws and plates hold me together; and apparently my right knee suffered some injury also, so that I now, after arthroscopic surgery—I who have always been so healthy! – must be aware of every step I take.

This makes going up and down the narrow wooden pull-down ladder in the garage attic a slow deliberate act. I wear my cell phone. I feel hindered in that I could hurt myself badly if I fall and no one would be there to hear the thud except our cat Phoebe, since Quentin is still working full time at his age of 76 as a proctologist, where he can work if he wants at his practice until his hands shake and his eyesight fails and his brain goes soft. I've studied him, wary about the brain part, but the rest of what he needs for all that rear-ended closeup work seems fine. As long as people have bums he'll have a job.

It is so quiet here at the house Quentin and I planned and had built. The land was impenetrable when we found it. As the heavy equipment yanked the many overgrown trees from the property to make room for the house and pool (and Quentin all but tied himself to each tree to prevent its loss), a rich dank rotting odor took over. We were having primal land ravaged here. Once while wearing knee-high rubber boots, I was held by the muck as I tried to walk through it, and I had to step out of the boots and walk barefoot to the hose. I even sat down hard when I pulled my boots out. The suction was a surprise. The aggravated land wanted to claim them.

And yet it was nothing personal, I knew. It was Florida, and the land always wins in the long run.

There are still so many trees that I have not been able to thrash my way to the rear of the one-acre yard. I'm sure there are plenty of snakes there. We have raccoons pattering away over our heads at night, and once there was an entire family that slept atop our porch until, exasperated, I took a hose to them.

Raccoons bite into our mangoes just before the fruit has ripened, compelling us to cut the still-green harvest and set the fruit on the kitchen windowsill. This land and animals force us into a way of living that, now I am in my little house with the green roof (and more about my new residence later) I do not miss at all.

We have no neighbors here, so if I did injure myself falling out of the attic nobody would hear my yelling over the cicadas. While I lived here there were days I would have only the trashmen to talk to.

Quentin loves it here. He is planning to work in the yard as soon as he retires. In the meantime he walked around the house every evening: "I spotted the stack of palmetto leaves out by the street."

"Yes, Quentin. After we were robbed twice I wanted to make sure we were not invisible from the road. Burglars like invisibility."

"Well, you just have to quit cutting things down."

"Look around, Quentin—I could use my saw all over this place and it wouldn't make a dent. These palms grow faster than I can keep them trimmed."

"Well, that's the *point*, isn't it? Don't trim them. Let nature be nature."

I have told him his tombstone will read: HE WAS A DOCTOR. Four words sum up his life. It is all he has wanted to do for a half-century. The two men I married in succession, first Robert Baldwin, then Quentin Forster II have focus, goals, no deviations, while I have spent my life wandering here and there like an ill-trained Samoyed, sniffing into odd corners, never sticking with anything for long.

Of course as a mental health counselor it's hard not to tinker with family; so I gave both husbands (in their turn) a personality questionnaire. Both came out the same—'independent, self-assured, can appear to be arrogant", although there are supposed to be only 5% of this type in the United States. So few, and I found *two* of them!

This husband will never trip and fall. He strides deliberately, never looking down, on extra-wide feet like snowshoes. I have forgotten what Robert's feet look like since musing about Quentin's for almost twenty years now.

Oh, Quentin—dependable, mild-mannered, kind to his patients and staff, oblivious to me unless I force him to look into my eyes, a man who retreats from altercation: oh, sometimes, irrationally, I miss the crazy excitement that Robert brought into my life! I'm wise enough now to know that a steady diet of Robert was downright dangerous. Still, *Quentin's* idea of excitement is to endure an entire day among the crowds at Disneyworld.

I was so exasperated to injure myself at age 73. I have for as long as I remember been in love with prime numbers, and it seemed unfair that this should happen to me then. Seventy-three should be a *prime* year, full of surprises and joys. And here I plod through this dull even year of being 74, waiting impatiently for a prime one again.

I have been in love with prime numbers ever since I was introduced to them in math class. It was love at first sight: "Hello, Joan—we're something clever you can rely on." Oh, these wonderful numbers that can only be divided by themselves or one (don't tell me nothing can be divided this way—this is my interpretation).

And 75! Another boring divisible number! Quentin is already 76. Pete is 44. Granddaughter Emily, 25. Susan—54—Excelsior—he would have been 36 this year. But as Miss Jean Brodie said, "Little gir-r-rls, I am in me prime."

So – how many prime years are left to me? My father died at age 72 and my mother at 69 and they were both heavy smokers, so I as a never-smoker except for all the second-hand nicotine that yellowed their final retirement village walls, showing me what my lungs might look like after inhaling those carcinogens as a youngster in our drafty Connecticut house—I should make it into my late nineties—79, 83, 89, 91, 97—only *five* prime years left if I live to 100. Not enough, not enough.

How many people my age do I know who look *forward* to another headstrong-numbered year?

... I found my journals in the attic. I had forgotten I had written them. What a do-gooder wimp I was then! And yet, looking back at the '60s and '70s, at Joan Baez, Erica Jong, , Simone de Beauvoir, Betty Friedan, Betty Ford of all people—Friedan letting us women know about "the problem that has no name" before we even believed we were feminists—what did we want? We wanted more.

Weeping, I had read Friedan's book —someone understood! I did not want the rest of my life to be spent with dishes and laundry and as the poem says, "waiting the boy who puts the groceries in my car to notice me".

Oh, that young naive Joan. I honestly believed back then that if I told my story in the third person I could achieve a kind of objectivity, but instead – !

Well. This was all Father Wolfe's fault. I never had kept a journal, but when I showed up at church, soggy from crying after Robert came home that time from Atlanta, he showed me into his office.

"So what's going on?" he asked, pulling at his collar. (If he were still alive today, how amused he would be to see Episcopal priests removing those white stiff collars, throwing them down on the altar, and announcing to startled congregations, "I cannot support a woman bishop and the whole gay issue!" before leaving the church and their nice pensions behind.

Anyway, Father Wolfe told me this was to be my homework before I met with him again. I still believed I must be moving into menopause, but blowing my nose on the way home I stopped at Eckerds and bought myself a notebook and, daringly, a lipstick in a darker shade: "Coka Moka".

I didn't know this would be the first of a dozen notebooks and how my life would shift as a result, these notebooks themselves my tectonic plates.

"You're a mental health counselor and you've never kept a journal?" he teased, while I relaxed from the pressure of his huge beefy hands on my shoulders.

"It's dangerous to keep notes," I sniffled. "If I were to be called into court to testify about a client—my mentor trained me not to keep notes."

"But this will be for you, not anyone else. Be your own client. Let the journal be your therapist. Get as wild as you want—isn't that what you allow your clients to do?"

✫ ✫ ✫

So now I sit in the garage on a fold-out chair amongst my old palmetto-bug-chewed musty papers, reading what I wrote over thirty years ago. Huh. This Joan (nee Gibson) Baldwin comes across as a fake-smiling, please-everyone marshmallow-soft clown.

But I must thank her for saving me, for I am sure if I were still with Robert I would be dead by now and Quentin would be reciting his dull and lengthy anal-fixated stories to some other woman.

Even so, knowing I escaped, reading these first pages Robert once *again* comes across as having all the answers to life even though we are only four months apart in age, damn him!

✫ ✫ ✫

When Robert was two years old his young mother became ill and both sets of grandmothers came to lay claim on him until she could get better.

My psychology books say that a male has a good chance of developing devil-may-care-like tendencies if at a young age there are two women vying for his attention. And while that explains the charm, I was certainly much more susceptible to it than my female friends were. As an adult Robert was tall, exercised to keep his weight down, showed a forbearance for chocolate whenever he saw his little paunch growing; he designed charts for my losing weight with graphs that looked like ski slopes downward, a trail of no-Hershey bars to the bottom of the trail where his idea of perfection awaited.

And I believed him. If only to please him I had been a little taller, or slimmer, or more blond or, or, or....how I looked for that magic button that I would press and make everything all right. I might as well have believed in the Easter bunny's laying all those colored eggs.

Susan's daughter Emily will not be mentioned in my old diaries, since she was not yet born. However, these new writings of mine, starting today, are all for her, since she is living with a man so like Robert. He is charming, yes, but when

Derreck and I are alone (which I try to avoid), he is *not* to me, although for her sake I hide my feelings. I will write this addendum and then leave it for Emily to find. Will she be able to see that she is setting herself up for heartbreak and pain, but that on the other side she will find herself? Or will she, like Susan, accuse me of meddling and controlling?

In the meantime I'm scared – he seems to be doing his best to kill me and make it look like an accident.

I am not mistaken that late last year, as I lay in pain, (you remember I wrote about my "tripping"), every movement to my crushed elbow a red-hot dance of pain, working my good left arm and hand into my purse for my cell phone, crawling and rolling in agony, I heard a "zip" sound of a wire being retracted behind me—the kind of sound you hear when you retract a metal measuring tape carelessly; and then the muffled laugh and the unmistakable roar of a sports car moving away from the other side of my building.

I know my enemy, me, Joan, the good girl who went out of her way to be friends with everyone. And where before with Robert I was defending my own life—this time I defend Emily's.

☆ ☆ ☆

You may think these are just the ramblings of an older woman who no longer bothers to dye her short gray hair light brown any more ("elderly" they call us in the newspapers), but I plead my case: It is ten months earlier. I am in my office waiting for a client I have not yet met. I only take a few clients now and I handpick those. The others I send off to younger, more enthusiastic therapists who are still convinced they can save the world one by one

I am standing out of view at my window when a red convertible pulls up, the top down. Over its jangling country music I hear and then see a young good-looking suntanned man. He is shouting at a pale young woman with long unwashed hair and she is ducking her head away from him and fumbling in her large cloth purse for—it turns out, a comb. He jumps from the driver's seat and leaves his car door ajar. He enters my waiting room—I hear the small announcing bell ring.

I watch through the window. What will the woman do? She pulls the comb through her straight hair and then fumbles for a tissue for her nose. This is all done with clumsy haste as she watches my front door, waiting for him to—return? Abandon her? She exits the car and closes its doors with much care, first hers, then his. She picks up the hem of her long peasant-style skirt and wipes down the places where she might have left prints. She still cannot see me, but I can now see her eyes—the eyes of a dumb, obedient, abused dog. She then enters my building.

I wait a few minutes, walk into the waiting room and escort the couple into my private office. I watch the young man frown at my beige loveseat, my desk, my rocking chair, my flowers and books. There is another chair behind my desk. I watch to see where they will sit. Still frowning, he sits at the end of the loveseat close to the door—so he can bolt if necessary?– and she, with her purse bumping against her knees, settles herself cautiously beside him.

"Good afternoon," I say. "I am Joan Forster. I see that you were referred by– " I glance at my notes– "Dr. Smythe."

"Damned witch doctor," says the young man, now winking at me.

I decide to leave that alone. "And you are– "

"Derreck. That's all you need to know for now." He stares at me with clear blue eyes and then smiles. Someone took good care of him as a youngster—his teeth have the evenness that come from many orthodontic appointments.

Derreck makes no mention of his companion's name and she does not offer it. Her long hair falls over her face, which is tilted toward the carpet, so she doesn't see me encourage her to speak.

"And you are– ?"

"Just call her Stupid," growls Derreck.

Leave it alone? Follow another path? No. "What is your name?" I repeat. No answer. A long pause. Derreck fidgets and pokes at the woman, so that she mumbles, "You can call me that."

"And what brings you here?" I ask.

"This room bugged?" Derreck scans the room.

"No," I say.

"Are you taking notes?"

"I might. I'd rather just talk with you for now– "

"*No notes.* Or if you have to, I get a copy."

So we are already jockeying for control. "All right. For now, no notes."

"Just so we got that clear." He leans in toward me as I sit in my rocking chair. "Okay. I belong to a government organization that is *so secret* the C.I.A. doesn't even know about it."

Shades of Colonel Flagg from "M*A*S*H"! Is Dr. Smythe having a joke at my expense? I don't smile. "Yes– ?"

"I could take you out if I wanted to." He doesn't smile, either. His eyes are now chilly.

"Take me out– " my god, does he want a date?

"Or her. I could take *her* out. She knows that." Derreck (his real name?) scowls in his companion's direction.

Oh!– take me out! *Kill!* Is *that* what he means? What have I let into my office? I am suddenly aware that I allowed my secretary to leave early—something about a friend's birthday party. I am alone with these two until my granddaughter Emily comes to take me to lunch. How could I have made this mistake, seeing a new unknown client with no backup? This is something the *old* Joan would have done, not me with all my experience.

"Does that bother you, what Derreck just said?" I ask the young woman, playing for time while I think of what to do next. She swings her hair, still hiding her face. "Naw. He talks to me like that all the time."

"If I started telling you everything I've done for the government," Derreck interjects, as though bored with the conversation getting away from a focus on him, "you would be sick as a dog—oh, yeah, I've also killed any animals that got in my way."

"You have."

"What? You wanna hear about my dog, the one went after my Pop's geese? You know a goose has a neck it can make stiff so it's like a piston– " he stiffens his left arm suddenly out and slams it across the woman's chest. She winces and then gives him a watery smile.

"Hang on there– !" I am startled to say

"Shit, she doesn't care. She loves it, don't you?" Derreck squeezes the woman's arm.

She nods. "I don't mind."

"He has just told you he could kill you."

"Naw—he says that all the time."

"Hey. You wanna hear about my dog or not?" Derreck demands. I nod. Here we sit, two nodding women, I think, while my mind races, wondering what I ever did to Dr. Smythe to inherit this client.

"Anyway, one time when I was a kid I got knocked down by this goose. So after I get my breath back I'm so mad I sic my dog on it and my dog *kills* that damn goose. So my Pop comes *roaring* out of the house, hopping mad—makes me laugh to see him—he misses the bottom step on the porch and falls flat, he's so mad! So I'm laughing and he's swearing, and then he gives me his gun and says I have to shoot my dog."

My god! "How old were you?" I ask, keeping my voice calm.

"Oh—I guess nine years old."

Nine—I think about Pete innocently going fishing when he was that age. "How did you feel, doing that?"

"Feel? *How did I feel?* Lady—it was just a dumb *dog.*"

I watch to see if he will cry at the memory. His girlfriend pats his hand and he pulls it away. "You know what I would have got if I hadn't obeyed my old man? Anyway, afterwards he gives me the gun. Says I can keep it. Best thing he ever gave me. Yeah. That was really something."

I'm feeling exhausted. "I'm still trying to find out what brings you to me."

"Yeah, well—that old horse-face Smythe says he can't help me. I think he's a fairy anyway, and we have ways of taking care of those guys—*if* they make it that far into this group I'm with."

Suddenly I remember the psychological seminar Dr. Smythe and I co-chaired. A young woman had asked a question about procedure and he stalled, smoothing his mustache while I waited for him to stop clearing his throat. So I gave what turned out to be an insightful solution.

Smythe with his pompous name-spelling, sounding it out ("It's with a *long* 'Y', you know") had frowned and narrowed his eyes at me.

Smythe, you bastard.

"Anyway, I want to know how to get Stupid here off my back. She's all the time crying, whining, "Where you going?" until I've had it!"

"Why don't you just tell her that?" I ask as the young tearful woman who clutches at her purse.

"Because I'm such a good guy," he smiles at me, and *now* I get the full brunt of his charm. Derreck is tall, muscled, obviously works out—when he smiles he looks as though it's you and me, just the two of us, babe, against the world.

Now the woman is whispering something and I lean closer to her. Something about a car. "Tell her I—bought you that car– "

"What car?" I'm not about to admit I spied on them. Now *that* would be an invitation to paranoia.

"I explained that to Stupid here already. It's too dangerous for me to have anything in my name that can be traced back to me." He turns to me. "She's paying you in cash, not a check. I don't carry those or a credit card, just in case– "

"Derreck says there are enemies all around." The woman whispers for my education. Then she rises. "Excuse me, but where is your washroom?"

"Right down the hall, the way you came in. It's marked– "

Derreck snorts, his breath coming out in a burst of derision. "I'm going with you."

They both stand. I do too. She sighs, picking up her purse, and heads carefully out of the room. He looks back at me. "Can't have her running off now," he winks.

As soon as they leave I grab my cell phone and put it in my pocket. Just in case. Then I hear my bell ring and I move into the hall also. And there is Emily, smiling, tying back her hair, moving toward me . Derreck appears without a sound and expertly interposes himself between us.

"Oh. I'm sorry," Emily says, "I'll just wait out here until you're ready– ." She sits on the waiting room sofa and picks up a magazine.

"Me too," agrees Derreck and now he is sitting next to my granddaughter— this sociopath with paranoid tendencies is breathing the same air my beautiful granddaughter is breathing!

"– nice car," Emily says. "Yours?"

"Belongs to the lady who's with your shrink," he says. "She's in the restroom. She brought me, but she can't take me home and I was wondering what I'd do. Are you by any chance heading downtown?"

Emily looks up at me. "Why– "

"She's going the other way," I say firmly.

Derreck puts his right hand up, palm facing Emily, and she does the same, little slap into his hand. "You're a good soldier," he smiles at her. "Another time then."

I hear the toilet flush and the bathroom door opens. A tiny sniffle behind me tells me the unnamed woman is waiting.

"We'll be okay while you finish up," Derreck says, dismissing the two of us with a flip of his hand and then turning back to Emily.

Smooth try, but there is no way I am leaving him out here alone with her .

"I'll need you both," I say in my therapist voice. He gives Emily a look of mock resignation, shrugs his shoulders in exaggeration, then follows his girl-friend and me back down the hall toward my office.

Smythe, you out and out s.o.b! If I were ever in hell going to see this client more than this one time, I'd have plenty to say to you. I know if I refer Derreck back to Smythe, it will be admitting defeat. I search my mind for a therapist I don't care for....

"Oops, now I gotta go," announces Derreck and before I can say anything he is out the door. The young woman sits silently on my loveseat for a few minutes, then whispers, "Mrs. Forster?"

"Yes?" I ask.

"Dr. Forster? Your husband? He was my doctor once?" She stands up and I am so sure she is going to bend over to show me how Quentin fixed her. "He was very nice to me. I had those hem-things."

We hear a roar and the sound of gravel hitting the building. Looking at each other, we return to the waiting room, which is now empty. "The car's gone, too," she says helpfully. "He does this—he loves to show it off."

"But it's *your* car."

"Well—it was 'til I signed it over to Derreck. He said something about my taxes would work out better this way."

What can I say? Emily has driven off with a dog-shooting, secret organization man who may or may not bring her back.

"Is he wearing a cell phone?" I ask. "Can we call him?"

"I guess. But I don't know the number. It's classified."

Frustrated—why haven't I asked Emily what *her* new cell phone number is?– I glance at the woman. She is pulling her hair out away from her face and now she looks familiar. "Excuse me," I say, "but have we met before– ?"

"I'm Charleen?" she nods. "LoRayne's grandbaby? Ev'rybody says I'm her spittin' image? She says she used to do your hair."

LoRayne—LoRayne's Beauty Parlour—LoRayne, who used to frizz my hair and color it odd shades of orange, until I left her for someone talented. Did *she* send this couple to me?

Joan– who's paranoid now?

"I used to see you when I was tidyin' up in my grandmama's store?" Shyly, "You had such nice fine hair."

Oh. That sunny young child, Charleen. What in life had happened to suck the joy out of her?

Standing with her now in my humid parking lot, listening to the wild distant screech of tires– "that's him now, that's how he drives?—see, he's coming back?– " I have no idea that I will never after this day see Charleen again; and I *will* see so much of Derreck that I will seriously consider—me, Joan!– methods of doing away with him before he can harm me or my beloved granddaughter Emily any more than I am sure he will be trying to do.

Susan, Emily and I all have that same accursed gene. We are all suckers for the kind of man that Sam Malone was when he stood in his bar in "Cheers" with his height, his easy way of wearing clothes, his grin, and little black book of phone numbers. Except Sam– Sam had some scruples.

☆ ☆ ☆

STORMY TIMES AHEAD

Citizens are asked to pick up free hurricane maps at the Town Hall.
Florida is in the start of its hurricane season,
and people should not be lulled into a false sense of security.
Be sure to tell area businessmen you saw their advertisement on the map.
—*Banana Bay Tribune, June 1, 1977*

Robert and Joan kneel at the rail of St. Barnabus' Episcopal Church in Banana Bay on the Sunday before their 21st anniversary. She has moved from her bench at the full-pedal, two-manual Baldwin electronic organ ("A Baldwin playing a Baldwin!" Joan had laughed) to join her husband.

She is wearing a white orchid that eleven-year-old son Pete bought her, after begging her to take him to Rhoda's Rose Shoppe on the mainland and then urging her not go into the store with him. The orchid tips are now browning and harassing her chin, but the gift is much appreciated. Apparently her best friend Fran had phoned Pete and told him she had a flower account there and she would go halves with him. Fran is like that.

Joan feels so *old* when she wears an orchid, like a bosomy middle-aged Hokinson matron in a New Yorker cartoon. But when she saw Pete's beaming lopsided grin as she pinned it on— !

And Pete, in white cassock, spotless (so far) above his scuffed sneakers, is one of the acolytes today. Standing almost hidden behind Father Wolfe he fidgets, looks up at the hand-hewn timbered heart pine beams, glances back at Robert and Joan in an expression of pride and "please don't embarrass me" .

They crouch uncomfortably on the lumpy cushions with two other couples, one young and new to the church, one many years married. The thick Episcopal Church Women-embroidered yarn imprints its Trinitarian logos into their knees.

The newlyweds clasp hands and gaze shiny-eyed at each other. The Scotts, apparently practiced in this kind of annual business, have helped each other bend.

Father Wolfe hovers over the elderly couple. He prays in a low voice, his huge hands on their heads. Father Wolfe likes to show off his hands, big as Little League baseball gloves, and to rest them heavily on parishioners' arms and shoulders.

Today it's heads. The Scotts' aging bodies are already stooped and those big paws seem determined to push the couple's chins into their chests.

This priest inserts many football references into his sermons, and refers parishioners back to his college days— when he made the decision to punt for the Lord instead of going pro. Tom "The Fox" Wolfe is so proud of this calling that Joan wonders if the pro teams didn't actually reject him. Anyway, he's a big sturdy man who is tending to let his abdominal muscles go to fat now, so when he folds those oversized hands he has a resting place for them on his stomach,which expands beneath his green robe.

Episcopalians can tell by the green (stoles and altar coverings as their colorful calendar) that they are in the long season of Trinity. Gone from Joan's youth are Whitsunday, Quinquagesima, Septuagesima, Sexagesima (she was reluctant to ask what any of those meant, since one of the words had "sex" in it and she was afraid both she and her Sunday School teacher would blush)...

"Amen!" Father Wolfe's tone is as hearty as that of a quarterback. He has taken so long with this couple that she figures they must give quite a bit of money to the church

Robert has told her that he, like a proper Baptist-turned-Episcopalian-because-he-loves-the-burning-candles, *tithes* his income. Since Joan is not allowed to look at his paycheck she actually has no idea how much money comes in and where it goes when it goes out. He gives her an allowance he has decided upon, for groceries and clothes for the kids, and frowns weekly when she says she needs some for gas, too. She has decided he is tithing contractually: "I've done this for You, Lord. Now You do something for me." She hopes he is getting a good deal from it.

Her own organist's small paycheck, he has decided generously like a paterfamilias of old, should be used for necessities for her—lipstick, Tampax, etc. He has no idea how much these things cost, but sounds quite certain about it all—and unyielding. Her clothing also. At the altar Joan starts to daydream about God owning a consignment shop–

Now Father Wolfe is standing over the young couple. "Oh, Lord," he commands in a voice calculated to reach the last row of the old Gothic-styled church, "we just want to thank you for– " he looks down at the man and woman working to straighten under the weight of his hands– "for John and Phyllis here, Lord, and we just want to praise Your name and thank You– " his voice goes softer as he segues into a personal prayer for just John, Phyllis, God and him.

Father Wolfe is fond of "just" prayers. Joan figures for those who do that, it works like an "uh": "We, uh, want to, uh, thank you for, uh, the rain and uh, the sunshine– " Insert "just" and you'll see what Joan means.

She needs to scratch her itchy chin. But the people sitting behind her would notice, and since they are perspiring and waiting to go home, any movement would be a welcome distraction and she doesn't feel like being a diversion for them..

"Amen!" booms Father Wolfe. "Amen," the churchgoers respond in unison. All have learned fast since the priest's blustery arrival this year (and his wife Margaret's baking of the coconut cake that choked old India Bayh, thus inadvertently giving the church enough inheritance money to replace the old reed pump organ with the one Joan now plays) they are to be the cheerleaders on his team, not the stars.

Joan wills her stomach not to growl. Then she hears in the musty thick air a cricketlike chirp. beepbeep.

"His watch is off," Robert whispers at her side.

"Sh-h-h-h."

"Father Wolfe's watch. I just heard it. His watch is *off*. *Mine* is right."

"Robert, please– " she hisses without looking at him.

"I'm going to tell him, too. *Mine* is the correct time."

"Not *now*." but as Joan whispers to Robert she feels the first hot flashes of panic wash over her. Once in Publix this had happened to her and she had hesitated, sure she was going to die, fearful she would *not*, while people wheeled past her and she had to leave her cart as she bolted outside for some gulps of fresh air. The cart was full and she'd been ready for the checkout aisle, and the thought of the frozen food defrosting was all that forced her, panting to quiet her thumping heart, to go back inside.

The cart was gone. She had no strength to fill it again. She drove home and had to go back the next day. There's just no way Joan has ever found to say, "Well, I've shopped for food. Never going to have to do *that* again."

Okay. Don't think about food. The thought of food always makes her dizzy. Her heart is pounding. What would happen if she jumped up and ran down the church aisle? Just jumped up? She *could*. But—Robert– Robert would be so *mad* at her– and everyone is watching her—and Pete is standing there–

Beepbeep.

"*That* was mine. The correct one." She glances at him. He wears the smug I AM PERFECT look she knows so well.

"Please, Robert– " My God, Robert, look at me. Get me out of here! Give me your arm, help me up, get me out!

Robert drones on beside her in a loud whisper, "Mine is the correct time. Mine is set to Greenwich time."

In Joan's panicked state she thinks she hears him say "Greenwich Village". Why would anyone want to set their time to that?

"A priest without the right time." Robert sniffs.

At the word "priest" Father Wolfe glances over at *Joan*, not Robert. Of course. "Amen!" he shouts.

"Amen," responds the congregation, fidgeting.

Now the football mitts fall on the Baldwins' heads. Now there is no way out. Robert shifts, scornful, justified, against her. "Oh, Lord, we just want to– "

Oh, Lord, Joan prays silently alongside. I just want to get through this without throwing up on Father Wolfe's chausable.

God will forgive me, I know. But the Altar Guild will not.

✡ ✡ ✡

At the door Father Wolfe chuckles, shakes hands, remembers names, birthdays, horoscope signs, moves the parishioners smoothly along like a born-again religious politician and motions Robert and Joan aside. "Wait. I want to talk with you two later."

"Good," says Robert to Joan as they move off the sidewalk. "I want to talk with him, too."

"I need to go get Excelsior from the nursery– "

"No, you don't. There's Pete. Make him do something useful for a change." Robert calls to Pete, who has been chasing two other acolyte boys his age around the lawn, mindless of the heat. "Pete, go get your nephew." Pete nods and moves in that direction.

"Make sure you get his diaper bag!" Joan calls. Robert frowns at her. She looks at the ground.

"Don't forget!" Father Wolfe calls to the remaining people, "if the weather turns bad during this hurricane season, for you who live beachside, St. Barnabus' is your home away from home!"

Several older women nod. They come here every Sunday. They don't drive, and their husbands are forced to sit in steamy cars for an hour at a time, under the ancient water oaks dripping with lichens, while Father Wolfe blesses their wives, who ask him to " please pray for my spouse, who could use it".

"One hurricane we stayed at the elementary school," one of them giggles.

"I heard about that!" No one can top Father Wolfe for news. "Strong men passing out from the smell of all those dirty diapers in the trashcans. No TV for football games! Those undersized bathrooms!"

One of the women smiles naughtily, lips together, as Father Wolfe mentions bodily functions.

"Oh, there'll never be a hurricane here, not a bad one, anyway," says another woman, fighting to keep her hand in Father Wolfe's. "There's a sandbar off the coast of Banana Bay Beach that keeps the hurricanes away." She looks at Joan then and simpers. He squeezes her hand expertly—he knows how long he can do this without getting in trouble with the other ladies, wristwatch or no wristwatch.

"Well, now, any sign of trouble, you be *here*! In God's house!" The woman, eyes wide, glows as though Father Wolfe has invited her into his bedroom. She moves slowly to her waiting car and sweaty husband.

Joan watches, laughing to herself. Will the husband lean on his horn to get his wife to hurry? Would he dare? And if anyone can be described as having a deliberately "mincing walk", this woman does

☆ ☆ ☆

Now Fr. Tom Wolfe smiles genially at Robert and Joan from across his massive oak desk. The couple are squeezed uncomfortably side by side on the ancient loveseat in his church office. Enough people have sat like this that the springs have lost their bounce, and as a result her hip rubs against Robert's, who tries to move away, but there is no room to do so, and the priest has piled the only remaining chair full of books, apparently to get couples to move closer together and perhaps make up before he has to get serious and personal with them.

Not that he would mind, Joan thinks. It would be like a locker room talk. You two whom God has joined together—get out there and show everybody you're a *team!*

"I wanted to ask you," Father Wolfe leans back, his oversized leather chair creaking beneath his ample body, "if you have had any news about Susan." He pauses. Joan can see he is savoring the moment. He pulls himself forward, regards them above his templed hands and smiles. "Because *I* have."

She is stunned. Ever since Susan ran away from home over two years before, leaving behind an angry note and her yowling infant Excelsior for the harassed new grandmother to find, they have not heard a word.

"She's all right?" Joan gasps, watching his face. "She is, isn't she?" Robert has not stirred beside her, although she can feel the muscles in his leg tighten.

"As of a week ago, she was," Father Wolfe continues. "In fact, Joan, it was the day I found you in church crying your eyes out." My goodness. That was the day she had begun her journal at his request.

"I'd just felt kind of—bad," Joan explains to Robert before he can question her and derail the subject of Susan.

"Well, apparently she frequents the Episcopal food kitchen in Deland, and some people who work there know me. Long story short, they got out of her that she used to go to St. Barnabus'. When they called and described her to me, I realized it had to be Susan. Only– "

"What?"

"Well—she's changed her name. I guess she wanted it to be something like that funny one she gave her kid—she never *would* let me baptize him, by the way– " he looks to heaven and then back at us.

"That was her request, and I honored it," says Robert in a stony voice. As a former Baptist he would not understand the need for infant christening, to make the baby God's own.

At least neither one asks why Joan was crying in church last week. Otherwise she might be forced to confess to both of them that one evening while she was holding the baby, several weeks after Susan had left and Excelsior was running a slight temperature and had a stuffy nose—he was just beginning to develop that *eyebrow* frown that he does so much now—and she was feeling so sorry for him, and so guilty that she hadn't been a better mother to Susan—for wasn't most of Susan's letter a diatribe against the way she herself had been mothered?– , that Joan impulsively dipped a finger into her cup of cooled tea and baptized the baby right then "in the name of the Father and the Son and the Holy Spirit", and she gave him the name "Excelsior Robert Baldwin", in case he should ever want to drop that stupid first name when the kids laughed at him on the playground.

But of course she couldn't tell anyone, since Susan had screamed at her, "You always need to *control everyone,* Mother!" the day before she disappeared. And Joan guesses maybe this *was* a sort of control, although she didn't want her first-born grandchild suffering the torments of hell as a result of Susan's stubbornness. With Robert backing his daughter on this all-important subject, for heaven's sake!

Not that Joan for a second believed that this innocent baby Excelsior (dreadful word!) would go to hell. But she was brought up in an era where she was taught:

The Japanese during World War II are poisoning Coca-Cola and Pepsi, so don't ask for any soda to drink; and don't give me that look, either, young lady,or your face will freeze that way;

and she didn't dare try it and see; and

if she didn't hold her breath as she ran past the Catholic church on her way to elementary school, the priest and the nuns would come streaming out of the church, grab her and drag her back into their sanctuary and make her a Catholic; and

if she didn't step off the sidewalk when two nuns walked toward her, they could shove Joan off into the gutter; and

if she was a towhead (she was), she was destined to die young; and

if she didn't wear a hat in church, that was a sure and certain trip to hell.

"– Joan?" Father Wolfe asks. Both men are looking at her.

"Please try to pay attention," Robert adds, as though the two men have decided to counsel her together.

"Uh—I was wondering what her name is now."

"I wrote it down. She calls herself 'Vronsky'. V-r-o-n-s-k-y. Some kind of Russian name."

"Joan." Robert's tone is one of forced patience. "What does the name matter?"

"I need to know what to call her when I go to Deland and get her back."

"And what makes you think she *wants* to come back?" Now Joan knows that Robert finds the house quieter since the yelling, scolding, defiant Susan/Vronsky moved out, but Joan is not about to say that in front of Father Wolfe. Also Robert took over Susan's bedroom to make it his den and she is aware of how he cherishes that cave of his, even to the point of putting his own lock on the door and not giving her a spare key. And what if there should be a fire in that room and she can't get anything of Robert's out, although she doesn't even know what is *in* there, but knows she would be blamed for anything going amiss.

"Robert, she's our *daughter!*"

"Yes, and she may not want to be found." Robert stands up. "We've heard all we need to."

"Actually," says Father Wolfe, "I thought I might take a drive up that way. I need to go visit an old friend who teaches at Stetson, and I thought I could sound out Susan, see if she'd like to come back and reclaim her son, or something like that. At least I could find out her plans *for* you."

"*If* you can find her– "

"Actually, Robert, I think she *wants* to be found. She talked freely to the kitchen people and gave them the name of our church."

"Oh, Robert. We have to let him. We have no legal rights with Excelsior and if anything should happen to him– "

Robert abruptly heads for the door, leaving Joan to pull herself out of the loveseat-sinkhole. He nearly collides with Pete, who stands outside, struggling to hold the heavy sleepy Excelsior in his arms.

"I'll be glad to see what I can do, " says Father Wolfe heartily, laying his catcher's mitt hand on Joan's shoulder, just missing the orchid. He then takes Excelsior from Pete and hefts the child easily. He smiles back at her. "Nice outfit, Joan. I've been musing about it since I saw you this morning—*I* know! My wife Margaret had one almost exactly like it!"

Not almost exactly, she thinks. *Exactly. I* have it now. And I can't believe I didn't know who its previous owner was, of all people, and I wore it to church and Margaret saw me—no wonder she looked at me the way she did, with my showing up wearing one of her castoffs from "Wear It Again, Sam-antha".

Oh, well—another reason to envy men. They can all wear the same suit and nobody cares.

"I'll give you a call," Father Wolfe's football stadium bass booms at them as he stuffs Excelsior into Robert's unready arms. "Don't want you crying about your lost lamb any more, Joan."

As they leave the office Robert pushes the young child at Joan. "Well, I hope you're satisfied," he mutters.

"I don't know *what* I am," she says.

"Susan is old enough to be on her own and she can just come back, pick this"– motioning to Excelsior– "up, and be on her merry way."

Pete chugs along, bouncing as though he is practicing layup shots with a phantom basketball into the water oaks. "Susan coming back?" he asks.

"Maybe," Joan says. "Our prodigal daughter may return."

"The prodigal *son* didn't come back kicking and screaming against his will," corrects Robert. He can't help it—it's his Baptist upbringing. "And Joan," he complains in his lecturing voice now, "You made me forget to tell Fr. Wolfe about his watch being wrong!"

✳ ✳ ✳

And so it comes to pass that five days later Joan, wearing a Goodwill store tee shirt and shorts, mops the kitchen floor. The front door opens, and there stands her only daughter, her elder child, a little taller than Joan, wearing an Army-Navy man's jacket, jeans with holes in both knees, no socks, men's castoff oxford shoes, and stringy unwashed purple hair. She is enveloped in a rank mildewed smell.

Joan, startled, looks into her daughter's sullen mascara-ringed eyes and goes to hug her. Susan hoists a heavy smelly duffel bag—maybe that's the odor – like the inside of an old canvas tent that's been left out in the rain for days– and blocks her mother's move by holding it in front of her. Behind her Father Wolfe beams. Mission Accomplished. Kicked one right through the goal posts. A real Hail Mary, Episcopal-style.

And all she can think of at this moment is that Fr. Wolfe is going to have to air out his Buick.

"*Susan!*" Joan exclaims. This vagabond daughter stands there just as defiantly as she did when she came home from running away pregnant, dropping totally out of sight, turning up months later grasping an infant son, staring at Joan like an angry Madonna, refusing to name the baby's father or tell anyone where she had been all that time. Joan wasn't sure if Excelsior had even had his round of vaccinations.

Joan starts to ask her, "Susan– "

"Vronsky," she corrects Joan. "Where's Excelsior? You haven't spoiled him rotten, have you?" She assesses the older woman in the same cool way Robert does. "Mother. Can't you do anything with your *hair*?"

Susan could work as a spy, Joan decides. You could torture her and she wouldn't give away any information. And that purple– ! what happened to change my beautiful happy little girl into this alien?

As she goes toward the front door Joan remembers to thank Father Wolfe. In the driveway she spots Margaret sitting in the Buick, watching and listening, her car window down in all this heat, ready to report her findings to the E.C.W. ladies, and so Joan waves to the priest's wife—could these also be *her* clothes Joan is wearing this morning?– just as she hears an old familiar scream: "MO-*THER*! What have you *done*? Where the hell is the key to my *room*?"

Joan reflexively heads away from this noise into the kitchen, slips on the wet floor and lands hard on her coccyx. She senses Father Wolfe's arms helping her to stand up, but she is confused and limp, seeing stars for the first time in her life from the pain.

"Margaret!" he calls. "Come and help!" The front door opens. "Don't slip!"

Margaret Wolfe is only too happy to enter Joan's kitchen and see her in this damp dazed condition—could Joan Baldwin be *drinking* and so early in the day?, Joan can hear her happily recounting to those same ladies whose husbands stay in their cars.

"My stars!" she utters. *My* stars, Joan thinks. She may have even bitten her lip when she fell. Oh Lord, this had to be the one day in the entire month that she didn't do the breakfast dishes! And there are still crumbs on Excelsior's highchair tray.

Father Wolfe plunks her onto a wooden kitchen chair. The pain of sitting so heavily makes her puff like a woman in labor. "There now, there now," he soothes. "This has to be a big moment for you."

Margaret pats Joan's hand absent-mindedly, looking around at the same time. Joan can tell she is taking note of everything that is out of place. She's going to have a lot to talk about.

"Do you want a drink of water?" she soothes. Anticipation is written all over Margaret's face, to open every cabinet door like Pandora, to see what will come flying out. Secrets! What secrets might I find!

Joan groans.

Suddenly a Susan obviously bent on war comes storming into the room with a bawling Excelsior on her narrow hip, ready to accuse her mother of some crime, but when everyone yells, "Don't slip!" and she sees they are not alone, she backs away and even the child stops crying.

He stretches out his arms for Joan, crying, "Doan! Doan!" and stares at Margaret, doing that odd eyebrow-twisting look that Joan finds rather off-putting. Then he and Susan retreat and the front door slams. Probably going to light a cigarette in front of the poor boy and blow smoke all over him, Joan thinks.

"He can't say his J's yet, so he calls me "Doan instead of Joan– " she explains.

A choked gasp. Joan looks up into Margaret's face. Fr. Wolfe's wife appears ready to cry. "What– ?" Joan starts to say, but Margaret fans her plump hands in front of herself, her palms before Joan's face, her lower lip trembling, and runs out, too. She does not slip and fall.

The priest regards Joan and drops a now-familiar hand onto her shoulder. "Oh, Lord, we just want to pray that you heal this woman, your servant Joan," he intones. "We just want to thank You for bringing her beautiful daughter, a lamb of Your own flock, home again. Lord, we just want to– "

Joan just wants to lie down. But she knows how long-winded the Father's prayers can be. She could go to the doctor's and be back before he's finished.

And that is why he is not going to see this part of her journal.

She'll just call it a sin of omission.

☆ ☆ ☆

JOAN FORSTER 2011

TWENTY-FOOT HIGH NORFOLK ISLAND PINE CENTERPIECE OF AWARD-WINNING YARD:

The Yard-Of-The-Month award for May
has gone to Mr. And Mrs. John Applebee of 714 Sabal Palm Drive.
The award is given by the Banana Bay Garden Club
and Homemakers Association. Mr. And Mrs. Applebee
will proudly display the Association's placard for the entire month.
To make nominations, please call Mrs. James Porter
at PArkway 7-9595.
—*Banana Bay Tribune, June 4, 1977*

These old newspaper clippings show the innocence of the era. But oh, we thought we were the bright white middle class people then with all the answers: just stay married, have children, keep the house tidy, have dinner on the table and be there for our husbands when they come home tired from a long day doing something we have no idea what it is at the office, serve their needs, keep any bad news away from them, have sex when they want, because that is what good wives do. We actually believed owning and polishing a complete silver tea service was something to be envied. Back then.

I wonder if we actually knew any of these female paragons or if this was something foisted on us by parents, society and TV. I remember even back then how annoyed I was by Lucy Ricardo—she had to go behind her husband's back every time she wanted to do something he told her not to do, and at the end of every 30-minute show he was always smiling indulgently at her as though she was an irrepressible youngster– "What can you do with kids nowadays?"

Why couldn't Lucy stand up for herself, do something on her own? And yet in 1977 did I?

Quentin. Quentin is A Safe Husband. Safe, I suppose, is a good thing and could keep me living longer than if I had stayed with Robert—I truly believe I would be dead by now if I had stayed with him—but is there nothing in between safe and dangerous in a man?

Quentin's way of treating sex is safe. I have learned that he acts rather embarrassed that I have a body that I from time to time present naked to him. And I have needs, and a positive aspect of his denial is that nothing has to be done about the problem if one keeps denying there *is* a problem. Therefore *I* am not a problem.

At 74 (oh, do quit protesting that older people are sexless— just trust that someday you will be 74 and you will not be all dried up and crotchety) I guess I should be grateful that there are hands that every now and then respond to me. And yes, I know where those medical fingers have been all day. But sometimes my body recalls my early married years with Robert and yearns for some wild groping and touching and heavy breathing and not getting enough sleep.

We even sleep in separate bedrooms like polite roommates. He says he needs his sleep so that he can get up fresh for work. He says I snore.

If I don't leave him soon my tombstone will read "Joan Baldwin Forster (nee Gibson), beloved wife of Quentin Forster II, M.D."

But *am* I beloved? I feel more like a discarded item that goes ignored unless stumbled over, and then the stumbler looks down and says, "What are you doing there?"

I wonder if Quentin would actively protect me if I told him Derreck is trying to kill me.

All right then. Robert.

I hardly noticed Robert in high school. I had my friends, all good-natured competitive geeks (I don't remember what "geeks" were called in those days). We were "brains" and we knew it, reveled in it. We felt set aside, special in a test-taking, awards-winning way. All my friends knew they were bound for college.

All of them knew it except for *me*. I had a mother who programmed me, "You can be a nurse, a teacher, a secretary, or a housewife, Joan. Pick one. The world out there is a dangerous place for a female and those are your only choices." She had never gone to college. For her life was *dangerous*.

And just several vulnerable years later was when I started going out with Robert.

He was in one of my English classes, but he always sat at the back of the room, his long legs sprawled across the aisle so that any girl going past him would have to get his attention and then put up with some veiled-sexy remark until she blushed; his work accomplished, he'd slide his feet back under his desk before Mrs. MacMillan could reprimand him..

He had grown taller over the summer between our junior and senior years and his wrist bones showed, thrusting themselves forward from his pink shirt that was all the young men's style (with charcoal gray slacks and scuffed white bucks).

And then one cold Connecticut winter day he showed up at the schoolyard door in a double-breasted camel's hair coat, and my knees went rubbery as I stared at that coat. There I was, my nose running, my eyes watering from the arctic air, searching frantically in my coat pockets for a tissue, and falling in love with Robert at that moment—and all because of his *coat!*

I have searched my memory for that identical tan coat from my childhood and nothing comes to mind. My parents never had anything so fine, or any of my relatives. A dog? No, we never had a dog, let alone one that color. No, Father Wolfe, we never had a camel, either.

My father smoked Camels! Did I get imprinted to that coat and stay with that man for all those years just because my father had a certain taste in cigarettes?

"ZO, FRAU BALDWIN, NOW VE GET SOMEPLACE. YOU HAF FIXATED ON A *COAT.*"

No, Doctor Freud. Sometimes a cigar is just a cigar, as you so famously rationalized. Sometimes camel's hair is just camel's hair.

But oh, I loved that coat. I went weak when I touched that coat. The palms of my hands still carry the memory.

He saw me watching him and he came over to me. "You're in my English class, aren't you?" he said, slouching against the brick school wall and peering down at me through those beautiful blue eyes. I kept my hands clenched in my pockets, I was so crazy-needy in my desire to run them over the camel's hair.

"I'm Robert Baldwin."

"Everybody knows who you are," I stuttered. "I saw you run the 440. You were good."

"You have to have the legs for it." He looked down at mine, which were covered up to my wool skirt hem in knee socks. I had made narrow elastic-band garters to keep the socks from falling and to my horror I saw that the left sock had slipped out of covering the elastic, and the white elastic clasped my leg, as though daring me to cover it up again.

"You got nice legs, too. For such a brain. You always beat me in the English tests— "

"How do you know?" I asked, intrigued.

"I know," he said as the bell rang. I jumped and ran for the door. "See ya in English," he said, and was gone. I rushed inside to the girls' room and some toilet paper for my nose.

I was not alone in there. "Saw you talking to *Rob*-ert," said a tough-looking senior who played basketball and spent much time on the bench for shoving the other girls. "Better watch it."

"Why?" I asked.

"He's been around. *If* you know what I mean." I didn't. My facts of life at this age were spotty indeed. This is what I had learned, overhearing the other girls in gym classes:

(1) Don't fool around with boys and get them aroused;

(2) If you do, they will get mad and you will have to do something (I had no idea what) about it, because when you get them all aroused it's *your* fault, not theirs;

(3) Be a virgin when you get married AND

(4) If you are not, it better be because of only one boy, and you'd better marry him, ESPECIALLY IF

(5) You are pregnant, which is worse than death, because everyone counts to nine AND

(6) The boy is honor-bound to marry you and the two of you will then live happily ever after UNLESS

(7) He blames you for everything that has happened (refer to numbers 4 and 5) and then you'd better spend your life making it up to him, which will be easy to do, since when you go to college you are just passing your time until you meet Mr. Wonderful, anyway. BECAUSE

(8) A girl who is serious about a career is either a lesbo (I didn't really know what that meant) or someone who will never marry, which is also a fate worse than death.

(9) This last one is my mother's—if you don't understand what sex is, you won't do it, and none of the above rules will matter. Just Don't Do It (whatever "It" was).

Don't laugh. I didn't make up those rules. Those were the Eisenhower Era/ White Protestant America/Walt Disney Unwritten Rules of 1955.

Information was hard to come by in those days. My mother had hidden away a book about the facts of life, but when I found it and read it, I saw it was dated 1902 and had to do with "abuse" causing blindness. In eighth grade Sunday school class our teacher said, "We are going to study the Ten Commandments." When we got to the seventh, I raised my hand and asked what the word "adultery" meant.

She looked down and said, "You're going to have to ask someone at home." I looked down and never did.

Which is why when, in ninth grade, I did a book report on Hawthorne's "Scarlet Letter" and stood reading it in front of the class, flushing in quiet pride at the power I had for putting sentences together, Mr. Conlin, our instructor said, "Miss Gibson, what does the 'A' stand for?"

I stood there, baffled. I just thought it was the first letter of the alphabet. I looked at my classmates. They had frozen into silence. No one even giggled.

"Adultery," he said. "*Oh*," I said. There was that word again. I *still* didn't fully understand.

And *I* was one of the *brains*!

Anyway, Robert asked me out. We went to a movie—one of those black and white "Beast From Outer Space" movies, where the boy gets to put a moist arm around his date while she's screeching at the movie screen (and I did and he did); and then we stopped for an ice cream soda at the local dairy bar.

Mine was so cold and I was so nervous that I kept burping and hiccuping while he tried to kiss me in his father's Plymouth and then he ended up reciting poetry to me: "— they fold their tents like the Arabs/ and silently steal away", while the engine idled and the heater blew hot air at us and I worried silently about carbon monoxide fumes.

I had to have a second date, because he hadn't worn the camel's hair coat on this one. See, that was my mistake (see rule number 1). He wore it on the second date. He had his father's 1953 car again and he kept kissing me and I kept smoothing my hands on that coat, and then he said, "I want you, Joanie."

"Oh. " (What does that mean?) "Okay. I want you, too, Rob—Bobby."

He sat up and pulled away from me. "Only my *mother* calls me Bobby. Don't do that ever again."

"Well, sorry—how about– Robby?"

"I am Robert and that is all I answer to."

"Sorry. I didn't know– "

"Listen. I've got this key I had made, back when I was a Boy Scout, so we can go to the Scout cabin in the woods and be alone." He laughed. "Don't worry. I'm a good Boy Scout—I came prepared."

I swear to you that I *still* did not know what he was talking about, but we drove to a cabin down some dark dirt road—I couldn't find it again if I had to— and in the pitch dark with a tiny slit of moon the only light, he fumbled with the lock, opened the door, led me up some creaking wooden stairs in the cold cold blackness, lay me down on a narrow bunk, fumbled with my skirt and then I heard the tearing open of a package and felt something wet and cold and rubbery on my leg, while our breaths came out in frost and I shivered, my skinny backside chafing against a scratchy blanket.

Then, not talking, we got up and put our clothes back on. Robert led me blind down the steep stairs, and out into the car. He turned the heat up to "high" and tuned the radio to WWVA, Wheeling, West Virginia, while I rubbed my goosefleshed legs. "You can get this station at night when the weather's just right," he said. He sang along to "Ah got tears in mah ears/ from lyin' in mah bed/ somethin' somethin'/ when ah cry over ye-ew– ".

Was this entire evening a dream? When I saw him at school the next day the basketball player girl was talking to him. He waved to me and when we got into English class he said, "New movie's here. Saturday?"

"Sure," I said. I was feeling bruised and sore, but I didn't dare tell anyone what had happened in the dark cabin. What would I say? Who would I tell? I had several girlfriends, but we'd never talked about stuff like this.

There was no way to tell my mother. She might pull out that 1902 book and warn me I was going to go blind.

After the movie Robert pulled me to him. He was wearing The Coat again. "How about it, Moonbeam?" he whispered in my ear.

Again? We're going to do whatever we did *again*? I wondered. What was the big deal? What did people get out of this? In the dark all my senses were blunted. Years later I heard a fellow therapist say, "Don't ever meet a date for the first time in a bar: it's too noisy and you can't hear him; it's too smoky and you can't smell him; and it's too dark and you can't *see* him."

I knew exactly what he meant.

However, those two times drew Robert to me as "an item". We were now known around our small school as a couple, going steady. I basked in the warmth of Robert's 440 fame. He pulled his legs out of the aisle only for me when I walked past his desk. We went to the Senior Prom together, where he wore on his belt a long chain which he twirled as he danced alone in the center of the gym, everyone making way for him because that chain looked lethal, and I clung to the wall, not wanting to steal the limelight from him.

Then he hid me with his buddies in the parking lot while they drank Schlitz with Southern Comfort mixed in– -I tried a sip when they all taunted me and it tasted like pine needles and sap—me with the camel's-hair coat now around my shoulders while their voices got louder and louder and I worried about being expelled before I could graduate.

– then on to college in Boston together, albeit different schools—he was there on his parents' money as their only child, and I was there on scholarships as the first one in our family who had ever gone to a higher-level school; and two years later I had to give the scholarships back when I became pregnant with Susan.

Robert and I were married (again, refer to rules 5 and 6) and on our way home from a rushed honeymoon after a rushed visit to a justice of the peace in New Hampshire, because Robert was "damned if I'm going to ask my parents' permission!" and he was too young at 20 to get married in Massachusetts, although I was not, we stopped at a grocery store to start stocking our tiny apartment in an ancient Brighton four-story walk-up.

I remember buying a broom and feeling trapped and also exultant as I held onto the stick. *Now* I was officially married. I'd never have to do anything with my life ever again, except make sure Robert was happy.

I had no idea what "happily ever after" meant, but I had every confidence that I could do it. This was a test . I was good at tests. I was going to get an A.

I stayed in college, swaying in a B.T.A. train to get to classes and praying not to throw up until I could reach a bathroom. My dorm mates gave me a post-wedding shower and I added their dishtowels and cookbooks to my kitchen supplies. When it was quite obvious that I was pregnant I dropped out of school, silent with shame, guilt and embarrassment.

Robert, of course, graduated with respectable grades. I attended his graduation with toddler Susan on my lap, his parents beside me like the two silent lions at the Boston Library, grim-faced with me and then cooing-face with Susan.

Robert did not kiss me in public when the ceremonies were over. I did grab his hand and congratulate him, basking in the warmth of being married to a man with a B.S. in Engineering.

I wouldn't need a degree, I told myself. I could borrow my husband's.

Smiling, I held up Susan's chubby dimpled hand to be shaken by him. "That kid needs to be changed," he said, turning away from us with his nose scrunched up. Robert's parents took him out to lunch to celebrate. By then Susan was fussy and tired. They dropped me off at the apartment so I could feed her and put her down for a nap. They promised to bring me back a doggy bag from the restaurant.

At lunch they mapped out his future with him. Susan and I had become his passengers, along for the ride, which would not include my own car until we moved to Florida five years later.

Where I would meet Fran and my life would ratchet in a corkscrew upward, the way the ancient Egyptians had raised water from the Nile.

And where, a half-century before Derreck would shove me into the slippery algaed bottom of the St. John's River water (only ten driving minutes away from the civilization of Sam's Club and the Olive Garden!), and as I clambered on hands and knees away from him, knowing he *would* hold my head under water and trying not to swallow any of the muck while listening, heart pounding in primal terror, to the grunting of a bull alligator, I would not have time to theorize as to why I had moved to this barbaric tropical wildness.

✡ ✡ ✡

DEB PARTY:

Mr. and Mrs. Edward "Eddy" Comstock on Saturday evening
hosted a Mexican Fiesta in honor of their Banana Bay
debutante daughter, Miss Annabella Comstock.
About 30 guests, including Fr. Tom Wolfe
and his wife Margaret, enjoyed a lavish buffet
(all prepared by Mrs. Comstock) of Mexican favorites,
such as "American-style" burritos, tacos and nachos, followed
by banana splits and sundaes for dessert.
Mr. Comstock entertained the guests by dancing
an authentic Mexican Hat Dance,
to the delight of all their guests, on a sombrero
he had recently purchased at South Of The Border.
—*Banana Bay Tribune, June 7, 1977*

There are so many divorces in this county that one judge calls it "Engineer's Syndrome". Banana Bay is close to Cape Kennedy, which used to be Cape Canaveral, an Indian name. The (almost all) men who work at the Cape are used to half-hour lunches, talking to each other in their own private scientific jargon about technical problems, and working in clean white rooms where there is no dust allowed.

Then they come home from the Cape to discover that children are messy, wives are tired, and the knobs have been pulled off their stereo sets. This is such a shocking disturbance to the engineers' orderly worlds where all they have to do is shoot other men into space, that they divorce, moving out into tiny apartments, leaving behind angry ex-wives and bewildered children.

From their apartments consisting of bed, sofa, and a new pristine hi-fi set, these engineers leave once more for their jobs, secure that everything will be in the same condition in the evening as they left it that morning.

Sometimes a well-meaning do-gooder will introduce a divorced engineer to an available woman, and if the engineer is not careful, he will marry this woman with (he believes) the absolutely clear understanding that she will always be there for him and will take as good care of his possessions as he does. He remains fixed in this state of delusion until the day he comes to play his favorite record, and finds that someone has scratched the needle across its surface, causing irreparable damage.

It is then that the delusion takes a sneaky turn and the man begins to believe that the first wife was not so bad.... Please note that at no time is anyone talking about reality. The engineer spends his time in the Land of Theory and does not even own a passport allowing himself into the Country of Actuality, where change occurs and cannot be halted.

Robert and Joan had been married for six years by 1963. Robert was such an innovative engineer at Hamilton Standard in Connecticut that he was searched out by a headhunter and given an offer by a small research and development company in Banana Bay, Florida, a town they had to hunt for on a map.

At that time small research companies dotted the Banana Bay area. One aspect of engineers (beside their perfectionism) is that they hate to take orders from anyone; they are also convinced that they have something unique to offer.

So they, like little satellites, launch themselves away from the Cape to start their own businesses. In general they lack basic "people" skills, but if they can find the right office manager/financial adviser, then they have a pretty good chance of succeeding. *And* if nobody at home is ripping the knobs off their components and threatening their tenuous sense of control.

If there were an engineer's handbook, Joan would not have to be explaining all this to you. If someone had explained it to her, she would not now be writing all this in her journal.

✲ ✲ ✲

Robert and Joan flew to Orlando, Florida in a twin-engine plane, puddle-jumping from Jacksonville to Daytona to Orlando. At that time, there was no way to take a plane into Banana Bay from Connecticut without going through extensive re-routing delays.

She doesn't know why she remembers that her first view of Florida was in the Jacksonville Airport , noticing all the men in uniforms from the Mayport Naval Base lounging around waiting for flights out, bleary eyes glued on the many small black and white TV sets rerunning "I Love Lucy".

They landed in Orlando at noon on a sweltering hot May day. Robert rented a car and then drove as though he knew where he was going. However, his Boy Scout training failed him, since there were no shadows at noon. He was forced to stop at a gas station and ask the attendant, "Am I going the right way to get to the east coast?"

Apparently he wasn't, since the service attendant looked at him and doubled up in laughter, while trying to catch his breath and pointing them in the opposite direction.

"Goddamned idiot," muttered Robert, doing a dangerous u-turn on Colonial Drive. They passed the four-story Jordan Marsh, where inside (as Joan would later experience), women in hats and gloves were drinking tea, eating petite sandwiches, and watching a daily fashion show, the models moving demurely from well-appointed table to table filled with shoppers.

"Well," she said, closing her eyes against the already-brutal sun, "it's nice that the first person we meet in Florida has a sense of humor."

A dank rotten-eggs smell assaulted their noses as they entered town. "What in the world– ?" Joan said, making sure her car window was closed. They would find out later that the Indian River is actually a lagoon and amasses much algae at certain times of the year, resulting in an odor not unlike decaying fish.

This was replaced by the smell of tar which clung to the air as they checked into the Holiday Inn, Robert cursing and narrowly avoiding the heavy machinery busy four-laning U.S. #1.

In the lobby of the Holiday Inn stood three men dressed identically in suits and waiting for Robert. He handed Joan his suitcase and the room key and left with them, all four of them stripping off their jackets and chatting as they walked out into the heat.

She found their room and turned the air conditioning on full blast, then sat on one of the double beds. Joan thought of calling her mother to make sure little Susan was all right, but the idea of her mother's guilt-inducing voice– *Florida's the end of the world!* They have *alligators* roaming the streets down there and there are no shoulders on the sides of the road, so if you drive off the road, you fall way down into a *ditch*! Snakes! Snakes in ditches!; but Joan tuned her out, needing to concentrate on her rising panic and the knowledge that she had left Susan behind for the first time in their lives. *And* that she had no idea where Robert was going and when he would return. Another wave of panic engulfed here.

Before she could give in to it there was a knock on the door. She opened it to find a smiling young woman who looked cool and tanned in a colorful sleeveless sundress. She was Joan's age, Joan's height, and had already had four children, as was the large-family custom during this era. Oh, Fran!– she should have been wearing wings, like a guardian angel. She would become Joan's best friend.

"Those boys leave you alone?" she chatted easily. "We're gonna get a nice lunch and I'm gonna show you around Banana Bay. I grew up here, back when it was just a dot in the sand!"

For Robert, it would be the title of Chief Engineer and the inflated paycheck that decided him to move here.

For Joan it would be *Fran*. Fran, who mentioned casually, "Got your degree? No? I'm planning to go back to college in my spare time. Spare time!" She laughed. "We could carpool together."

"Down here?" Joan gasped, expecting this to be a collegiate wilderness. "Wh-where?"

"There's a local community college. It's not a bad drive. "

"Your husband lets you borrow his *car*– ?"

"You kidding? I have my *own* car." Oh, Fran, Joan's new hero, her Sacajawea out of the choking aloneness Joan had felt while polishing the furniture one more time or finding creative uses for leftover meat loaf. Even playing with Susan hadn't eased the solitary pain that she couldn't even put a name to. She didn't know much about women's liberation then, except that a Connecticut neighbor, hanging her clothes outside on a line and listening to Joan complain about boredom, took a wooden clothespin from her mouth and said, "You just have to get used to it, Joan. *We* all have."

And Fran had her own car! "But," Joan asked, trying to understand, "why do you want to go to college?"

Fran shoved her over a little on the bed, as though they had known each other all their lives. "Because, honey-chile, every woman is just one man away from being a bag lady."

"Oh," Joan began explaining to this stranger, "I have *Robert*." Joan smiled, remembering how he'd made all these traveling plans, how certain he was that Florida was their future, how nonchalant he was about leaving family and friends behind to further his career goals, how dismissingly he had waved aside her concerns about moving so far away. "See, so I don't have to worry about– "

"Hey," she replied. "Who writes the checks and pays the bills in your house? Do you have your own checking account? Do you have your own savings account?

Do you know how much your husband earns? When's the last time you took a look at his paycheck? Do you have your own car, or at least a driver's license? Do people call you by your first name or are you 'Mrs. Robert Baldwin'? Do you have a will? Do you know if he has insurance?"

Joan gulped.

"Does your husband order for you in restaurants, as though you're not allowed to give the waiter your order directly? Do you have to wait until he opens a door for you? Would he feel less like a man if you opened a door for *him*? And when you drive, does he sit in the passenger seat without correcting every little move you make? Can you initiate sex, or does it always have to be his idea? *And* do you know what you're going to do after your children are grown?"

Joan— she was Eve in the Garden of Florida and this new acquaintance Fran was bouncing an apple off Joan's head! She had never heard talk like this before, and she was both alarmed and curious. "Uh—one. I—we have just the one child. Susan. She's six— excuse me a minute, please." And Joan ran for the bathroom to sit on the toilet seat and put her head between her legs.

"Come on. We have a lot to see. I'll go get my car. It's out front. I'll turn the AC on for you. Your makeup looks fine," called Fran, knocking on the bathroom door. "I'm gonna drive you over to Banana Bay Beach, where Ken and I live, and give you a guided tour of some model homes, see what you like. There are some really nice ones for $29,000—aqua appliances, four bedrooms, three baths, two-car garages— . Then I thought we could toot up to Cocoa Beach and eat at Bernard's Surf, where the astronauts eat. Maybe we'll get to see one. Then we'll drive out onto the beach. You ever had fried conch? Oh, and key lime pie!"

In the little tiled room that smelled of chlorine, Joan's stomach turned over.

"I knew a woman at the Yacht Club," Fran went on, "who bragged that she'd spent the night with an astronaut. Then another woman said, "Well, lordy, who *hasn't?*"

Suddenly Joan screamed as something fast and green zoomed across the sink counter. "A baby alligator!" she yelled.

To Joan's surprise Fran opened the door and laughed. "Lizard," she said. "Lots of those around. Chameleons. They're cute. They change color to match the background. Don't know how that one would ever manage to turn *white* in here, though." She scooped it up casually and took it outside, where she set it down in the stiff St. Augustine grass. Oddly, the lizard fright had arrested Joan's panic attack and she followed her new friend on shaky legs.

"Now just you wait until you see your first *palmetto* bug!" She took Joan's arm in hers, patting her with the hand that had just touched the lizard. "Those guys can get *big*. Some of them stink when you squash them. And when you go to the beach, remember to wear flip-flops. If you step on a sandspur in your bare feet just *one* time, you'll never do it again. It's like stepping on needles."

Fran handed Joan her purse and motel key and Joan breathed in the hot fecund Florida air. Chameleons, palmetto bugs, sandspurs—what alien world had they entered?

You know how people remember the first time they got drunk or laid? *Joan* remembers the first time she went to the Banana Bay beach and stepped barefoot onto a sandspur. The pain brought tears to her eyes. Fran was right. And if she was right about sandspurs– that's when Joan really started to trust her new friend with her life.

Joan never did get used to the palmetto bugs.

"What—what's the smell?"

"Smell?" Fran sniffed. "Oh. Rotting algae in the Indian River. You get used to it."

They drove across the Indian River on a wooden bridge that seemed rickety, the boards slightly uneven, and stopped in the middle near a man outside a small building. " Opening the drawbridge for a barge to go through. That's a drum over there," Fran said and pointed, and they watched a crowd of people on the bridge who had all left their parked cars to gawk at an immense, grotesque fish that someone had just caught. "Those black drum, they're hollow inside. Got worms. Now watch the water and you'll see the mullet jump. Nobody knows why they do that. Some say they've got lice on their backs and they're jumping to knock them off." Joan held off on an impulse to scratch herself.

And sure enough there were fish hurling themselves up out of the Indian River lagoon and slapping themselves against it as they fell back . "Nobody knows why they do that," Fran said again, putting the car in gear to drive over the now-closed bridge– the metal mesh hummed under the tires. "And look up there." Again she pointed, this time to the north. "Raining there, but not down here. You can see it coming."

"You can see so *far!*" Joan exclaimed. Where she had grown up in Connecticut there were overarching trees hugging the roads, blocking out the sky. Here in Florida the sky stretched horizon to horizon, so big she could not take it in with one glance. She gaped at a small bushy island just off the bridge. An artesian well was shooting a spray of water high into the air as though it were a landlocked whale.

Fran looked over at Joan and smiled. "It'll be gone some day soon. These little spoil islands pop up and then they submerge. We could take a boat over to it and have a picnic when you come back. Nice, huh?" Joan nodded. Would that island be lizard-free? "Florida's a jungle. It's just polite enough to let us live here, as long as we respect it. But as soon as we're gone, the jungle will take over the streets and the houses and soon nobody'll know we were ever here. It's kind of humbling."

Fran caught Joan's stare at the trees along the road. "Australian pines. Not native. Shallow roots. They blow over in a hurricane. Don't worry about hurricanes, they come so seldom. Now beachside where I'm taking you used to be a sandbar billions of years ago. And billions of years from now it'll be a sandbar under water and Banana Bay mainland will be the beachside. You and I need to stick around and watch the fun." She nodded her head toward the river. "Bet you couldn't guess there are sharks not twenty feet from you."

Robert and one of the men who turned out to be Fran's husband Ken, a big loose-limbed guy who reminded Joan of a friendly Saint Bernard, came back early in the afternoon. Fran (mostly) and Joan had talked all that time. They had walked through several new homes with wet cement smells, jalousied windows and new (to Joan) terrazzo flooring. "Your feet will get bigger," Fran warned. "It's from walking on concrete instead of wood over a basement, like you have up north."

After the men arrived, Joan and Robert were given a tour through Fran's house, the house Joan was to know so well over the years. It was like the one the Baldwins would eventually buy, listening to Ken and Fran's advice about buying in Banana Bay Beach. "It's only a mile wide and not much bigger north to south, so you'll get to know all your neighbors. And good schools. There's talk of de-segregating."

Dinner while the sun was still shining high in the sky was full of new foods to Joan. She stared at the Florida lobster– "It doesn't have any *claws!*" and then wrinkled her nose at some slimy-looking green pieces of something strange in her salad.

"Avocado," Fran said. "You've never had *avocado?*"

Joan shook her head.

"Well, if you're not going to eat it– " and Fran speared a section of it from Joan's salad and ate it. "You'll grow to like it, Joan, I promise." Joan tried not to gulp.

Robert and Joan bought a new house on a short palmswept block containing thirty children, all shouting and playing in the road and yelling at the one teenager on the street, "Slow down, doofus!" when he made them run onto the prickly St. Augustine lawns as he drove by without putting on his brakes.

(Joan had only Susan at the time, Susan who learned to dash outside and play ball with the others, not even crying when she skinned a knee. Joan was embarrassed in the company of these people with their four and five children, that they might think she and Robert weren't even *trying*.)

Fran added again, "Down here you learn to *sweat*."

Permission to sweat! Of course Robert would have to wear more deodorant. And Joan's mother would never approve of this move.

Fran and Ken left them at the motel, promising to come back and get them in the morning and take the Baldwins out to a real southern breakfast with grits. Robert lay down on the bed near the air conditioner without taking off his shoes. "This is a good career move for me," he said.

"Oh, Robert," Joan said passionately, lying down beside him and sweating, "I want to go back to *school*!"

"You're nuts. A day with that talky Fran and she's got you thinking women's lib. She's good-looking, though, for someone so radical. She had *chipped* nail polish on her toes."

Joan hadn't noticed. "So how about it? What do you think? Did you know the schools down here are *segregated*? Fran says she's part of a committee fighting it. Would you help take care of Susan, so I could go back to school?"

"Forget it." He yawned and patted her hair automatically. " I'm not paying for something so unnecessary. You've got *me* for anything you need. We'll buy a house down here and that will keep you busy."

"We're leaving Connecticut?" Her heart sank—twelve hundred miles from home! "Is that for sure?"

"They want me as soon as possible. I might come down here and start working while you're up there packing and selling the house."

"Oh, Robert! I can't do that without you!"

"We'll get a realtor. Quit worrying. Think you'd never moved in your life."

"I haven't. Not far, anyway—" Oh. Joan groaned. Their first home together, their little Cape Cod. Robert and Joan had just papered Susan's bedroom in blue cornflowers. And what about all those marks on the woodwork beside the kitchen door to show their daughter's growth? And Joan had just planted zinnias. Wonder if you could buy wallpaper down here?

But if Robert had already told them yes, she'd have to move. To this jungle, so out of bounds, so incapable of being controlled. It was as though she could see in her mind's eye the vines encroaching on the roads as she breathed, the foliage demanding to reclaim what was naturally its own.

No more winters, no more white Christmases, no sanding the icy driveway, no dark nights when it wasn't even suppertime yet. Then she groaned again. Dad would understand. But *Mother*! How could she explain this to *her*?

"Robert," she said tentatively. He grunted, close to sleep. Joan tried to think of the many important things she would have to do before moving down to this tropical overgrowth of an area. "Do you think I should redeem my books of Green Stamps?"

There was no answer. Robert slept, probably already at his new desk solving new technical problems while she wrestled with the domestic ones.

✳ ✳ ✳

So back in Connecticut she hurriedly cashed in her stamp books, all eight of them, not yet enough to get the vacuum cleaner she'd been saving for. Then after they moved here she found out that the same trading stamps were being used at the stores in Banana Bay and Banana Bay Beach. This place just seemed so far from—civilization! They ate odd food down here: those yucky-looking avocados, for instance. Who would want to eat something a funny green and kind of – oozy? It took Joan a year before she would try one (and wonder why she'd waited so long).

Joan realizes that today in 1977 this reads like fiction, but she swears it's true: in 1963 if you were a housewife dedicated to helping your husband get ahead (and every woman Joan knew was), you wore your green-tinted fingers with pride. You weren't just pasting little stamps in books that became wet and curled before they were full and you could trade them in for crockery or a baby swing—no, you were serving your family and for all you knew, the economy of the entire *United States*!

(When Fran told Joan she didn't bother saving stamps, Joan was aghast. It was like discovering your best friend was a member of the Mafia.)

The downside to moving to a warm climate was that Robert never again wore his camel-hair coat. For *Joan*. There was never a need to wear it in Florida.

He just kept it to wear when he traveled north on business, which was often. Joan was spared, for some years at least, from knowing how many other women also found its touch alluring.

✳ ✳ ✳

STINGRAYS INVADE BANANA BAY BEACH WATERS:

Bathers can escape
the stinging tails by shuffling their feet
as they walk through the water, a technique
that sends the stingrays scurrying away.
Jack "The Jock" Wolfe, a Banana Bay Beach
lifeguard who was interviewed, agreed
with this, and also told swimmers to "bring
meat tenderizer to use in case of jellyfish stings".
Jack is the son of Father and Mrs. Tom "The Fox" Wolfe
and will enter his junior year at Florida State
in Tallahassee, where he plays third-string
football with the Seminoles.
—*Banana Bay Tribune, June 10, 1976*

Fran and Joan, after years of carpooling, finally in 1976 earned their Masters' degrees in counseling, and agreed to share office space so that they could cut down on expenses while they built their client base.

Joan gave that psychology major much thought. She had been an American Lit major at Boston University originally because she admired her roommate Harriet and that was *her* major. Now she was ready for something different.

So Joan thought about her life experiences and how adept she had become at reading Robert's moods and listening to him without interrupting; how she could ask him questions without trying to draw attention to herself, and, if he didn't want to ask her about her day, she figured he had that right, since he was the wage earner and was paying her an allowance. Her day wasn't that important anyway, she guessed—the usual laundry, dishes, cooking, ironing, stocking the freezer, studying, going to classes, taking tests, arranging for a babysitter, being pregnant with Pete and giving birth to him—women's conversation with which a tired husband should not have to burden his mind.

So, she listed her assets (beside breast-feeding, which she found she was good at, but which did not seem to be marketable outside of her superfluous milk the hospital took to help preemie infants thrive).

She had honed her talents though the art of housewifery.

She wrote down carefully:

1.   Listen and Be useful; Give Advice without appearing to; Multi-task;
2.   Pay exquisite attention to another's body language, words, facial expressions, tone of voice, posture, gestures;
3.   Ask questions without drawing attention to myself—not have to be the Center of Attention..

There was only one career choice (besides wife), given those qualifications, where Joan would be able to use the above talents—she should become a mental health counselor.

Also, Fran was her best friend and that was *her* major.

So they rented office space from Doctor Ernest Griffin, a middle-aged dentist regarded as being somewhat out of the mainstream because he told his patients that the silver fillings in their mouths were leaching lead into their systems and slowly poisoning them, and for a reasonable fee he could remove the offending amalgams and replace them with something safer.

Since he warned this to people while they were staring up at his buzzing drill from a reclining position, they nodded "yes" to whatever he was saying, and then they managed to escape without making another appointment, even when Mrs. Griffin, his office manager wife, phoned them repeatedly.

Doctor Griffin hoped to get a double benefit from Fran and Joan: besides collecting rent for a tiny room (which smelled faintly of eugenol) at the far end of his office, he wanted to offer their clients a dental discount if they would come to him for a checkup and teeth cleaning.

But Fran and Joan knew the grim-faced Mrs. Griffin to be a busybody and a snoop who could not be trusted to guard the privacy of their clients. So the two novice therapists agreed to see clients only on Wednesdays and Fridays, which were Doctor Griffin's days off, until they could build up bigger caseloads.

Mrs. Griffin's face grew dark when she heard these plans, since she wanted to find out whom the new therapists were seeing so she could report it in majestic glory to her bridge club, but she couldn't let Fran or Joan know her purpose; *their* plan included asking clients to park around back. Then nobody could see their cars from the street.

The clients only had to do this for two weeks before Mrs. Griffin, in a freak accident, tripped over her Pomeranian and broke her left leg, which kept her then at home furiously scissoring articles for her husband from his dental journals and recipes for herself from Better Homes and Gardens.

By the time she and her prize-winning dog were recovered she had lost interest in Fran and Joan, as well as losing her job, since Doctor Griffin had been forced to hire Mitzi Sommers, a pretty but dim young woman just out of high school to replace his wife, explaining, "I can't very well be answering the phone while I have my hand in somebody's mouth, now can I?"

Mitzi took no interest in the two therapists. Possibly it would have hurt her concentration on herself to do so. She sat with her back to the waiting room and even moved her desk so that Doctor Griffin's patients had to repeatedly ring the little bell beside the sliding window before she would look up from her movie magazine

No one in Banana Bay was too surprised when Mitzi and the much older Doctor Griffin took a trip together to St. Louis, calling it a "dental seminar". The incident flipped Mrs. Griffin into a close-mouthed bridge player and not as much fun as when she had been an established gossip.

✻ ✻ ✻

Oh, mea culpa—Joan was so ashamed of this fact of her new career : she only had *one* client. She kept this a secret from everyone but Fran. Robert would say, "I told you so," if he knew. Fortunately if he were to ask her anything about her practice, she was ready to simply say, "Sorry. Confidentiality."

Not that he asked. He had quit the group who had originally hired him and had begun his own company in 1976– "declaring my *own* independence, dammit. Thought they could tell *me* what to do." Joan stayed in the dark about his finances. All those questions Fran had asked her about financial education when they first met remained unanswered. If Joan had been forced to take a test in how Robert handled money, she would have flunked. For example–

ROBERT : "We're going to Miami. Get Susan to babysit."

JOAN: A vacation! "Oh, boy!" And then in Miami–

ROBERT : "See that shop over there? I've bought a motorcycle. "

JOAN: (stunned) "A *motorcycle*? What for? What about our *vacation*?"

ROBERT (pulling a leather jacket, helmet and goggles from the trunk): "You drive the car back home. Go under the speed limit and stay in the right lane. I don't want anything to happen to my MGB. I'm riding the motorcycle."

On the Turnpike—driving by herself on the *Turnpike,* dear Lord!– he pulled away from her while young women, their hair whipping in the wind, waved to him from their convertibles. He did, however, stop at the toll booth south of Vero Beach and pay the toll for the car. Joan had kept the MGB out of all accidents and had cut the speed down to 35 when a sudden thunderstorm had blackened the sky. She worried about Robert—was he *dead?* Rain-slicked road, a sudden skid, motorcycle out of control sliding under the wheels of a tractor trailer!– , but when they met at home, Pete jumping up and down wanting a turn to sit on the BMW seat, Robert was dry. Not even rain dared touch this impervious man. Joan's legs were so shaky from an attack of agoraphobia that it took her a few moments to pry her fingers from the steering wheel.

He kept upping the ante–

ROBERT: "We're going to Ft. Pierce."

JOAN (warily): "A vacation?"

ROBERT: "We'll take Susan and Pete."

JOAN: "Wonderful! I'll go pack."

ROBERT: "There won't be room in my car for anything extra."

JOAN: "We're taking the MGB? The kids will be stuffed in the back seat. They hate that. They– "

ROBERT: "It's a *treat.* They're just going to have to learn some discipline."

Then after a tense 90-minute ride, Susan hissing angrily in her mother's ear and Pete trying not to make any body contact with his older sister–

ROBERT (In Ft. Pierce, at an airport, pointing) : "See that blue plane over there? I've bought it. It's a Cessna 175."

JOAN "An *airplane?* But you don't know how to *fly–* !"

ROBERT (pulling his motorcyle helmet and goggles from his car trunk): "I've been taking lessons. Pete, want to fly with me?"

PETE : "Oh boy oh boy oh boy! Can I, Mom?"

SUSAN : "Hey! He gets to do *everything*! Mom, why can't I ever– !"

ROBERT (to Joan, ignoring her shocked expression): "You girls take the car back home. Stay under the speed limit. Stay in the right lane. Susan, make sure your mother doesn't take her eyes off the road. This MGB is going to be an antique someday and worth a lot of money. Meet us at the Banana Bay Airport where the private planes are parked. I've got a hangar there."

SUSAN : "Why can't *I* drive your car?"

ROBERT: "You are only fifteen. Be reasonable." He had now donned, Joan was startled to see, a pale blue silk scarf around his throat. He strode toward the plane, five-year-old Pete (her *baby*!) charging after him like a puppy.

Joan, tense and gulping air, moved into the driver's seat. The keys dangled from the ignition. Susan flung herself into the passenger seat and slammed her door shut. Joan fought another panic attack. She took some deep breaths and waited to stop shaking.

SUSAN (actually *snorting* in her frustration): "This is all *your* fault, Mother!"

And finally, four months later—

ROBERT: "We're going to Fort Lauderdale. Get a babysitter."

JOAN (on guard): "How come?"

ROBERT: "Geeze. How about some enthusiasm? You've been wanting to go someplace, haven't you?"

JOAN (gratefully): "Oh yes! Yes, fine! Thank you, Robert!"

ROBERT (at a Fort Lauderdale harbor, pointing): "I bought that boat over there. Sleeps six. I'm sailing her back. You bring the car. You should know by now how to be careful with it. I'll phone you when I'm back and you can meet me at the Banana Bay Yacht Club."

JOAN: "A *boat*? But we're not members—*Robert*! A boat– ? You don't know *how* to sail."

ROBERT (opening the trunk): "As of yesterday yes, we are members. And for your information I've been taking lessons."

JOAN: "But– " (This was said into the wind and Robert's back as he arranged a captain's hat on his head and marched toward a white sailboat bobbing in the water).

Did Joan spot someone wave to him from his new boat? She couldn't be sure, since she wasn't certain which boat was his. She sighed and walked around the car to the driver's side , where she moved the seat forward. She carefully adjusted the mirrors. She put her head down on the steering wheel and sobbed.

When she finally lifted her head and blew her nose, a white sailboat with the name "SEE LEGS" freshly painted in gilt on its backside was heading away from shore.

Somehow Joan just didn't have the same strength he did. Getting through school, every night before an exam she could count on Robert's starting an argument. An example:

ROBERT (standing in the doorway to their bedroom): "Where is my new shirt?"

JOAN (putting down her calculus notes): "It should be in the closet."

ROBERT (without smiling): "It isn't. And I need it."

JOAN: "Well, maybe it's in the laundry room. If it is, I'll iron it when I'm through studying. Okay?"

ROBERT: "Not okay. Seriously *not* okay. I *need* that shirt."

JOAN (her eyes on her notes, trying to concentrate): "Just give me ten more minutes– "

ROBERT: "I told you. I need it *now*."

SUSAN (sweetly, entering the room): "*I* found your shirt, Daddy. It was in the *dryer*." (smiling triumphantly at poor old confused Mother, who can't do anything right.)

ROBERT: "Well, good for you. At least someone is looking out for me. Jeeze, look at these *wrinkles*!"

SUSAN: "*I'll* iron it for you right now, Daddy. We can't bother Mother while she's *studying*."

JOAN (cornered, two to one): "Are you going out, Robert?"

ROBERT "No. But I need that shirt. Jeeze, does everything have to be about *you*? Boy, you'd love to have me out of here so you could do your precious studying. Well, just for that, I *am* leaving. You can have all the time you want to *study*."

Robert and Susan walked out to the hall, Robert telling Susan he'd pay her for the ironing job. Teenaged Susan, who tended to wear something once and then dropped it onto her littered floor or kicked it under her bed and then stormed through the house when she couldn't find what she wanted. Susan, who should be studying, herself, or she'd flunk another course. Susan, who looked at Joan a *little* too long with a trace of a smirk on her lips like a flouncy downstairs housemaid in a Victorian movie. Susan who smelled of tobacco, although Joan couldn't find any traces of cigarettes when she searched Susan's satchel while her daughter was in the bathroom.

One evening Robert got Joan so riled that she drove to class wearing two different shoes. Looking down halfway through class she decided she would tell people it was a sorority ritual if they asked.

However, since she was the oldest in her class and therefore rather invisible, no one did

Getting pregnant with Pete and then raising him to the age of eleven is why it took Joan until this year, 1976, to finish her courses to the level of Master's Degree, write an extended graduate paper on "The Personality Differences of Identical Twins Raised Apart". She thought this was an answerless subject, but since her instructor was a twin who compulsively believed his brother was his mother's favorite, she took it on, slanted it in his favor, and got an A.

Her one, her *only* client—Joan even disliked writing that name here: Annabella Comstock, the debutante college dropout who had already seen three other therapists in Orlando before her parents dumped her here—Joan thought, looking back, that she could have had more success treating an ax murderer.

Fran and Joan had joyfully decorated their office with a new beige sofa which Fran paid for until Joan could pay her half, a desk with separate file drawers that locked for each of them, a bookcase, a throw rug, a couple of inexpensive framed prints, and a comfortable dark tan leather therapist's chair. It made her happy to know that when she wasn't sitting in that chair, Fran was.

Joan liked sitting here and roaming around the room with her eyes. "Oh yes, oh yes—how nice."

The first time Annabella entered the office, she glanced around and then climbed onto the sofa, so that her shoes were on the seat cushions and her firm bottom on the sofa back.

"In this office, I don't allow people to sit on the sofa that way," Joan said to her, sitting in her/their chair.

Annabella sniffed, glared at Joan—oh, shades of Susan!— and shinnied down, planting her sneakers on an armrest as she shifted her slim young body into a pose of comfort.

"And I don't allow people to put their shoes on the sofa, either."

"You sure seem to care a lot about this cruddy sofa," said Annabella, amiably enough. "So can I put my *feet* on your precious piece of furniture if my feet are clean?"

Joan thought about this. There had been no mention of "feet on case goods" in any of her psychology books. "How about if you wear a clean pair of socks? Then I wouldn't mind."

"Shoot, I'll *buy* a new pair of socks every week if it gets you off my back." And that is what she did for the next interminably long year of Joan's life with her—50 weeks!—a million hours!— , holding up a packaged pair of white socks for the therapist to see, ripping open the plastic with a professionally honed manicured finger, slipping the sterile socks onto her size six feet, and shoving them onto the sofa cushions.

Now at their first meeting Joan asked the question she'd learned to ask, courtesy of the Psych 101 classes: "What brings you here?"

"Oh, *you* know. I'm bored with my life." Annabella yawned, peeked at Joan, and stretched her tanned arms up to the ceiling.

"Will you tell me about that?"

"Look, Mrs. Baldwin— "

"Ms. Baldwin." Joan hadn't learned some women's lib along the way without wanting her new title. The two fledgling counselors , heady with a degree, had even discussed getting their Ph.Ds! *Doctor* Baldwin! How impressive was that– !

"*Miz-z* Baldwin. Okay, here you are. I *have* to be here. My mother said If I don't get counseling and figure out what I want to do with my life, that my Daddy's going to kick my rear end out of the house, although between you and me he wouldn't dare do it. So. I'll come here and sit on your stupid couch and you can collect the money from my Daddy and we'll both be happy, okay?"

That might have been tempting if she had not been Joan's first (and only) client. But Joan wanted to put all those notes she'd taken in class after class to good use. "Look, Annabella– "

"How come you get to call me by *my* first name and I have to call you '*Miz-z-z*'?" This word was spoken through beautifully perfect white teeth that Joan was sure Doctor Griffin had never been allowed to lay an explorer on, but rather some specialist in Orlando.

"I'll be glad to call you Miss Comstock if you like."

"Nah. In fact," she brightened, "I've been thinking of calling myself by a different letter of the alphabet every time I come see you. That way I can keep track of how long we've been together: Annabella, Barabella, Carabella, Dorabella– "

Joan halted the 26-name recitation, although she was curious about the letter Z and if it would be Zellabella—no. Surely they'd be done here be done before they ever got to Z. "How come you left your last therapist?"

"Huh." Annabella seemed to notice Joan. She scowled. "He told me he was retiring. I didn't believe that for a minute."

"You think you have the power to make someone retire?"

"Oh, yes. O-o-oh, ye-e-s."

Joan felt exhausted and here she had only been working with her client for— she glanced at the clock—*seven* minutes!

She had underestimated Annabella, who saw Joan's glance and said, "So you're bored already, too, huh?"

"No. I wanted to make sure we have enough time."

"*Sure* you did. I can tell you already hate me." This was said in a detached manner. Seven minutes and she was already challenging Joan for who would be in charge, the way an expert fisherman would play a fish.

Well, Joan would show her this was one counselor who was no fish! "Tell me your interests."

"I'm interested in why you hate me."

"I don't know you."

"Oh, that's right. You weren't on the guest list for my fabulous debutante party, were you?"

"I read about it in the paper. Your dress looked very nice."

"It was a black top and skirt. I've already given it to the thrift shop. I need *much* more room in my closet. Anyway," Annabella waved the memory of the party away, "rest assured that when you get to know me better you'll hate me. Except I'm not going to let you get to know me better."

"Then I can't hate you." That sounded like a good double bind to Joan. Okay! They were starting to move along now. She picked up her notebook and pen.

Annabella grimaced. "Are you going to take notes about what I tell you?"

"Would that bother you?"

"Hell, no. I *like* people hanging on my every word. But when you hate me and I leave here, I *want those notes!*" Her sudden fury startled Joan, who tried not to show it. "Can't have you writing a book about me now, can I?"

"How about for now I don't take any notes." She laid down the pen and paper. Annabella smiled that lazy "I win this round" smile Joan would get to know so well. "So. How do you get people to hate you?" Joan asked, congratulating herself for asking this.

"Oh—I show up late. I say the wrong things and insult people just for the fun of it."

"Like– ?"

"Like– why should I listen to anything you have to say to me? You're only a waitress."

Okay, that one stung. Joan's face reddened and she imagined a pizza odor coming from her clothing as Annabella shot her verbal arrow and hit the bulls-eye. How to explain this to a rich man's only daughter? And was an explanation called for?

When Robert had refused to cover any of Joan's college courses, she had first sobbed and felt depressed until Fran found her a job as the only lunch waitress at the nearby Italian restaurant. Joan worked so fast between noon and one o'clock that she would afterward stare, dazed and flushed, at the several dozen tables full of dirty dishes left by the now back-to-work patrons. People had rushed in and eaten lunch and she didn't even remember serving them, the pace was so frenzied. And all this for a *quarter* tip per customer! And this, with piano teaching and church organ playing, got Joan through college.

Robert pretended she didn't work there. In the year she was working at Tony's he never once entered the place, although he would send Pete to get a pizza to take home once a week. Pete would smile at his Mom in her red-white-and-green apron and she would fill his pockets with quarters to take home and count. Tony, the owner, would present Pete with a piece of sugary Italian pastry, "All-a for you. Don't share it."

At least Pete had been proud of his mother. *Joan* needed to be proud of having done that work. It was honest labor. It had paid for her books and tuition. She had earned all those quarters so that she could now sit in this leather chair and not react to her only client, who had probably never held a job herself.

Annabella had made waitressing sound like something shoddy. Joan had to get the upper hand again.

Have you ever had to work for something you wanted, Annabella?"

"No and so what? Maybe I'll grow up someday, but so far I just like to have a good time. Hey, you know what I really like?" She held the question out like a bowl of water for a panting dog

"What?" Joan jumped at it, glad to be away from the waitress topic of conversation.

"*Roller coasters!* I go *cah-razy* over roller coasters. I want to go around the country and ride on every one there is. It makes me feel alive!"

Robert and Joan have not been on a roller coaster since high school, when an acquaintance of his dared him to eat five hot dogs in a row. Just thinking about it brought back the whiteness of Robert's face.

"Also, I like to drive around with my car full of junk. I have a suitcase packed for if I decide to take off on the spur of the moment, and I always throw my car keys in the back seat when I get out and then I have to hunt for them—like a scavenger hunt." She beamed at Joan—aren't I a good student, Ms. Baldwin? What're you gonna do with *that* bit of wisdom?

"Okay, so here's your homework for next session. Fill up a trash bag with the contents of your car, and look them over and decide what to keep and what to throw out."

"It's gonna take more than one trash bag. And that sounds boring. Besides, it's mostly old hamburger wrappers from Wendy's, old milk shake cups, that kind of thing. "

"Well—doesn't your car— *smell*? Doesn't that bother you?"

Uh uh. Joan, don't ask two questions in a row. It makes a client crazy, deciding which one to answer first.

Annabella apparently didn't notice. "Yes, it smells and no, it doesn't bother me."

"What if you want to drive your friends around?"

"What friends?" Now she put her head down and sniffed. Was that a tear? Had Joan gotten through to her somehow? Oh, how smart Joan felt! She was going to succeed where other, more seasoned therapists had failed!She was going to use her powerful intuition and make Annabella Compton all better!

But first Joan had to deal with a queasy feeling of agoraphobia. She could not shake the olfactory memories of Robert sick from the roller coaster, the greasy hamburger wrappers and old milk shakes mildewing the floor of Annabella's car, all threatening to make the therapist need to run out of the room.

"Listen," Annabella waved one foot in the air, around and around and around— "I hope we're going to talk about sex. I have a lot to say about it and maybe that's where my hangups are, but I don't think so, and why shouldn't a woman have the same freedom a man does, don't you think?"

Joan looked at Annabella's forehead. She had read that if you did that, the person you were looking at could not tell you weren't making eye contact, and she needed a moment to quiet her reeling senses.

"How come you're staring at my forehead?"

"Was I?" Okay, that didn't work.

It was then that Annabella gave Joan some free, unasked-for information. She was to learn that this was another trait of her client, much like the baited-hook trick: "I ride roller coasters because I haven't decided if I want to be dead or alive, and the ride makes me feel alive." She looked across at the therapist. She smiled— see how straight I'm being with you, Miz Baldy?

"Okay." Okay, let's get this out in the open. "Do I need a no-suicide contract with you, Anabella?"

"If you want." She shrugged. "The other guys did. I told them I wouldn't commit suicide. But so what? If I wanted to I would. Right now I don't want to. Probably never will." She held up her right hand. "Got a Bible here? Want me to take an oath?"

She held out her slim wrists. "I tried to cut these once. With a butter knife. I was just testing, to see what it would feel like." Joan studied them. She had two little marks. On the back of her wrists.

"And one time Daddy insisted I work at a nursing home and I took some old lady's pain medicine to see if it would kill me, but somebody'd been there before me and taken it already, and refilled the bottle with water." She saw Joan's startled look—Annabella knows how to *work*! "It was for extra credit so I wouldn't flunk out of high school. Daddy arranged it."

"What about the old lady—the patient? In pain? You took her medicine, medicine that was hers."

"Hey, it wasn't *my* fault. Blame the one ahead of me." There was no evidence of contrition on that young face. "So do you hate me yet?"

All at once a light flashed on in Joan's head. Borderline. Wow. She was going to have to do some fast reading. Why did the college make her take a *statistics* course and not bother much with borderline personalities? That was what Joan now suspected Annabella was. These were rare, and here was one as a first client. Borderlines loved you or hated you. They didn't just *dislike* you. They actively *loathed* you. They didn't just *like* you. They craved to inhabit you, to *possess* you. And they could turn on a dime between those two black and white emotions.

Maybe Joan could ask Fran for her insights before next week and Annabella's next session. They were supposed to start their careers easy as therapists, maybe talk with somebody who just wanted to change jobs or move someplace else. Not a *borderline*. Borderlines could squeeze the life out of you like a python taking your last breath away.

Now inwardly Joan shuddered, betting the last counselor hadn't retired. Oh no. He'd simply changed his name and gone into hiding after a few sessions with Annabella. Might she have to do the same?

"So, hey." Annabella leaned over and removed the socks. She got up and tossed them carelessly toward Joan's wastebasket. "This was fun. Maybe we could do this *twice* a week."

FELINE FLIES ITS COOP; AIRLINES SENDS IT HOME

The passengers aboard Eastern Airlines Flight 423
got free drinks and the Alberts got a free bottle of wine
after the Alberts' cat Irving was discovered wandering
in a Connecticut airport.
The plump Himalayan cat escaped from his carrying case
while being placed in the cargo hold of Flight 423
from Bradley Field to Banana Bay. That delayed the flight
more than an hour, sent airport workers on a frantic feline
search and gave Irving's owners, Mr. And Mrs. Frank Albert
of Banana Bay, a big scare.
Irving was allowed his own first class seat
as a result and flew home with his owners—
in a carrying case, but this time by a window seat.
—*Banana Bay Tribune, July 1, 1977*

T hat's the flight Joan's mother took, which brings her to the Baldwin home for the first time since Robert and Joan moved to Banana Bay Beach in 1963.

"I've never *had* such a frightful time!" are her first words. It is fortunate she is talking, because Joan is shocked to see how old and thin her mother appears. Gladys has always been compulsive about dieting, but this seems a very unhealthy weight for her to be carrying. When Joan hugs her she feels bony, almost wispy.

"You know I'm allergic to cats," Joan's mother goes on as her daughter and a silent Pete pick up her luggage—matched, white, with thick clear plastic zippered liners to keep the pristine suitcases from being scuffed—like plastic slipcovers on the sofa in the seldom-used living room when Joan was young.

"Irving," she scoffs as she follows Joan to the car. "Who names a cat 'Irving'"? She stops. "Where is Robert?" She turns around and notices Pete, who has been trudging in her wake with one of the suitcases. "Peter," she says, holding out her hand. "I am your Grandmama." She gives it a Gallic pronunciation. "You must never call me by any other name." Pete looks away and digs at a sore spot on his hand.

She scowls at Joan. "Is he—all right? Nothing—slow about the boy?"

"He's just a little overwhelmed," Joan says, smiling at Pete, who hasn't wanted to come. "He's never seen you before."

"Well, *photographs*, to be sure—you shouldn't have moved so far away." She settles herself into the passenger seat. Pete scoots into the back seat and buckles his seat belt. Joan reaches across her mother and fastens hers.

"Well, if you're driving I suppose I'll have to use this thing. It doesn't leave a mark on clothing, does it? And when did *you* learn to drive? I suppose I'll have to get used to *that,* too."

She looks ahead, lips pursed, at the palm trees. "Well, I guess I'll just have to get used to a Fourth of July without any hometown parade." Her voice shakes a little. "You can't have everything you want."

At home Pete becomes talkative showing her around. "This is the guest bedroom. We changed the sheets and there's a blanket if you need it. You'll have to share my bathroom, but I'm mostly out playing." Joan's mother Gladys does not answer him. She looks around, but does not seem to be taking anything in.

What is wrong here? She seems so—old. Well, of course she *is.* Joan is 43, so that makes her– 69. At this time 69 sounds quite aged, although she knows 80-year-old women in Banana Bay who exercise by walking together around their neighborhood every morning. Maybe Mother would want to join them.

Maybe not. Joan thinks of her tripping, breaking a hip, and being laid up with them for months.

Pete, ever-helpful now, keeps introducing Gladys to the house. "That's Dad's den that used to be Susan's room, and this is the one I share with The Shaver—I mean, Excelsior." Joan's mother clucks disapprovingly. "I call him The Shaver because 'excelsior' means 'shavings', even though Susan says it means something else. Mom and Dad's room is on the other side of the house. You can get in the swimming pool from your sliding glass door here—see?– and I could show you where I fish off the causeway, and the beach– "

Pete is acting as polite as an adult. Joan feels proud to be his mother. *Her* mother, however, ignores his talk and says, "I could use a drink before dinner. Make me a Scotch and water while I freshen up."

Pete and Joan stare at her narrow back as she turns toward the guest room. "Is she your *real* mother?" Pete whispers. "'fraid so," Joan whispers back.

She mixes two drinks, the weaker for herself, and checks the dinner. Mother is planning to stay with them for two weeks. Joan wonders now why she had agreed to that much time. Maybe she felt guilty about only seeing her mother twice a decade (at her mother's Connecticut home, where she always greeted Robert and Joan tearfully and said good-by the same way,) since they had moved down here.

You know what's funny, Mom?" Pete says. "She doesn't seem interested in anything. I mean, she's never been to Florida and never seen our house, and she's never met me—"

"Don't take it poysonally, kid," Joan fluffs up his hair and talks cartoon-style to him. "When she gets a load of Excelsior she'll go nuts. No, actually, she's always been this way."

Gladys enters the kitchen."So what have you done with Robert? I need to have a talk with him." She takes a cigarette from her pocket.

What about? Joan wonders. "He took Excelsior and they went to get the oil changed in his car. They'll be back soon. And Mother—we don't allow smoking inside." With relief, turning from her mother's disapproving look, she hears the garage door open and close. "And there they are now."

Robert enters the house with Excelsior on his shoulder. Mind the child!, Joan thinks, running to hold the youngster's head down, the way the police do when they load a suspect into the back of their car, to make sure he doesn't hit his head on the top of the door frame.

Three-year-old Excelsior pounds on the back of Robert's neck :"Fwench fwies! Fwench fwies!"

"You let that child eat French fries?" demands Joan's mother as she kisses Robert and carefully pats Excelsior, who looks grimier than usual. The child frowns at her and bursts into tears.

"Where did he get that dreadful habit of moving his eyebrow like that?" Gladys demands to know.

"He just sees TV ads for French fries." Joan picks up the howling Excelsior from the floor, where Robert dumped him when he started to cry. "I'll give him a bath and some supper."

"Good." Joan's mother waves her hand at Pete and picks up a drink. "You go with your mother, Peter, that's a good boy. Your father and I need to get re-acquainted."

Excelsior calms down in the warm bath water. "Can I go find my friends, Mom?" Pete asks. "Half an hour," Joan answers. "Then come home for dinner."

"Hey, Shaver, look at that <u>water</u>! You got yourself as dirty as Pigpen!" Pete runs out as Excelsior dutifully looks down and splashes Joan, who picks up the squirming boy and, pushing her nose into his chubby neck, sings, "Who's a good boy? Who's a good boy?" while the child yawns and clings to her. She decides she'll give him oatmeal for his supper, with a banana—easy-to-eat foods, since he is already drooping with fatigue. Mother doesn't seem inclined to socialize with him tonight, anyway. And she hasn't asked anything about Susan, which means she will spring the subject later when Joan is at her most vulnerable.

Joan suddenly wonders if Mother suffers from agoraphobia too. Maybe it's inherited, the panic attacks!

When Dad came for a visit she refused to come with him—afraid of leaving home?

Mother and Robert are sitting on the screened-in patio, the ice tinkling in their glasses. He is leaning toward her, trying to make her understand something—what? Joan feeds Excelsior, gets him ready for bed, and lays him down in his crib. They'll have to get him a bed. He's too big for this crib now.

She kisses him good night. She hears the door slam and knows Pete is back home. She finishes making dinner. She has the start of a headache. She yearns to be be sitting with Fran, talking with her, taking comfort from her common sense. She'll have to find some private time to phone her friend.

"Joan," says Mother at dinner, pushing a meager amount of food around on her plate, and refusing seconds– "I've asked Robert to help me with some business dealings. You know it takes a man to understand these things."

Robert eats methodically, not even nodding agreement. He has recently joined a bicycle club and is using this means of exercise to stay in shape. Joan notices that the back of his head is losing hair.

After dinner Joan does the dishes while the two other adults resume their talking. She knows Mother had resigned herself to Joan's marrying Robert– "I like him, even under *these* dreadful circumstances that you brought upon yourself, Joan,"– meaning the pregnancy with Susan– but this is something new.

Gladys has had a second drink during dinner and now Robert is mixing her a third. "Do you think that's wise?" Joan asks him quietly.

"She *knows* what she wants, Joan," he answers. "And by the way, I'm going back to the office tonight."

"By the way, I'm going back to the office" has become something of a family joke. Pete and Joan hike their shoulders up in an exaggerated way when Robert starts a sentence with "By the way– ". He doesn't think they're funny, sees it as their ganging up on him. "*Somebody* has to earn a living around here," he says sternly.

Now he frowns at Joan's facial expression of disappointment. "Do you good to sit and talk with your mother, Joan. You don't need me for that. " As he heads for his car, Joan hears her mother's alarmed call, "Joan! Joan ! I think I heard an *alligator* in your yard and it could be heading for your pool!"

Thirteen days to go.

She tries inviting everyone they know for a Fourth of July picnic. All have other plans. Joan had hoped someone would come magically along, lift her mother from this funk she is in, and (truthfully) give Joan a breather.

Even Annabella lets her down. She is going scuba diving in Acapulco with her parents– "Like I need to be anywhere *near* them. But they'll pay my way and I'll go out to the bars at night. God, your mother must be a *saint*. How do you stand to be around *anyone* old for two weeks?"

Joan studies her client, wondering if she herself is included in the "old" category, but Annabella is busy buffing her nails and shoving those feet in their brand-new white socks into the sofa cushions.

Joan knows things have gotten desperate if she is looking for Annabella's company, even for an hour a week. She can't get away from Mother long enough to visit Fran, and if she tries to talk on the phone, Mother listens in. Fran is busy with her four, anyway, and in charge of the vacation Bible school at her church.

"What do you do for enjoyment around here in this godforsaken land?" Mother asks. She sits at the kitchen table, having refused to help with the breakfast dishes. She had come out to breakfast late and had not allowed Joan to make her a meal. "Just toast and coffee," she says. "That's all I ever have."

Joan dries her hands. "You haven't asked me about Susan," she says, taking a deep breath. In this case she figures a good offense is better than being caught off guard.

"I asked Robert. He told me how you *chased* her away and made her abandon her baby. Do you think I want to sit here listening to your story, letting you fictionalize what you did?"

"But that's not at all what happened– !"

"You forget I know you. You have been self-centered all your life, Joan."

"How can you say that?"

"When your father and I were ready to go to Bermuda, who cried and carried on and wouldn't let us go have a good time?" She goes on in a high-pitched voice, 'I want my mother! I want my *mother*!'"

"I had *measles!* I was *sick!*" Joan is sounding like an eight-year-old again despite herself.

"We had a perfectly good babysitter for you. But no, your father sided with you. Ruined a perfectly planned trip."

"I'm sorry– ."

"You have such a good husband there and you treat him like dirt, running off at night to class, trying to compete with him earning a living." She wipes at her eyes. Joan thinks about her one client and the fact that she paid for her own college education. "Oh, I miss your father. I *know* what a good man is like. I should have died with him."

She points a thin finger at Joan. "You know you drove him to an early grave. You made him go out on that awful night and get you some medicine. You could have waited until morning, but oh, no. And then he comes down with a cold and the cancer followed right behind– "

"Now, that's just not fair. When he came down here three years ago he was fine. We went to Disneyworld together and had a great time." Where had all the woman's quiet venom come from? Had Gladys harbored all this resentment toward her daughter for years? "You could have come with him."

Gladys sniffs. "As if he'd want *me* around, with you to joke with. And I had no need to spend time with some silly cartoon characters."

Joan now smiles, remembering—Dad at Disney. February, 1973—she can still hear his voice:

"Come *on*, Joanie, let's go. Who knows when we'll get this chance again?"

"But Dad, it's cold out. It's raining– "

"So? We'll have the place to ourselves. You get the car out and I'll get the umbrellas. One for Pete, too."

"Pete? He just went to school!"

"We'll pull him out. It's a holiday– Grandpa time, eh?"

So Joan, her father and an excited Pete joined the cold wet crowd at Disneyworld. Their sneakers were wet through by the time they reached the Haunted Castle. The two males read the fake tombstones together. "This's the one, Pete, old boy! This's the place I came to see!"

He exclaimed about the elevator, imitated the spooky sounds around them, and insisted on sitting by himself in one of the black moving hooded chairs. The line of soggy people separated Joan and Pete from him and they flung themselves into another chair five seats behind.

Well, at least she could sit and relax for a moment. Her father was as thrilled as Pete to have this adventure, Pete acting as guide to point out the sights. They had gone through "Small World Adventure" twice before Joan's father had reluctantly opted for another, different ride.

But— something was wrong up ahead, she thought as they disembarked their Haunted Mansion ride. Disney attendants were scurrying back and forth, herding curious sightseers to the exit. The moving chairs had halted. When Joan and Pete walked forward, she looked inside the first chair—and to her horror there was her father, his head back, his eyes closed.

Joan panicked. "That's my *Dad*!" Oh Lord, had the scary parts of the ride actually given him a heart attack and *killed* him? "Is he—dead?"

Before Pete could start crying, her father opened his eyes and grinned. "Surprise!" he said.

There was an instant change in mood as the Disney attendants switched from caregivers to betrayed victims. "Get out!" one ordered (Joan didn't think they were allowed to show anything but toothy happiness) with a warning: "– and don't you *ever* come back here!"

"Well, *that* was fun," her Dad said in an unrepentant chuckle, striding beside her as she, redfaced and humiliated, opened her umbrella. "Right, Pete? What'll we do next?"

Pete looked up at Joan as if to gauge what his response should be. He tried to hide a grin.

"Dad, I have to *live* here."

"Orlando?"

"In Florida. What if they recognize me and kick me out the next time Pete is with me?" There was a frown from Pete.

"Joanie, Joanie—you care too doggoned much about what others think of you. Don't get like your mother now. You inherited your sense of humor from me, y'know. And– wasn't that even a *teensy* bit hilarious?" Then he did a little Gene Kelly and umbrella dance in the rain.

"But– ," Joan could not let him off the hook yet– "why did you pretend you were *dead?*"

"Oh—just practicing for the future, I guess." He began to sing in a loud voice, "It's a *world* of *laugh*-ter– ".

She moved away from him. He continued to sing, "*It's* a *small* world *after* all– " and a group of tourists joined in. The brain-boggling words and tune followed her all the way to the Country Bear Jamboree.

Pete came back from school the next day: "They gave me an unexcused absence."

Joan was surprised. "Because you'd been to Disneyworld?"

"They said if I'd been sick it would have been excused."

"So if your mother had *lied* they would have accepted that?" Joan's father looked ready to do battle to save his daughter and grandson.

"Guess so." Pete looked at the floor.

"Well, here's a conundrum—a puzzle, Pete. What should your mother do then—lie or tell the truth?"

"Well—Mom never lies– "

Joan's face flushed at this. Her father nodded. "Right. Be like her. That's the way to be. Integrity is worth an unexcused absence."

"But—weren't you lying to the people at the Haunted Mansion when you pretended to be dead?"

Joan's father studied his grandson seriously. "The important thing is—I wasn't lying to *myself*."

Joan blinks. Gladys is scowling at her, using an unlit cigarette as a pointer:

"– as I was saying, Joan– I got a letter from Susan. Oh, yes– you're surprised, aren't you? And there I was thinking of coming down here finally, even though you *know* how I hate to fly. Then I got the letter from that poor girl, and I could almost see tear stains on the pages! At least she knew where she could turn, poor lamb. You remember how I took such good care of her when you ran off to Florida to force Robert to move away from me, to pressure the people down here to give him a better job."

Joan feels as though she is flying a plane into a 45-degree wind and has to keep adjusting for the weather in order to get straight to her destination. (Robert, mentioning his ground school lessons, had explained that much to her.)

"Mother, Susan had a fight with me the day before she ran away, but I can assure you it was nothing out of the ordinary. She argued with me a lot. She was a teenager."

"Nothing out of the ordinary for you, perhaps. But did you ever consider that she might have been suffering from post-partum depression?"

Joan considers. Joan has never seen Susan down and discouraged. She is more like a rubber ball that you can't hold under water. As soon as you let go it's sproing! to the surface.

"Okay, Mother, now wait just a *minute*!—Excelsior was almost a year old! She was out most nights drinking and seeing I don't know who– "

"Whom. She wrote that you changed the locks on the doors."

"I sure did! She had some scruffy friends on drugs, and she kept losing her house key, and I was afraid they had stolen her keys and Robert traveled a lot and we were all going to be murdered in our beds while he was out of town. So I asked her to knock when she came home, no matter what time, and I'd let her in."

Shut up, Joan, shut up. Pull yourself together and quit acting like a schoolgirl being questioned by the principal.

"Well," her mother says, a tiny smile playing at the corners of her mouth, "we won't talk about it any more. I can see how it all upsets you."

"What upsets me is that I am your daughter and you aren't giving me any credit for the hell that went on around here– !"

Gladys puts a finger to her lips, the little smile a bit bigger. Now that she has passed her emotions on to her daughter and Joan is more passionately involved than she, Gladys can sit back and let someone else handle the feelings of frustration for both while–

– while she can stay calm. *Robert*! Joan suddenly realizes. Robert is also good at doing this. And Susan, *and* Annabella. Joan thinks, what is she, an emotional lightning rod for people, a sponge, a piece of damned *Velcro,* that others' craziness should stick to her while they walk away unscathed?

Joan takes a deep breath. "Mother," she says, "I'm curious. Are you aware you're siding with someone who is not here? And not siding with me, when I *am* here?"

The response is a surprise. Gladys sniffles and tears fill her eyes. "Oh, yes, pick on me with your psychological jargon. You and your father were so good at putting your heads together together against me." She lets a few tears fall. "Oh, I miss him so much! I don't know how I've gotten along these past few years." She dabs at her eyes again with the paper napkin she had placed in her lap to catch toast crumbs. "At least I've had Robert to confer with– "

"Robert? You've had *Robert*?" It is Joan's turn to be surprised

"I will not say anything more. I can see I've upset you. Robert told me you were easily upset these days." And before Joan can respond, Excelsior runs into the kitchen and throws his arms around her legs.

"Doan, cookie, Doan. cookie!"

Joan's mother arches an eyebrow at her daughter and nods—you've confused this child, also. Joan kneels down and picks him up as Gladys walks ramrod-stiff from the room. Excelsior takes Joan's chin and moves it so their eyes met.

"Doan—look." He holds up his two index fingers. She sets him down and gets out the package of butter cookies, each round and scalloped with a hole in the center. Joan takes two cookies from the package and rings one on each outstretched finger. He grins and takes off for the screened patio.

"Watch out for all those alligators," Joan murmurs.

She takes a cookie and sticks it on her thumb. This might prevent her from sucking it, which she very much wants to do at this moment. The cookie smells like vanilla and tastes soothing. She can hear her father's voice: "Don't argue with her, Joanie. I've found it's easier that way."

✡ ✡ ✡

Gladys Gibson walks out of the kitchen, away from her daughter and her great-grandson (she refuses to admit to anyone she has a great-grandchild—it makes her sound so *old*) and is around the corner and out of sight before she has a spell of dizziness. She leans against the hallway wall to catch her breath. She listens, but no one comes to look after her. Not that anyone would. You have to take care of yourself, because nobody else will. And didn't her own husband up and die and leave her?

She decides that perhaps she will concede to her doctor and try doing something about her shortness of breath, when she gets back home. Although she knows there is absolutely nothing wrong with her. It is just that family members *arguing* with her always get her so unnerved. All their fault.

She decided long ago to trust no one but Robert, Robert who is so kind to her, who takes her out to dinner and drinks whenever he is in town, who shows up in his expensive suits and his camel's-hair coat that reminds her of some movie star, and doesn't she enjoy sauntering into a restaurant on his *arm*!, who just hated to ask her for money, it was against all his principles, but he wanted to start up his own business and he had some phenomenal ideas to make them all rich, and it was just a matter of time, and with what her husband had left her—Gladys, after several drinks had bragged about how he had left her a millionaire- -surely $500,000 would multiply itself and make her a *multi*-millionaire!- only he is having trouble paying her back and she needs the money now, but he is so kind saying he will get it to her as soon as possible.

But now she is having her doubts—no, don't think that. He is her only hope.

She should never have come.

※ ※ ※

On the plane back to Connecticut she feels faint. Probably a little constipation, the way her daughter cooks. Nose twitching, she pushes her way up the narrow aisle to the unoccupied bathroom, where she sits down amidst the roaring airplane engine noise and dies. A stewardess finds her and quietly alerts a doctor she knows is on board, who pronounces the undernourished elderly woman dead of an apparent heart attack. They both agree to leave her where she is and not distress the passengers.

The young stewardess, excited that she will have a story to tell her buddies in the bar after they land, leaves the "occupied" sign on to deter the other passengers from using that bathroom until the plane is on the ground at Bradley and they can notify the next of kin.

* * *

Robert hides his feelings of elation from Joan. He is suddenly, providentially free of the obligation to pay Gladys back!

Outwardly he shows his wife proper behaviors, such as patting her and offering to take them all to MacDonald's, so Joan will not have to make dinner the night she is informed about her mother's death. And can't she see how happy he is making Pete and Excelsior at dinner, letting them choose anything they want, even French fries which his wife for some strange reason never lets them have, while Joan looks out the fast-food restaurant window at the darkening sky and weeps.

What *really* matters, what matters above all else, is that the money is now his. Never to have to pay back.

He should, he decides silently, take the entire day off from work on Gladys' funeral day, to be held (convenient for him) in Banana Bay. Not out of respect for his mother-in-law so much as the fact that Joan has asked him to be by her side, and this is a trump card he can use in the future with her if he needs. He is sure any business associates watching him at the graveside will understand his not working that day.

Maybe if Joan and Father Wolfe decide on a service early enough in the day, he can get in a little sailing. The weather should hold. Morning showers maybe, but no thunderstorms building up until late in the afternoon. Too bad Annabella's in Acapulco. He will tell Joan, if she protests, that he needs to be alone with his grief.

* * *

What makes Joan cry uncontrollably on Fran's shoulder is, "Having to turn around and travel right back here on a plane, in the cargo hold! She *hated* flying."

Joan's father's ashes had been sprinkled on Long Island Sound, so there is no previously agreed-upon gravesite for the few remaining family members. The funeral service, it is decided, will be held at St. Barnabus' Church, since Joan's mother had no living relatives in Connecticut. Interment is behind the church, where Gladys' cremated remains join those of old India Bayh, who has just been placed at rest.

Fran finds the grieving daughter a black blouse and slacks to wear from Joan's closet of "Wear It Again, Sam-antha" outfits. Joan bursts into tears when she realizes to her horror the blouse had last been seen in Joan's office on Annabella and that she, Joan, has not had a brand-new piece of clothing in *years*. Thus does even funeral attire come full circle, whether it means to or not.

Joan is crying too much to think about playing for the service and from seemingly nowhere appears Mrs. Griffin, the hanky-pankying dentist's wife, to sit at the organ and play rather well for a Methodist.

There has been no way of contacting Susan to let her know about her grandmother's death. Pete and Excelsior wander around the back of the church looking for lizards while Father Wolfe intones, "Rest eternal grant to Gladys, O Lord, and let light perpetual shine upon her."

Joan likes the comfort of "light perpetual". Her mother had always been afraid of the dark. She does not even argue with Robert as the sparse crowd heads back to the parish hall for a brunch prepared by Margaret Wolfe and the E.C.W. He has just murmured, "By the way...." into her ear. Right now she is too numb to notice what follows those words.

Joan has nightmares for months afterward about alligators thrashing about on her mother's grave.

✳ ✳ ✳

HAVE TEETH, WILL TRAVEL

The resurgence of the alligator in Florida reflects
the success of state and federal efforts to protect
a species that just 20 years ago seemed marked
for extinction. The growth of the human population
and the need for golf courses means that man and
alligator must find ways to co-exist. "Most golf courses
in Florida have alligators, and after years of watching
golfers come and go those big lizards occasionally can get real bold,"
reports David Quinn, greens keeper at Banana Bay
Golf Course. "If you see an alligator basking on the edge
of a water hazard and you are a club's length from him,
the best thing to do is take the stroke penalty."
—*Banana Bay Tribune, July 15, 1977*

There is something quite profound about losing one's parents and realizing
that one is next in line as the now-oldest generation, for death.

Joan, writing in solitude while Robert sailed and Fran took Pete and
Excelsior to her house so Joan could rest, looked at that sentence and thought,
profound, hell: death could happen at any time. She knew it from her own
family.

Her father died two years ago. He had never been in good health and her
mother made no secret of her resentment at having to take care of her husband.
He had been born a twin (he had a brother, and perhaps this is why Joan chose the
twin subject for her master's degree paper), and *his* mother died when they were
born. Illnesses were kept either so secret or so general ("consumption") in those
days that Joan was unable to uncover any more information.

Anyway, the widower had two sisters who said they could each raise *one* of the boys, but not two. So this is how it was decided to choose a baby— the sleeping infants were placed on the same bed where they had been born a week before. The aunts darkened the room. Then they drew straws and each in turn felt her way into the room and chose a baby in the dark.

Joan's father went to his Aunt Hilda and Uncle Bert. His brother went to Aunt Lucille and Uncle Edmond, who had a farm a town away. By the time her father was old enough to hear the story of his twin-ness and separation, his brother had already had a fatal accident on the farm—something involving a bucket of hot water or being stepped on by a cow; nobody in the family had the story clear. Joan's father told her that he never felt quite whole all his short life. "I always knew a piece of me was missing," he would tell her. She wondered if his humor was a defense and he grieved himself to death.

As to *his* own father, after he lost a wife and then his two sons, he left the area and no one heard from him again. So Joan's father was essentially an orphan from infancy.

Robert lost his parents when he was still a young man. They both had cancer and died within months of each other when Robert and Joan were in their thirties. She personally suspected they choked to death on their own bile, but that was her private thought.

Robert's parents actively opposed the young couple's marriage. Robert was an only child and they had great plans for him. He had told them once when he was in grade school, "I intend to establish the first engineering camp on the moon!" and, so thrilled were they at their son's big words and aspirations (and having little common sense about how this could be accomplished in Robert's lifetime, also believing that "camp" meant their son, already a Boy Scout, would be pitching tents up there), they set out to make sure he had all the opportunities he needed.

This even gave his mother a chance to be the center of attention at her mah jong club meetings: "Yes, someday my Bobby will be going to the *moon*!" and she would dab at her eyes while they clucked over her while quietly deciding to query their own sons once they got home, in order to have something more portentous to report at the next meeting, like making camp on *Mars*.

It's a good thing for parents when their only child has such a far-fetched idea. Then they don't have to worry about losing him, except to his passion. They were fortunate he didn't want to be a race-car driver, for instance. He could have really worried them with that dream.

He never told them he had thought up that idea in an attempt to get as far away from them as possible. He had an insatiable need to protect his privacy.

Joan, still in love with a coat, didn't know this at the time. Would she have married him, knowing all she does now? That's a philosophical question with no answer. At that time, 1956, (re-read those rules from farther back in Joan's journal) marriage was their only solution.

Anyway, moonstruck, his parents got downright nasty when Robert and Joan turned up on his parents' doorstep one week end and announced they were getting married. Yes, they would continue their college educations. No, this would not even make a blip in anyone's lives. Yes, it would be even *better now,* because now they would be together, studying together, eating better, not having to go out on dates–

"You're *expecting,* aren't you?" demanded Robert's mother. Joan hesitated. That was all Cecelia Baldwin needed. She shrieked, threw herself onto the family sofa and sobbed. "How could you have *done* this to Bobby and me?" she wept, over and over into the cushions, coming up only for air and to fix her red-rimmed gaze on the skinny teenaged girl.

Robert stood next to his father, the two men each patting one of Cecelia's chubby shoulders as they had done for years every time she was thwarted. Joan stood across the room by herself, not sure what to say. Had Robert's mother thought this was a *virgin* birth? she was tempted to say , but her morning sickness kicked in—or maybe her agoraphobia—and she ran out of the room for the guest bath, where she knew she would not be allowed to use the fancy tiny towels that were there just for show.

Robert's mother had, Joan saw, looking up from the tiled floor, apparently been to a mah jong tournament and stayed at a fancy hotel, because Cecelia had carefully folded the trailing end of the toilet paper into a V-shape.

Joan was careful to do the same to it after she had used that V-square and more.

When she came back into the living room Robert's mother was now standing. She held her son in a tight "my precious baby" embrace. "...you'll finish college and then on to a master's degree and Ph. D and then– "

His father interrupted her. "Robert. Find yourself an apartment, nothing expensive, in the Boston area, and I'll cover the rent and utilities. He turned and noticed Joan. Joan, the obvious cause of all their woe, "Perhaps—uh– "

"Joan," she helped him.

They'd known her for three years now and still acted as though they hadn't been introduced. Stanley Baldwin frowned and Robert shook his head at her– this is no time for levity– "Perhaps *your* mother could come up with grocery money and– " he cleared his throat and tried not to stare at Joan's still-flat stomach– "incidentals."

Robert's parents refused to come to the wedding. Even Gladys begged off with a "sick headache" on that day, and that is why only their college friends were there, Robert's M.I.T. roommates joking and slapping him on the back, Joan's B.U. girlfriends whispering to each other their concern for her .

Afterward they said they thought it was "a very good mixer". Several of them made dates as a result, although none ever got serious. Robert's roommates were too studious for Joan's friends, who preferred Doris Day movies to Attacks From Outer Space.

Robert and Joan went on an abbreviated honeymoon (they both had big exams the following Monday and neither had studied). Robert wanted to make love Saturday night at the motel in Maine and then again on Sunday morning and then *again* on Sunday after breakfast, before they had to turn the key in; and then again when they got to their apartment, Joan with her new broom, Sunday evening.

This was to her a new, almost needy, side of Robert. Her morning sickness feelings kept her not as enthusiastic as he wanted her to be. "Robert, I think I'll feel better if I have a cracker or something."

"Leave them by the side of the bed. You can munch on them while I lie on you."

Of course she did as he said—he *had* rescued her from a fate worse than death, hadn't she?– but she hated the idea of having cracker crumbs in the bed.

As she got bigger and more uncomfortable it became harder and harder for him to make love.

"I have *needs,* you know," he would grouse.

"I'm sorry, Robert—it's just so awkward for me." Where was the pleasure *Joan* was supposed to feel?

She wasn't. This was 1957. She was supposed to give her husband pleasure. His was a necessity. Hers was a luxury. They had no room for luxuries.

And while she refused Robert, he still had needs. Still had needs. And *he* could fit behind the steering wheel of their 1957 red and black Plymouth (an overly-generous gift of his parents).

"I can't study with you here, getting in my way! I need to go study in the library on campus. Where are my car keys?"

He could get away, even then, even that early in their marriage, privately, while she studied alone and waited for him to come back to their chilly fourth floor walk-up apartment.

He didn't let Joan go to his parents' funerals. "They never liked you, Joan. What's the point?" Besides, he pointed out quite reasonably, there was Susan to watch. It never occurred to Joan that he might be in someone else's bed being comforted in his grief those separate nights in Connecticut, would never have occurred to her there might be someone else witnessing the tears of mourning he never allowed her to see. Would never have occurred to her that his pumping away at someone else would reduce any need to mourn.

Was he as marmoreal with others as with Joan? She would not have known to ask herself that question.

✿ ✿ ✿

DRIVERS LACK LOVE FOR BUGS

The annual invasion of love bugs has hit
the Banana Bay area, leaving residents less than thrilled.
"They're just horrible," stated Mrs. Andrew Scott.
"I guess their only purpose is to mate." The love bugs,
also known as honeymoon bugs, made their entrance
into Florida via Escambia County in 1947 and are now
found in much of the state. The bugs don't sting or bite,
but they make a mess of motorists' windshields and car grills.
Some people have tried smearing the grills with
cooking oil, to keep the bugs from sticking.
It is not recommended that you do this to your windshield.
—*Banana Bay Tribune, July 29, 1977*

Robert surveyed the city of Columbus from his ninth floor room at the Marriott. He disliked coming to cities for the first time—having to find his way from the airport in a strange car, making wrong turns, having to backtrack—Robert did not find getting lost amusing, the way Joan did. "We're together," she would say, "and that's all that matters."

Well, it wasn't. She was wrong. Doing something perfectly the first time was what mattered.

Good thing he wasn't chauffeuring the engineers he was supposed to meet. Sometimes at lunch they all piled into his rental car, saying, "Gas is on *you,* Baldwin," and chatting about who knew what, football or something else trivial while he tried to negotiate his way in traffic, hardly helped by some man sitting smoking in the passenger seat, who would be turned halfway around to talk with his fellow workers, and yell at the last second, "Gotta turn left there, Bob!"

If he were going to work with them on a long-time basis, he would have to let them know in no uncertain terms that his name was Robert, not Bob, thank you very much—but for the most part, after he visited a city once, then all their work was done over the phone, and he didn't much care what they called him then, as long as they paid him for his consulting.

If Robert had a flaw—and he would simply call it a "preference"– it was that he did not like to do anything for the first time. All of life, he believed, should happen from the second time forward, so that there was no chance of things being out of control, with possible shame or embarrassment ensuing.

He calculated how long it would be before he could be relieved of his business duties, go down to the bar alone, and find a woman to talk with—the goal being to get her into his bed. This was the way to live, he said to himself again. No encumbrances. And didn't he deserve this? Look at how *hard* he was working, for God's sake. A man *needed* to get away as often as possible.

No encumbrances. Just a hotel room in a new city, having the benefit of even being able to give a fake name; he always introduced himself as "James Bonde with an e"—he suspected the women he slept with could not *all* be named Susie Smith—and then board a plane, be served a meal and a drink and a chat with an attractive stewardess, and have his MGB waiting for him in Banana Bay, so that he could see his latest female "friend"– right now Annabella– before having to go home.

He'd learned a long time ago from his father not to tell Joan exactly when he'd be home. He'd also learned she would not ask for a phone number where he would be, or even the city.

"What if I need to get in touch with you?" she would protest. But she'd never follow through and demand he tell her his plans. No, his father was right:

"If you tell 'em, there they are at the window, where they've been lookin' through the curtains for you for hours. Ever see a dog waitin' for its master? That's what a wife looks like. It's too late for me, Bobby. Watch it doesn't happen to you. In the movies they say, 'It's curtains for you.' Well, that's what curtains *mean*: they're waitin' at home 'til you show up, to check your balls and see if you really need two of 'em, or if they're entitled to keep one for themselves. *Don't* tell 'em when you're comin' home!"

Stanley Baldwin always ended his paternal homilies with "And that means no disrespect at all to your mama."

So, no disrespect, Joan, but I am not telling you when I'm coming home.

Robert ground his teeth remembering—that one time Joan needed his car and picked him up at the airport, just because *her* car was in the shop! Or so she said. Maybe she was on to him. She'd sit there so innocently, and then out of the blue she'd say something that would make his heart skip a beat: "Your car smells different, like perfume." It was then that he'd have to think fast and swear, "Dammit all to hell! The shop must have sprayed it when I took it in for an oil change! I tell them every time– !"

Then she'd just smile and go back to writing in her notebook.

Was she writing about him? Was she taking notes so she could take him to court and screw him?

Worse, was anyone calling the house looking for him? Had some disgruntled female in some city taken his fingerprints off a bar glass behind his back to find out who he really was? What would that do to his standing in the community, president of his company, vestryman at St. Barnabus'?

He never told Joan where he was going. He didn't even like to tell her *when* he was going. It kept him from having to answer all kinds of useless questions. It wasn't as though she couldn't take the kids with her to Publix instead of counting on him to be there at night so she could go then.

The information about his trips really made no difference in her life, anyway. Oh, sure, she would cry sometimes and say, "Pete could be dead and buried before you came home and found out," but that was a specious argument. She could get so emotional over nothing.

He would have to talk to her about how she and Pete acted when he said , "By the way, I'm going out of town on business." The way they shrugged up their shoulders together and looked no-neck! Easy to tell they were related.

Robert hoped Pete wasn't turning out to be a sissy. Pete had to be the man of the house when Robert was gone. He'd told that to his son enough times. And then Joan met him at the door that one time with, "I had an emergency—Pete dislocated his shoulder and I was at the hospital, and I phoned your *secretary!* She was crying. *Crying,* Robert! She said she had an important call for you and she didn't know where you were!"

But Joan would never go so far as to demand that he leave a phone number. That wasn't her style—to demand. He'd spent too many years getting her trained that way.

That damned secretary of his. Okay, lesson learned—don't screw your secretary, although Sheila had told him that was not the reason she was so mad at him; she just wanted a bigger paycheck. Then she threatened to tell Joan. That was when he got—*wary* about playing in home waters. He wasn't about to give up the chasing he'd loved since junior high school. He'd just be more– careful.

Fortunately Sheila's husband got a job offer up north and they were moving. Funny how his life kept working out so well for him. And he *deserved* to have it running smoothly—look at all the hours he put in at work, and who cared? Joan? Fat chance. She didn't even know exactly what he *did* in business.

Now as he looked out at the Columbus skyline, he thought of a movie Joan had told him she'd like him to take her to when he got home, and when it was convenient for him. It sounded somewhat scary. Robert decided to look in the local newspaper, and if it was playing nearby, to go and see it before he went home and had to take Joan. Hey—there it was. Maybe he could take in a matinee tomorrow.

That was part of his plan not to do something for the first time. That way, if she got startled and grabbed his hand during the movie, he could smile across to her in the dark and not be sweating himself.

She told him she had panic attacks and she needed to sit on the aisle, in case she felt jumpy and had to leave all of a sudden and walk around in the lobby. What a sissy she was, making something out of nothing—all she had to do was pull herself together and not give in to her emotions and she'd be the better for it. He himself had never met a woman who had panic attacks and he bet she was making the whole thing up, just to get his attention.

He scowled. This whole college and then counseling crap. She seemed to be getting different. Not so willing to take his word for everything. And getting herself a car! A used one, sure, but still—his mother would never have gone behind his father's back like that. Fran—Fran had helped her. He was certain of it.

He was looking forward to that drink and the idea of cruising around the bar downstairs with his eyes, as though it was some kind of a pick-up buffet. He was well aware that lonely women came to bars when *their* husbands went out of town.

You'd never see Joan in a bar, though. Straight arrow, Joan. Naive. He'd had no idea she was a virgin back then when he talked her into going to the Scout cabin. He thought she was as eager as he was. That came as a shock, that she had never had any experience with anyone else.

But that was how he preferred it, Robert nodded to himself. That way Joan had no one to compare with. The hell with these women who had "experience": "What are you *doing*? I don't like it when you *do* that!" Or

"Move yourself like this." Or

"That scratches when you do that."Or

"Ouch! Haven't you ever been with a *woman* before?"

That was the worst thing a bitch could say to Robert. What made them so damned cruel and cocky?

A man should be just that, a man. He'd honed his technique a long time ago. It was a good one, one that gave him pleasure, and as far as he was concerned, that was that. Then like a dancer with his moves memorized to perfection, he'd go at sex like a dance– pick out someone he wanted to move around the floor with, and she'd jolly well better move in step with his steps and that was the end of it.

If he was in a good enough mood and the woman seemed less apt to take things personally, he'd let her teach him a thing or two (never letting on that he'd never done this before), to take home and try on Joan as a sort of present to bring her. His Mama had taught him that women are satisfied with simple things—a piece of colored paper with a four-line second grade poem in crayon which hung, framed, in the kitchen until she died ("My Mama is sweet/My Mama is deer/ I'm happy wenever /My Mama is neer"); a ride with him in his first teenage car to the grocery store where his Mama would buy her customary prune juice and toilet paper; or, if he was feeling particularly generous, a drive to his Mama's mah jong group, with her sitting in his car beside him, waving her hand like the Queen and leaning across him– her fat breasts shoving against him in an unintended way and threatening to have him grow a forbidden erec-tion– to honk the horn so her friends would come to the window and see her wonderful son.

Yes, women liked simple things. Leave the expensive dinners and the expen-sive jewelry to the ones he picked up in bars, the ones who demanded payment for services rendered.

He tried to picture Joan with jewelry and failed. In the land of stiletto heels she was strictly loafers.

When he finally phoned home Joan was frantic. "Oh, Robert, where *are* you? Are you on your way home? You *have* to come home!"

He did not like to be told what to do. "I'm still out of town. I just called to make sure you take my blue suit to the cleaner's– "

"Robert! Listen! You have to come home as fast as possible! Something *awful* has happened!"

Robert could hear other voices behind hers, raised voices. A man was now on the phone. "Robert. This is Tom Wolfe. There's been a bit of a mishap here– " Robert thought he could hear Joan crying in the background. "Now don't get alarmed, but it's your office, nobody hurt– "

Father Wolfe stopped speaking. Apparently Joan had grabbed the phone back. "Robert! The *firemen* were there at your office. They called me and then none of us could *find* you! They say it looks like you had a lot of paperwork stored above the acoustic tiles and when the fire started it just whooshed through the whole building– !"

She had to be making this up, Robert thought, although how could she know where he was storing all his reams of computer print-outs? No, she had to be kidding, having some cruel joke on him. Dammit, if Sheila had called her, blown the whistle— but who would think to make up a *fire?*

"Robert!" Joan was sobbing. "It's dreadful! Your office, your equipment! Everybody's here from church and they've got prayer groups going for us— !"

He said the first thing that came into his head: "Did *you* start it?"

"*Robert!*" Joan sounded distraught. "Robert, please, please come home! We need you! How soon can you be here? Robert— !" She stopped talking and he could hear her sobs.

Father Wolfe came back on the line "They saved your M.I.T. chair, the black one with the cherry wood arms, and some of your books. There's been a lot of water damage, of course. When the fire cools down they're going to let Joan and me put on hardhats and go with them through the building." He sounded excited and eager. Robert could hear Pete shouting in the background, "Me! *Me*! I want to go, too!"

"So get here as soon as you can, Robert. Where did you say you are— ?"

Robert carefully set the phone on its hook in the darkened phone booth. He was aware that there was at this very moment a beautiful blonde-haired naked young woman who desired him as she lay on the bunk in his boat "SEE LEGS". She'd lit a candle and he could see its glow. She would set his *boat* on fire for all she cared. He stepped onto the deserted dock , turned and looked down the river . Yes, he imagined he could make out a plume of smoke to the south about three miles, in Banana Bay.

He'd told them he was still out of town. He'd have to think, to plan. For the first time in his life since puberty he was not interested in sex.

INDIA BAYH'S FABULOUS COLLARDS

Ingredients: Collard leaves, smoked pork meat, sugar, Accent.
Directions: Select small or medium-sized leaves.
Check leaves carefully for worms or bugs; if you find any,
throw the leaves away. Wash greens several times until
there is no sand in sink bottom. Don't add water or salt. Add pork.
Turn burner on high, then at boil, turn down to medium heat
for two hours. When greens are almost cooked,
add a pinch of sugar and a little Accent.
Greens are best cooked the day prior to serving.
—*Banana Bay Tribune, May 2, 1975*

"I have a recipe we need to try," said 18-year-old Susan, yawning, coming into the kitchen at 11:00 am. She started pulling out flour, sugar, a large Tupperware container, bread, butter, jam and orange juice.

"Looks like an interesting recipe," Joan replied carefully, stifling her housewife's moan, since she'd just cleaned the kitchen. She had also looked in on Susan(sound asleep) and had taken Excelsior (sobbing and totally drenched in urine) to be changed and given a bottle. Now he was asleep and Joan was looking forward to working on her Master's thesis.

"Well, part of this is for my breakfast."

"I'm going to serve lunch in an hour, Susan."

"Well, there is no way in hell I am going to wait an hour to eat! Honestly, Mother! You tell me I'm too thin and when I tell you I'll eat you *forbid* me to!"

"Okay. Okay," Joan said. "Sorry. What's the recipe?"

"Well," she mumbled through a piece of mushed-up bread– "Want toast?" Joan asked. "Mm-mm," she responded. "Not yet. Later, maybe."

Joan poured her daughter a glass of juice before she could spill the quart of it on the counter. Susan took the glass and poured half of it in the sink.

"You always give me too much," she said. "So okay, this is called 'Amish Sweet Bread', and it's really delicious. I had it the other night at the Wolfe's and Mrs. Wolfe gave me the recipe– "

"You had dinner with Father and Mrs. Wolfe?" Joan asked, surprised, although she should not have been surprised by anything that Susan did or that she told her mother.

"I took Excelsior. They wanted to see him."

"They wanted to see Excelsior? I thought you were going to MacDonald's. Did they talk you into another name for that boy?"

Okay, Joan should know when to keep her mouth shut. Maybe she should have stuffed a piece of bread into it the way Susan did hers. Only no matter how full her mouth, her daughter could still get the words out.

As she did now. "Mother! I have told you time and time again why I named my baby Excelsior!" Susan struck an aggrieved pose beside the sink. "It's a Greek word and it means 'Upward and Onward', and *that's* what I mean for Excelsior to do. And I'll thank you to keep Pete from calling my baby 'The Shaver'!"

"All Pete is saying is that excelsior is also the name of shavings. I think it's kind of cute."

Apparently Joan's thoughts were not to be considered with any gravity.

"Well, you just make him stop! You're his *mother*! What a nickname for a child when he enters school! They'll think he carries a switchblade!" She took another piece of bread and this time slathered it with jam. Then she stuck the jam knife into the butter, piecing uneven pats of Land O'Lakes on top of the jam. She folded the bread over and took a large bite. Jam squished out onto the counter.

Joan ripped off a piece of paper towel and cleaned the counter. "Honestly, Mother. You are *so* anal!"

"Really?"she said, wiping. "I thought I was more an oral type."

Her daughter snorted. "Obsessive-compulsive about your kitchen."

"Okay. Sorry. It's just that the jam stains the white surface and then I have to get out the bleach, and I worry about Excelsior inhaling it– "

"He's smelling ammonia diapers and poop all day long. I don't think a little Clorox will bother him."

"Let me see what your recipe is," Joan said, wanting to return to some safe ground. And Joan was not about to be incautious enough to remind Susan that this grandmother was the one changing him and paying for diapers out of her grocery allowance.

"Okay," Susan said, opening the refrigerator door wide and leaving it that way while she assessed its contents. "Do you have any yeast?"

"I have an unopened jar on the pantry shelf." Joan got the yeast out.

"Check the expiration date. This recipe calls for unexpired yeast. It *has* to be fresh!"

"Expires June 1977—two years from from now."

"All right. That's good. Now the flour has to be fresh, too."

"I just bought it this week." Susan nodded. The flour passed muster.

Joan stopped, ear cocked. "Did you hear Excelsior? Maybe I should go check on him– " she headed for the bedroom.

Susan meanwhile had brought out milk and eggs. "He'll be all right! Honestly, Mother, it's a wonder Pete and I grew up normal, what with all your *fussing*."

"Well, I just don't want to be in the midst of all this and then we have to stop and pick him up."

"*I'll* pick him up. Quit worrying. Now, the first thing to do is crack two eggs into a large bowl —is this the largest bowl you've got? Because it has to be *large*."

"How much does this make?" Joan asked, fishing out some shards of eggshell while Susan was looking for the salt. Or the pepper. She was examining both.

"Funny how we use up salt faster than we do pepper," she mused. "Now, I need a teaspoon measure. *And* a measuring cup. Oh, and you have to sift the flour. I've never done that, so you do that part."

"Could I see what this is going to make?" Joan asked, sifting. "More," Susan said. "Keep sifting. It looks like fun, anyway."

"Well, it is," Joan smiled. "I'm enjoying working with you on this—what? Amish something?"

"Amish Sweet Bread. And this starter makes enough to go around, so after it's sat on the counter for a week, you can give it to all your neighbors. See, the Amish share the starter, and that's why it's called Amish Sw– "

"A week? It sits on the counter for a *week*? With eggs and milk in it?" Shades of botulism danced before Joan's eyes. Was she going to infect the entire neighborhood? Those crafty Amish. What a way to bring down Episcopalians. "Where's the rest of the recipe—what it makes? Bread? And how much bread? I may not have enough pans."

"Don't *worry* about that. I don't have the recipe with me right now. I think I left it at the Wolfe's. But you can call Mrs. Wolfe and she'll give it to you. *Watch now*! This part is *important*!"

But Joan had heard crying. She knew that when Excelsior woke up, he woke up hungry. Howling hungry. "I think, Susan, I need to go change– "

"Mother! I'm not going to tell you again to leave-my-baby-alone!"

Joan desisted. Maybe if she hurried this starter business along, they could get to Excelsior before he turned blue from crying. He was still thankfully too young to be able to work the crib across the terrazzo. When Susan was a baby she could rattle her crib all the way across the floor

"Watch now. Watch! You're not watching! You put in the flour and sugar and salt, then the yeast, and you add enough milk—wait, was the milk supposed to be heated? I forget. Maybe you'd better heat it a little. Wait, wait. The milk goes in *first,* and then the yeast goes in a little hole in the flour after you add the flour. I remember it had to be in a hole. I don't think the milk should be cold. We'll heat it some."

Joan got out a pan and did so, her ears straining for nursery sounds of calamity.

"Maybe cinnamon. No, I mean vanilla. I think that's it. It's what makes the sweet bread sweet."

Halfway to the spice rack she changed her mind. "We can always add that later. This is the *best* recipe, no kidding!"

She took the milk from the stove, poured it into the mess she had started—ah, Joan thought, that's what a starter is. She starts it and I finish it by cleaning up the kitchen. Start-or- finish, take your pick.

"Now, do you think you can do this? Because this is so good you're going to want to keep making it. Okay, now you get a bunch of Baggies out, because after a week you pour this starter into each Baggie and take it to the neighbors. They'll love it! When you get the recipe from Mrs. Wolfe, I guess you'd better make copies."

"Do I cover it tightly?" Joan stared down at the grayish mixture. Bubbles were starting to froth at the edges. She leaned over and sniffed it. It didn't smell bad. She cautiously tasted it with a finger. Okay, maybe this was going to be all—

"*Mother*!" screeched Susan. Joan stopped dead, her finger still in her mouth. "Did you just put your *dirty finger* in that starter?"

"It was a clean finger," Joan protested. "You've been watching me wash my hands over and over– "

"I cannot *believe* you!" Joan knew this tone of voice. Susan was getting wound up, the way she did only with her mother and only in her presence, with no witnesses. Where was Joan's tape recorder? Outsiders would never believe this. Had she used this voice the night she got pregnant? It's a wonder the father, whoever he was, since she'd never uttered a name except Robert Redford's, and Joan had her doubts about *that* being Excelsior's parentage, would have been able to—

"You ruin *everything!* You have to *control* everything and you *ruin* everything! Ever since I came home with my baby you've done nothing but pick at me and tear me down and belittle me– !" Joan didn't know how she did it, but when Susan was angry, words came to her effortlessly. It was as though she had memorized them for her Big Scene With Mother.

Two weeks home and they were already seriously fighting—at least Susan was trying to engage in war, oblivious to Joan's white flag of a paper towel.

You would think Joan would have been immured to this by now. But no. Every time Susan catapulted herself into this mode was a fresh one for her mother and it left her speechless. Joan stood her ground (*her* kitchen), thinking of different therapeutic alternatives:

(1) I could hug her. No. She would kill me; she could shift from mild to mad so fast that I knew she was dredging up old junk from somewhere. Or

(2) I could sit down, so that she was above me and we were not at eye level. No. She would think I had given up and rolled over, exposing my underbelly and she would kill me. Or

(3) I could walk out of the room. No. She would run after me and kill me.

Since all Joan's ideas ended with the assumption that she would be killed, she waited to see if her daughter would run down. Joan doubted it, but it might be a new alternative.

Actually, as Joan read these words later—Susan sounded a lot like Joan's mother Gladys.

Susan had been sunny until she hit puberty. Might she have ADD or ADHD? Joan wondered. Hm-m–

and was ADHD neurological or behavioral– ?

"– and you're not even *listening* to me!" Joan blinked. Susan was so close to her she was actually spitting on her mother. Joan took a step back and that's when they both heard the heartbroken wailing sound.

"Well, you *got* what you *wanted*!" Susan wheeled away from Joan and dashed out the front door. She heard it bang several times, trying to catch, as she went down the hall to the baby. Joan heard Susan's old secondhand car grind away from the driveway. She was shaking so hard that she had to lean against the door for a few moments while the caterwauling Excelsior demanded an end to his abandonment.

All afternoon Joan waited for Susan to come back so that she could apologize for her careless finger. Her purse was still here, Joan saw when she studied the messy room Susan shared with her baby and his crib. No drugs in her purse. A little money. Driver's license—something *else* to worry about.

Robert was once more out of town, so Joan fixed toasted cheese sandwiches for Pete and herself for supper. The starter was now smelling very yeasty and a slightly sickening odor was permeating the house, so Joan snapped the lid shut on the oversized Tupperware container and burped it the way she'd been taught at Tupperware parties.

"Good," said Pete, holding his nose.

Pete, Excelsior and Joan watched TV until both boys got sleepy and she put them to bed. She left the porch light on. She didn't know if Susan had taken her house key, so decided she would wait up. By now she was feeling panicky, but had no idea where Robert was and how to locate him. Why didn't she insist he tell her where he was when he went out of town? She had asked him once, and he said, "If I do, you'll just keep calling me, and I'm on business, not available for trivia."

Well, *Susan* wasn't trivia, and Joan sure could use another, clear-headed adult to keep her calm. She would have phoned Fran, but expected Susan at any time, so put it off until it was too late to call, past 10:00 pm.

She lay down on the family room sofa and tried to read. Sometime later she fell asleep. In the midst of her sleep she heard a "pop", but couldn't rouse herself. When she next woke up and looked at her watch, it was three something. She went into Susan and Excelsior's room, but only the infant was there, flung out on his back, sweating a little at his forehead. She smoothed his hair and went into the kitchen; and that's when she found the note on the table: "I'm leaving Excelsior with you, since your a better mother than I am. You know you always have to control EVERYTHING and you always have to BE RIGHT. Tell him not to forget his REAL MOTHER. DO NOT EVER CHANGE HIS NAME!!!!!" There was no signature, not even a crude drawing of a middle finger..

Noting that she had spelled "you're" wrong (*did* Joan always have to control and be right? And if she did, was that a sin?) Joan went back to the bedroom and turned on a light. Susan's purse was gone, as well as a small suitcase and the gold hoop earrings Robert had given her on her 13th birthday ("Today you are a woman," he had told her. How little they knew). She turned the light off before Excelsior woke.

She was now aware that the smell in the kitchen was overpowering. She saw why: the "pop" she had heard in her middle-of-the-night stupor was the lid blowing off the Tupperware bowl. Amish Sweet Bread starter oozed over the counter, into the drawers and onto the floor. Tiny ants had come from hidden parts of the house and were now swimming helplessly in the wet yeasty sticky mixture.

Joan gave herself five minutes to cry, from frustration and lack of sleeping in her own bed (where would Susan sleep tonight? She wondered fearfully) and because she hated ants, but at least they weren't Palmetto bugs. Then she cleaned the kitchen for the second time in less than 24 hours and was able to make herself a cup of coffee before the crying of a hungry, wet, and now motherless baby started up again.

How could Joan have predicted it would be *two years* before they would hear from Susan again?

Like Mary, Joan could have used a message from an angel, who did not just thrust Jesus upon her overnight, but gave her a little time to go to Publix-Israel and buy more diapers.

You know reading this far that Susan came back. We later found out who Excelsior's father was. We two women kept an uneasy truce until that poor child died in an accident. I trust he is prancing around in heaven now and I will see him in another couple of decades. More of that later. I have larger, closer to home things to worry about.

I am about to meddle, big time. Susan is turning a deaf ear to me about the danger of Derreck—she thinks he's *cute*!– and her new husband Timmy, who is Emily's stepfather and as such claims not much interest in her, is no help. Emily's father—well, this time Susan is not making the mistake of telling me who he is, for fear of my getting in her way.

You remember Derreck, whom I labeled a charming somewhat paranoid sociopath—and those are only the words I use when I am feeling some kindness toward him!– Derreck has entered our lives by way of first dating and then living with Emily. In my consternated and lone-juror way, I console myself by picturing him as not being able to have sex.

I haven't yet described Emily. I will, without bragging about my only granddaughter, without photos to pass around: she is intelligent intellectually, although easily flattered (I am finding) about men. She is 25, tall and slender, with long fingers that cry out to be placed lovingly on piano keys. I put my stubby ones against hers and bewail the loss, since she has no interest in a keyboard.

Her eyes are Robert's, that unusual blue somewhere between the sky and the water-blue.

She went through the local community college, thought she wanted to be a nurse, fainted at the sight of her first tonsillectomy, and is now working as a secretary to a local lawyer. She's going to school nights and online to become a paralegal. She should go all the way and become a lawyer herself. But she's been sidetracked by Derreck and the thrill of his attention to her.

Her heart is without limits. If she worked at the animal shelter she would bring home all the strays.

But with Derreck around, a stray dog or cat wouldn't stand a chance.

Before you think I'm just a worrying grandmother, let me tell you that Charleen has gone missing: Charleen who bought a sports car for Derreck (which he still enjoys, the stereo blasting, the tires screaming around corners), Charleen who also has/had a huge heart. That's the kind of woman he attracts.

I hope Charleen has run off to somewhere safe. I doubt it, however. Banana Bay and its outskirts are full of mucky deep dark ponds and impenetrable woods. There are plenty of wild Florida animals that would know what to do with a dead body.

After I sent Derreck and Charleen to Dr. Reed, Ph.D, I phoned to tell him what I had done and to give me a call when they showed up. I finally called *him*. He'd seen no sign of them. He's a huge man, an ex-Marine, and I figured he could take care of himself; but there was no need.

So I invited Susan and her husband and Emily and Derreck for dinner. Maybe he would be such a slob that Emily would be turned off by his table manners. Odder things have happened.

I wished Pete and his wife didn't live so far away in Georgia. It would have been reassuring with them here.

Quentin came home from his office and seemed dazed by the smells in the kitchen and the table set for more than the two of us. "What's going on?" he said, kicking off his shoes and plunking them on the stairs.

"Company for dinner. I told you last week and then again this morning."

"Do I have to change?"

"No. But you could put your shoes where nobody will trip over them."

Quentin looked around, located his shoes, said mildly, "Now how'd *they* get there?" and sat down with the newspaper.

"Your *shoes*, Quentin."

"Oh. Nobody's going upstairs, are they? They're okay, out of the way there. Who's coming again?"

All four guests then showed up at the same time, so I was spared the same recital I had given him that morning. Don't ask me if Quentin will be on my side—he *likes* Derreck. This makes me feel like the paranoid one.

Dinner conversation was lively: Emily wanted to talk about their new apartment, her classes and her job, and Derreck doted on her and let her finish sentence after sentence without seeming to need the spotlight on him. "Just wait," I thought. "He'll crack."

Sure enough, Emily said, "Announcement! We're thinking of planning a small wedding."

Susan glowed. Her daughter getting married! To such a cute guy! Timmy drank some more wine. Quentin looked as though he hadn't heard where the conversation was going. I tried to think of something pleasant to say. And Derreck:

"Now honey, we don't want to bore everyone with our ideas."

"*I* want to hear them," I said. He narrowed his eyes at me for a second, then,

"Actually, we want to take our time. Get to know each other. Gotta let my relatives know so they can start making plans to come down. My Pop's gonna want to– "

"Isn't your Pop in the *C.I.A.*?" I asked daringly.

Now he stared me down. "You've gotta be confusing it with the F.B.I. Actually, he was one of J. Edgar Hoover's right-hand men."

All eyes turned to Derreck in interest. "But it's confidential stuff. He never wanted to talk about it with me, even. But I *can* tell you he protected most of the presidents. You see those guys running alongside the president's car, looking for any trouble? My Pop did that."

Take that, his look said to me.

"Derreck was offered a Rhodes scholarship," Emily bragged. "But he had to give it up."

"Yeah—my Mom had a rare form of liver disease and my Pop was off on a secret mission, so I stayed home with her. And you know once they offer you that scholarship and you don't take it, you can never get another one."

Emily patted his hand and Susan said, "How about having it at St. Barnabus'?"

"It?" Derreck said.

"The wedding. And Mom, we've already talked it over. Derreck doesn't believe in formal religion. We *could* get married on the beach."

Timmy, who I knew from experience really wanted a stronger drink than wine, hoisted himself up off his chair. "Let's toast the happy couple," he said, pouring his wine glass to the brim, threatening my linen tablecloth. We all stood and raised our glasses. Derreck squinted at me over his.

He insisted on helping with the dishes, urging Susan and Emily to go "rest yourselves." As we stood side by side at the sink he muttered, "What's up with you, lady? What're you trying to pull?"

"Where's Charleen?" I said boldly.

"Gone. Went to visit her family. Not coming back. Why? You want to *join* her? On a kind of permanent vacation?"

This was the first time I was truly scared, and realized he could be dangerous, although he had a frilly dishtowel tucked into his belt, which had only endeared him to Susan, I could tell.

"Stay out of my face, lady," he was smiling. In case anyone was watching? "I know you wrote down what I said in your office that night. You were alone with Charleen. Those notes better be destroyed. Or I can break in and burn them myself and you'd never know I was there, I'm that good. While I'm burning other stuff." No one could hear our conversation over the clattering of the dishes and probably the pounding of my heart.

"I took no notes."

"Sure you did. What about after I was gone? I— let's say I *interrogated* Charleen about it, military style, and she finally admitted it. She said you wrote down all kinds of things about me. You're saving them to show Emily and have a big laugh at my expense. But let me tell you—the group I work for doesn't have a sense of humor. I told them about seeing you. They threatened to dump me someplace unless I —oh, and I want your tape recorder, too. And Charleen's cell phone. She told me she texted messages to somebody and then hid it under your cushions. *I want that cell phone.* And I want those notes for myself or— "

"Or— ?" I tried to keep my voice from shaking. He leaned past my hands, which rested in soapy water, put his hands beside mine underneath the water. grabbed a steak knife there before I knew what he was doing, and while still smiling, sliced the back of my right hand.

I gasped as the dishwater turned a murky color.

"– Or your granddaughter pays a high price." He turned as Emily came up behind him and wrapped her arms around his waist. I was wincing in pain from the snakelike suddenness of the attack.

"Now look what your nice grandmama just did," he said, taking his dishtowel and wrapping it around my hand. "You need to be more careful," he said to me. "*Much* more careful."

"Oh, Grandma," exclaimed Emily, looking woozy at the sight of my blood, "let me finish those dishes! Go get a bandage. Quentin!" she called.

My husband, who had been dozing in his chair, looked up, saw my hand in a towel, and asked,

"Anything wrong?"

Yes. Much is wrong. And I'm the only one who is aware of it. Therefore, I'm the one who will have to take care of the matter. The very next week was when

Emily urged me to take a drive with them on an old unused road which suddenly ended at the St. Johns River.

We all left the car, me to stretch after a cramped ride in the briefcase-sized back seat, and Emily to stand fifty feet away studying some birds, neither of us noticing as Derreck suddenly ran up to me and hit me across the backs of my legs, leaving me gasping on my hands and knees like a terrified beached fish until he, staring at me without emotion, reached out a hand and said, "Aw. Careless of you to slip, just when you were enjoying the wonders of nature. Now you're gonna have to get changed before we go eat. Emily! Come on over here! Your grandmama *wet* herself!"

The rotted smell of that muddy bank is still in my nostrils.

Last Sunday on my way to church a squirrel ran under my car before I could react and for the first time in my life that I know of I killed a little innocent animal. Then I made the mistake of looking in my rearview mirror to make sure it had escaped and no, there it was, lying back there in the road, its tail twitching frantically as its life ran out.

I haven't dared to drive down that particular road since then and face my crime. And *I'm* thinking of doing away with a large human being, his psychopathic rage now zeroed in on *me?*

LIGHTS OUT! LOGGERHEAD TURTLES ON THE RISE

Our county's beaches are the largest nesting site
for the loggerhead turtle in the western hemisphere,
with more than 20,000 nests a year along our shoreline.
Remember—if you go out at night to watch Mama sea turtle
come up from the ocean to lay her eggs, do not disturb her
with lights or noise, or she will go back out to sea
with her eggs not laid, which could harm the
sea turtle population. As the turtle is digging her nest
in the sand along the dunes she may appear to weep.
This is due simply due to exertion as she uses
her powerful flippers to dig a hole in the sand for her babies.
—*Banana Bay Tribune, August 7, 1977*

This part of the year remains a blur to Joan. Susan returned, bringing her attitude with her. Fran and Joan graduated with their Master's degrees in counseling and have opened their office for private practice. Joan is able finally to start paying her for half of the sofa.

Pete turned eleven. He spends his vacation time with the Roosters Little League team, where he invariably swings at all the balls, good or bad. The other boys' fathers practice with their sons.

Robert does not enjoy sports. "I see no reason why I have to encourage Pete in something he'll never make a living at, anyway," he said when Joan asked him to go out into the side yard and throw a few balls to Pete. "And it digs up the grass." So *she* tried, but she throws like a girl. She worries about hitting her struggling son with one of her pitches gone awry.

Robert has just opened his own private consulting work after telling Joan in one short sentence that fire insurance paid all the bills and workers' salaries. Joan is not privy to the financial side of all this. You know that line close to the end of "The Godfather" movie where Michael Corleone says to his wife Diane Keaton, "One question. You can ask me one question." That's how Joan feels.

She honestly does not know how she managed to finish school while caring for her grandson and grieving over Susan's departure. Not knowing where Susan was and if she was dead or alive kept Joan crazy with worry. Now some days she has fears in the opposite direction, that Susan will *never* leave them.

But she only tells this to Fran. Only Fran keeps her going. "So rejoice that you've got Susan back. That kid is like a cork," Fran says. "Push her down under water, you've got to keep your hand there. Because as soon as you let your hand go, she bobs to the surface again. And look—you've got some free time again, away from babysitting."

Joan nods agreement and picks up her teacup. She looks around. Fran's kitchen is sunny and peaceful. No high chair. No dried-up blobs of cereal heaved at the curtains.

"It's even better than that," Fran continues in a way that only an old trusted friend can, "it's like she's got *needles* on the top of her head. If you try to hold her down, *you're* the one who gets hurt, while up she bounces again, because who can keep their hand pressing down on *needles*?"

She leans back and studies Joan. Fran has gained no weight in the years since Joan has known her, and she looks marvelous. She plays tennis and works in the yard, and her tan is enviable. Her sun-bleached hair is pulled back into a ponytail and she's wearing just a dab of lipstick. She exudes health. Joan envies the way she and Ken can laugh at some private family joke. Joan is about to learn there is a big difference between privacy and secrecy.

Joan, at the same time, has lost weight so that when she hitches Excelsior to her hip she fears he can feel the sharp hipbone through the little flesh she has there. She is wearing her hair short—LoRayne at the beauty shop just about curses every time she cuts it—but she doesn't have time for extensive hair care. Excelsior has developed a rash that won't go away and she keeps taking him to the doctor for allergy tests.

Robert has once more come through another ordeal, the fire, unscathed. His consulting business has now taken over Susan's old bedroom completely, leaving Susan with the guest room and Pete sharing a room with Excelsior. And when Robert is working at his table-sized computer, it blocks the phone lines so that if Pete or Susan were to call, needing Joan, they wouldn't be able to get through.

This worries her so that she has a hard time eating, but when she dares to say anything, Robert turns to her and says, "*Whose* office burned ? *Who* has to make all the sacrifices? *Who* is doing everything possible to keep food on this family's table?" Then he goes out to lunch with business contacts while Joan roams the aisles at Publix, hungry and yet unable to eat.

Or, worse—he does *not* turn to Joan. He keeps his back to her and mutters at her to go away, he'll talk to her later. He has, as she's stated, installed a lock on his "office" door– "to keep the kids from my things"– and yet, even while they are in school, Pete a sixth-grader almost as tall as his mother, and Excelsior in a special daycare now three mornings a week, he *still* locks the door while he works inside.

Except. Except for those half-hour interruptions in her morning when he works at home and wants sex. Then she must stop what she is doing—washing windows, vacuuming the pool, penning a grocery list– and make herself available to this man who is putting food on the table and who persuades her that she must keep him motivated to do so.

Joan's routine has been so compromised that she no longer makes their bed, aware, on Excelsior-at-school days, of what one of her marital duties will be.

Maybe she could also enjoy sex if her mind were not so preoccupied, she tells Fran.

"Bull," she says. "He's got everything *he* wants. How about *you?*

"Well," Joan starts counting my blessings, "Pete. He's a joy." Fran agrees readily. Pete is almost *too* good, given the circumstances of having had to abandon his room. "There was the time last year right after the boys were rooming together, when Excelsior took off his diapers and smeared his poop all over his crib and the wall while Pete was asleep. I had to let Pete sleep on the couch the next night while the room aired out – "

"– and did Robert help you clean it?"

"You can guess the answer. No. He was busy with something at his computer, and he looked at me and said, "Get rid of that damn stink," while I was hosing down Excelsior– "

"– and then later he wanted sex, right?"

"Well, he works hard– " Fran raises a hand to stop Joan from explaining Robert to her.

"Hey, you know what we can do?" she says. "He's out of town, right? You're here at my house and the kids are taken care of. Pete's going to his Scout leader's house with the other boys for lunch. So let's us go lie by the pool at the Yacht Club and I'll buy you a drink and lunch."

"I have to pick up Excelsior at noon–"

"They'll feed him lunch if you call, and they'll put him down for a nap. Come *on*!"

"I don't have a suit."

"Borrow one of mine." Joan has to wear an old one, a smaller-sized one, of Fran's. Fran eyes her friend's body with concern. "Joan, what's happened to you? You've lost a bunch of weight, and for anyone else that would be a good thing, but *you*— "

"I just—can't eat. I have to eat a little all the time, like a cracker or a piece of banana, and if I don't, then I seem to—shut down and it's physically impossible for me to eat anything."

"Yeah, well, if I didn't know you hate to throw up, I'd say you were bulimic." Joan frowns. "Have you had your thyroid checked? And your blood sugar? Seriously, what are we going to do about you? Has Robert gotten worried?"

"He spends about a third of his time on business trips. He's really busy, building his business back up— he's out of town now." Which is why I'm at your house instead of in bed with him in the middle of the morning, Joan could have added.

"Joan, Joan." Fran takes her friend's face in her hands and Joan almost weeps at her kind touch. "This is *not* how a marriage is supposed to be. Better or worse, remember? Richer or poorer— "

"Sickness or health. I know."

"A partnership, not master and slave!" Fran shakes Joan's head up and down to assure agreement, then laughs. "Oh, listen to me." She drops her hands. "Okay. Towels, suntan lotion, car keys, eat poolside, charge it all to my account—a perfect day. Go—call the preschool."

An hour later they lie on the aqua-colored lounge chairs, the only women at the pool. Pleasantly, the lagoon on the beach side of Banana Bay never accumulates algae the way the mainland does, so the air smells clean, although hot.

"Hey, this is so nice," Fran says, idly looking at the river over the top of her sunglasses. "The place to ourselves." Suddenly she sits up and her voice changes. "Joan. My god. Didn't you say Robert is out of town on a business trip?"

"Uh huh."

"Well then, somebody's stealing his boat."

Joan sits up and makes a porch with her hands to shut out the glare of sun on the water. The SEE LEGS is out of its slip and heading for the open river, toward the causeway. Fran and Joan stare, then look at each other. "That bastard," she says before Joan can react. "Come on."

They clamber into Fran's car and head toward the causeway. "Wh-what are we going to do?" Joan asks, fastening the seat belt while Fran is moving. All she can think is that they have to save Robert's boat before he comes home and blames her. "Shouldn't we call the police? Harbor patrol?"

"We're going to chase a sail." Fran's face is determined. "Get the binoculars out of the glove compartment."

Joan is too bewildered to wonder why someone would keep binoculars in the car. "Ken likes to birdwatch on Merritt Island," she says, as though reading her friend's mind. "—there it is!"

The SEE LEGS has now tacked and is heading north toward Cocoa. "Want a race, do you?" Fran says. They drive over the causeway and turn right onto U.S.1, keeping the sails in sight.

Joan feels as though she is in a dream, but the sun is glaring bright and when she rolls down the window to put the binoculars into the open air, the metal on the side of the car is hot to the touch of her forearm. No, this is no dream.

"North of Banana Bay is an old unused dock and an abandoned house. I'll bet you that's where he's going."

Joan gapes at Fran. "How do you– ?"

"Ken and I used to park there and make out when we were in high school. I know all the make-out spots in this area."

"But—but why would Robert have to– ?"

Fran pulls the car up near the edge of the river underneath some pines. This way the car is mostly hidden. "I hope to hell I'm wrong."

"Wrong– "

"Just keep your head down and watch and when you have to slap mosquitoes do it quietly. Ken and I used to come home covered with bites– " Fran laughs quietly– "but boy, it was worth it."

They each have time to take a drink of water from Fran's thermos when they spot the SEE LEGS pull up close to the dock. Joan takes in the scene: a broken-down dock, lots of old pine trees blocking the view from the road, a rusting phone booth that leans a little to the left, a ramshackle old settler's house with pine siding and tin roof. They can be seen from the road, but not the river.

They watch a man Robert's height and weight wearing Robert's captain's cap tie the boat to the dock. They watch him go to the phone booth, yank the broken door open as though he has done this before, and place a call. ("I'm surprised the phone company hasn't shut that thing off by now," whispers Fran to Joan.)

Joan doesn't answer. She's fascinated, seeing a side of Robert she had never seen before. It's like coming across a coiled-up rattler and needing to get out of its way, but being hypnotized by it at the same time. She has to switch her mind around to seeing this familiar person as someone altogether different, and the picture is making her rather dizzy.

"Still think he's out of town?" Fran whispers once more, as the man heads back to the boat, swinging himself a little stiffly onto its deck. The two women look at each other. Now they can hear giggling coming from the interior of the SEE LEGS.

"You ever been out on that boat?" Fran asks.

"I'm not a really good sailor, and Robert says it's only for business contacts. He says if I came aboard, he wouldn't be able to get a tax deduction– "

Fran stares at her a moment, squashes a mosquito, and then puts the car in reverse. "Let's go. You're in shock. Shut your window." Joan sits, uncomprehending. "*Joan.* Close your window. I'm turning on the AC."

They drive back down U.S. #1. Joan is tallying the cars that come toward them. If there are three white cars in a row, she decides, then all this is a dream and she will wake up.

"Honey, I'm so sorry," Fran says, her hands gripping the steering wheel so that her tan whitens, "I never would have gone on that chase if I'd known—oh, I suspected, but—*you* knew, too, didn't you? You guessed he was messing around, right?"

Joan puts the binoculars away carefully in the glove compartment after wrapping the cord around it carefully several times. "Fran," she says finally, "Fran—*I* give him sex whenever he wants."

"He's a sexaholic, Joan," Fran says. "You remember that from our psych sex class?"

"A what?"

"He defines himself by his conquests. He doesn't feel adequate unless he's having sex."

Joan laughs tightly and shakes her head no. "Not *Robert.* "

"Okay. But from all you've told me, I bet it's true." They drive in silence to Fran's house. Joan goes to her heated car.

"Joan. No," Fran says.

"What?"

"You can't sit on that seat without a towel or something." Joan hasn't felt the singeing leather until Fran points it out."

"I'll be ok. Uh– I'll return your bathing suit to you."

"Keep it. I'll never fit in it again." She looks at Joan's face and is apparently startled enough to say, "Joan. I'm going home with you. Somebody needs to stay with you a while."

Joan is too drained to argue, and that is why, coming into her kitchen and pushing "rewind" and then "play" on the answer phone in case there is a message about Pete or Excelsior, they hear Robert talking in his smooth-as-custard voice that matches his face, "I'm delayed out of town. Bad weather. See you in two days. Don't let the kids get into any of my things. And keep them the hell out of my car." She hangs up the phone. He really should not say "hell" where the kids could overhear, she thinks.

"Where *is* his car, Joan?" says Fran. "He sounded like he was in a hurry, or he would have realized– "

"I—it should be at the airport. "

"Then how could they get into it? Come on. Bring your key to his car."

"I don't know where he put it."

"Then we'll look until we find it!"

Okay, now Joan realizes she *is* in shock, because she doesn't react to the sight of Fran in her bedroom rummaging through the closet.

"What's this?" she says, holding out a little date book. "It was stuffed in a sock on the top shelf in your closet. There's a metal box up here, too, shoved way back." She opens it. "Not locked. How careless of the man. He must know you're not the snooping type. Huh. Some kind of legal papers."

She hands the book and the box to Joan, who stares dumbly at what she has in her hands. How impressive– Fran is *good* at finding things! "I've never seen these before." Joan opens the book.

She sits down on her side of the bed and starts to read, oblivious to Fran's continued rummaging through dresser drawers.

The book is in Robert's careful handwriting and is full of entries about *her*! Joan reads at random: "12/10– Good day—sex twice, morning, bedtime; 12/11– bad day—Joan says headache. Don't believe her; 12/12—Joan sick. Temp 102 Sex good, Joan nice hot . Joan says sick. Sex bedtime. 12/13– "

She can't read any more. She remembers those couple of days when she was burning with fever and had no strength to prevent Robert from having sex, how she was headachy and unable to eat, and wondered if she was just imagining his cool body on her fevered one. She is ashamed for some reason at the memory.

She stuffs the little books back into Robert's sock and opens the metal box. She pulls out a stiff piece of paper at random. A will. She starts to read, her hands trembling–

"Found it!" Fran holds up an MGB key. "Let's go!"

✿ ✿ ✿

Fran circles the airport parking lot until they find Robert's car, carefully parked in the shade. They unlock the driver's side door. "What are we going to do?" Joan asks, scared. What if Robert returns and finds them? She has no idea of the depth of his anger. "Robert– "

"Uh uh. He's out of town for two days, remember?"

"But—what are we doing?"

"We're looking for clues," says Fran. "Aha!" She holds up a garage door opener.

"That's not ours," Joan says, puzzled. Is she talking slowly, like one drowning in thick sludge? She can't command her brain to make sense of anything. Fran grabs her arm.

"Lock Robert's door. Take the key. I've got the opener. We'll bring it back when we're done."

"What– ?"

"Think of me as Hercule Poirot. And you, ma chere Hastings, are my confidante."

They drive up and down the streets of Banana Bay beachside– "he'd never be stupid enough to have sex with a *mainland* woman," says Fran. "They'd be too low-class for him. *And* they could beat him up, especially the ones from west Banana Bay—they're cattle people and they have *muscles*."

Recalling Fran grew up on the Banana Bay mainland, Joan thinks maybe she is talking about her own youth, but she doesn't respond. It's a good thing that beachside is only a mile wide with just several dozen streets, because Joan is now a little seasick from all the slow swerving Fran is doing. Fran slows down at every house and aims the door opener at each garage. This is a needle in a haystack, Joan thinks, bringing back the image of Susan as a cork with prickly things in her hair.

Joan is so tired! She is looking at her wristwatch and wondering why she can't concentrate long enough to read its face and if there will be time to get home before Pete leaves the Little League lunch when– "Bingo!" yells Fran.

She stops the car. They stare across the street at a large pink stucco house with a pecky cypress garage door. The door is moving up and down, up and down, at Fran's command. There are no cars inside.

"We got it!" Fran is elated. Joan looks at the cacti on the manicured zoysia grass lawn, the brown smiling ceramic burro wearing a colorful serape which contrasts crazily with the set of pink plastic flamingos. A small fountain splashes in the sunlight, with a miniature humpback bridge over the cement front yard fish pond. A glazed ceramic boy looking like Huck Finn with a toy fishing pole sits on top of the bridge.

"Whose– ?"

"Oh, ma fois. Quel dommage– you've never been to the Comstock's house?" Fran says, moving her car faster now up the street and back toward the airport. "Well, unless Mrs. Comstock has grown tired of watching her husband dance on his hat, *your* husband, ma chere Hastings, is screwing *your* only client , the beautiful and most dysfunctional Annabella."

✡ ✡ ✡

They have left the garage door opener in Robert's car and Joan is now back at her house. Fran has picked up Excelsior from daycare and taken him home with her for the afternoon– "We'll go swimming together, won't we, honeypie?" she has cooed to the delighted child. She has asked Joan several times how she is doing. "Fine," is the only word Joan can think of.

Pete has gone to a friend's house to swim. "Your mom's not feeling well and just needs to have some quiet time," Fran has explained before he can wonder why Joan is not talking, not even reminding him to wear sunscreen.

Fran's voice, "That bastard. Oh, that bastard," echoes in her head. It was like a hymn that Fran had chanted all the way home. If they were Poirot and Hastings (the helper always the last to figure something out!) shouldn't it be "batarde"?

The house is silent now. Joan leaves untouched the sandwich Fran made for her and enters the master bedroom. She opens the metal box again. She unfolds the stiff paper: her mother's will. She reads, glancing guiltily up often, waiting to hear Robert's car and see his accusing face—what is she doing with *his* personal belongings!

So. *This* is the difference between privacy and secrecy—secrecy is when your husband is your mother's executor and says nothing about it to you. This must be what they were discussing when she was here. But why couldn't he tell his own wife, Gladys' own daughter?

She reads the will. It is not long, since Gladys had few possessions other than her money, and fewer family members to inherit anything. The upshot is that "since I lent Robert Baldwin, my son-in-law, the sum of $500,000– " Joan gasps at this– "I consider it to be his family's inheritance. He is to disperse all the money, after he has paid his business expenses, to my daughter Joan Gibson Baldwin.

"She is also to have my jewelry– " Joan stops and searches through the box,where there is no sign of Mother's expensive brooch or diamond earrings or her antique wedding ring set– " and any other money from my estate is to go to the Order of the Saints Abroad, which was my husband's favorite charity. Robert is also to oversee the sale of my home with all its furnishings, after Joan removes what she wants. The proceeds are to go to Joan Gibson Baldwin, my only daughter."

Robert ! *Robert* got half a million dollars from Joan's mother! The giggling woman on the SEE LEGS (how Joan hates that name) pales in her memory for a moment. Then she blinks: Did he use her money—oh yes, from *her* mother to her, it is *her* money!– to buy that boat? How much of anything he told her has been true? Their marriage! Has it all been built on *lies*?

She returns the box and the little book to their hiding places. She is numb. She lies down and turns on the TV set. A soap opera comes on. She watches it unseeing.

Her life is a soap opera and she is not even the lead actress.

And why, oh why, does a joke Robert once told her come to her now? – A burglar breaks into a house where a man and his wife are sleeping. The burglar decides to have sex with the unwilling wife. He draws a circle on the bedroom carpet.

"You have to stay in that circle," he tells the husband. "If you move out of the circle, I will kill you and your wife."

He then has sex with the wife. Then he turns to the husband.

"Ha ha," he says. "I just had sex with your wife."

"Ha ha yourself," says the husband. "Every time you weren't looking, I stepped out of the circle."

✭ ✭ ✭

BAD WIND BLOWS GOOD TIMES

Hurricane Clancy, a Category One blowhard,
roared at record speed through Banana Bay Friday night,
leaving trees down and many homes without power.
Among the families opting not to leave beachside
were Mr. And Mrs. Edward Comstock, who entertained
Father and Mrs. Tom Wolfe, as well as several
other St. Barnabus' parishioners, in their well appointed
home. A good time was had by all, with FatherWolfe
preparing his famous "Episcopalian Excess" chili.
Mr. Comstock performed, by popular demand,
his Mexican Hat Dance.
Hats off to our intrepid partygoers!
—*Banana Bay Tribune, August 15, 1977*

Joan is a coward. She writes it a second time and this time she underlines it.
JOAN IS A COWARD.

There. She is afraid to confront Robert. What if he throws her out of the
house, locks the doors and won't let her have Excelsior and Pete? She's told this to
Fran, and Fran has been kind enough not to push at her to do anything; but Joan
can see that Fran seethes every time she has to talk to Robert.

Annabella is on an extended vacation, roaming the Riviera or something.
Her absence has made Joan's life easier, since as a therapist she is not sure what to
say to her young client, either. Joan may be the only one who knows how fragile
Annabella is. She has bragged in confidence about male conquests she has had,
and Joan, listening and wanting to respond, "Does your mother know what you
are doing, young lady?" the way she would like to talk to Susan if she dared ,

thought she was making it all up. Now Joan wonders if Annabella has been having fun at her counselor's expense.

Was that really *Robert* on his boat? Maybe she needs glasses. She can't really be *sure*...and she wouldn't want to accuse anyone unless she was certain. If you put a captain's cap on a man, a colleague of Robert's, of course they would look similar from a distance.

Especially awkward if she were to accuse and then have to allow Robert to take her by the hand to the optometrist and wait, tapping his foot ("Joan, you have screwed up again") while the doctor examined her and adjudged her to be almost totally blind. Robert nodding I told you so.

But how about the garage door opener? Joan almost laughs when she thinks of sitcoms where the same opener opens several garage doors and hilarity ensues. Sure, that could happen. And Robert found the garage door opener and was going to turn it in when he got back from his trip. There, that made sense.

Anyway, she can't just storm at Annabella, who would doubtless burst into tears and leave. So far she doesn't have another client, and that wouldn't be very professional, either. So until Annabella returns for more sessions Joan is paying her half of the monthly rent check to Doctor Griffin from her piano teaching earnings.

This is the other job Joan had while she was putting herself through college: she would go to Tony's Italian Restaurant at 10:00 am, get things ready for the lunch crowd, clean up afterward (tidying the bathrooms was included in her job description—she had never before been in a men's room), and then run home before Pete came home from first grade. She would give him a snack, say "hello" to the babysitter, who would keep him busy coloring or watching TV in the other end of the house, while Joan taught piano students not much older than Pete for the rest of the afternoon.

Then she would make dinner, mostly for Pete and herself, since Robert was so often out of town. Many times dinner was courtesy of Tony, the restaurant owner, who would fix her some pasta covered with aromatic sauce and put it in a round cardboard container with crimped-edge aluminum on top.

"You gotta *eat* more, Joan," he would tell her. "I don't want-a no skinny waitress waiting on my customers—they gonna think my food is no good."

Tony's kindness kept her going, because she harbored a heart full of resentment toward her students. Oh, outwardly she was good to them, but inwardly—they would come down the street singing, chatting, friends walking with them, being so—carefree!– and she would be struggling to make enough money to keep herself going to school at night. Oh, how Joan wanted to be young and carefree herself again, and not carry around a pizza smell in her hair and thrift-shop clothing!

Any anger she felt toward Robert for not helping her with money for her college courses she swallowed: she had to agree she was doing something considered a luxury (even selfish), while he was taking care of all their necessities. He, with his hand on the checkbook and knowing their monetary situation, had every right to deny her financial backing. "Do it yourself the way we *all* had to, Joan," he lectured. "It will make you a stronger person."

Ah, so in his own way he *was* helping her! By not helping, in some Zen way, he was showing his love toward Joan. (The elephant in the room was that his way had been paid through M.I.T. by his father. But men—men *needed* a higher education. Betty Friedan aside, college for Joan, which she loved, still seemed like something housewives would be free to do after they got all their other chores finished.)

And then any resentment would melt away at the sight of those small fingers touching Joan's piano keys. Sometimes—okay, most times– she wasn't that strict a teacher—a student would just sit by her side on the piano bench and talk with her about what was going on at school or even what trouble he or she was having at home with siblings, and it was here that Joan realized how good she was at listening without judgment.

This same listening without judgment is not helping her with Robert, however. " I saw your boat on the river," she says cautiously, a few days after Fran's and Joan's Mad Toad's Ride.

"Oh yeah? When?" He does not look up from behind his engineering journal.

"Eight days ago. August seventh." The date is seared into Joan's brain.

"Couldn't have been. You know I was out of town."

This is her cue to drop the subject. It is now a contest between his truth, his reality, or Joan's. Only the image of that grinning ceramic donkey on the fake-looking lawn keeps her going: "Uh—Fran and I both saw it. On the river. Near an old dock– "

Now his eyes bore into her as he calmly lays down his magazine, first placing his finger to mark the page he has been reading. "August seventh" he repeats her words. She watches his face, an amateur Hastings ready to report her findings to Fran, Joan's Poirot. Huh. Not a frown or wrinkle mars that custard skin.

" August seventh. Oh, *you* must have seen Arnold Probst."

"Who's Arnold Probst?"

"He's a guy who comes to town every now and then, a marketing rep. I lend him the boat, figure it's good business. He looks like me—same height, same hair color. I thought I'd locked up my captain's hat—he told me once he likes to wear it. But what were *you* doing? "

Joan studies his face closely. He could win at poker every time—not a trace of emotion flits across that visage. Well, M. Poirot, I tried.

"Well—you told me you were out of town and we noticed the boat from the Yacht Club– "

"And what the hell were you doing at the Yacht Club?"

"Fran invited me."

"*Fran.*" The name is said with such disgust that Joan ends the conversation, not eager to have her dearest and most trusted friend vilified.

Robert returns to his fingered page. "Don't you have dinner ready *yet?*"

Later she picks up the journal while Robert is outside. The journal contains an article by Arnold Probst, Ph. D.

✫ ✫ ✫

A larger issue suddenly takes precedence: Hurricane Clancy is coming. Toward Banana Bay. Father Wolfe has given his usual speech about "everyone gather in the parish hall to wait it out. We'll have a great time together!Make sure you come now and bring some food for all to share. We'll have a regular *hurricane* party!"

Joan has decided the family needs to do this. She needs to be with other people, not just Robert. She is aware that the last hurricane they went through was a fluke, in that nothing happened to them except for a few water oak limbs breaking off, and a schefflera that had grown too tall too fast fell into their pool. Pete made an afternoon out of it, pulling out only one umbrella-type leaf at a time so he could keep diving underneath the soggy plant as though he were a fish in an aquarium.

Joan is making a huge pot of tomato sauce for the crowd which will be gathering in St. Barnabus' parish hall. She'll take the linguine and cook it there, she thinks. Father Wolfe has raved over her sauce in the past and the recipe is one of her favorites. Nothing like Tony's, but even so....

"What's going on?" says Susan, coming into the kitchen and lounging against the counter.

"I'm making spaghetti sauce to take to church while we wait out the hurricane there."

"Not me," yawns Susan. (Joan is writing "Susan" here instead of her preferred new name "Vronsky" because Joan doesn't care for it and is not sure how to spell it.) "I'm not going anywhere."

"You have to! You can't stay here!" Already the wind is whipping through the trees. They have the TV set on and the local weather reporters are beside themselves with glee—a third hurricane this summer! Maybe they'll be able to report something terrific instead of that minuscule one that sauntered through last month—that fizzled-out pretender "Benjamin"! "Look, they're telling everyone to prepare for Category *Two*!"

"They don't know what they're talking about half the time." Susan dismisses the newscasters. "Anyway, *if* it comes, I figure I'll take Excelsior and go stay with some friends in Orlando." She peels a banana, abandons it to the counter, and goes to the pantry. "Isn't there anything *good* to eat in this house?"

"I am trying to get ready for a *hurricane* here!" Joan tells her, stirring the sauce and adding more anise seed. "Find whatever you can." It tastes good. A little more red wine should do it. Then she'll put it in containers, leave some here for the freezer, praying that the electricity stays on, and pack most of it in ice for the trip to the church–

"What *smells* in here?" says Pete, entering the kitchen.

"Mom's taking you to church for the hurricane. You're going to stay with the old geezers."

"No!" protests Pete.

"I told you to get your sleeping bag and a suitcase ready," Joan tells him.

"I thought we were going to wait it out at some *fun* place! With TV!" howls Pete, sounding at this moment like Excelsior.

"*I'm* going to Orlando," smirks Susan.

"No fair! I want to go with Su– with *Vronsky*!" Oh, Pete can be a sly one. Susan shakes her head "no". He slams the wall oven door open and shut a few times in his frustration before his mother can stop him. "Then I'm staying *here*." Joan frowns at him, lowering her head slightly. He reads her expression correctly, gives the oven door one more "bang" and skulks out of the room. Ever since Susan moved back home he has been moody.

Joan senses he's miffed about having to share a room with Excelsior. Robert refuses to give up his den/office/Susan's old bedroom or the lock to it. Joan has no idea what is in there anymore. He also keeps the blinds drawn– "sunlight is not good for a computer."

"Get your things ready!" she calls after her son.

Robert comes in. He has been at the Yacht Club, making sure SEE LEGS is shipshape and bound up so tight she can't float down the river. He says to Susan without saying hello to his wife, "You should see the way some of the landlubbers are tying up their boats. They'll be fishing them from the bottom of the river tomorrow." Susan nods.

"Are you packed to go?" Joan asks him. He does not respond. Robert has seemed in a more pensive frame of mind since giving her the Arnold Probst information. He's quieter than usual. She hasn't wanted to ask him about her mother's will, fearing a major blow-up, and now she is distracted by the hurricane.

"It won't come, anyway," says Susan, mushing her peeled banana onto the counter absent-mindedly.

"There's a sandbar off the coast of Banana Bay in the ocean, and it keeps hurricanes from coming here. *Everyone* knows that." Joan sighs. "Well, gotta get ready for the trek to Orlando." She leaves the kitchen as her mother wipes up the banana.

"You're not going with us? You're not leaving *Excelsior* with us!" Robert calls after her.

"She's taking him with her," Joan explains.

"Good," Robert says, more to himself than to his wife. "That kid gets on my nerves." Since Robert never takes any notice of his grandchild unless someone is watching, "getting on my nerves" means "I don't want to be reminded of his existence".

Pete is already outside when they bring out their supplies, Robert with an overnight case and Joan with pillows, sheets, sleeping bags, extra clothing, toothpaste and toothbrushes, soap, towels, shampoo (although there are no showers at church), extra toilet paper, Parmesan cheese, linguine and the spaghetti sauce.

Both Baldwin males wait while she hauls all this into the car, Pete taking his cue from his father. "I hate to leave before Susan does," Joan says. "She always forgets to lock one door or the other." Joan has stuffed more towels down by each door in case the wind blows rain under the frames,and has turned off the AC. She has set the refrigerator and freezer as low as they will go, and she has filled the bathtubs halfway with water, because she has heard that is what you're supposed to do if there's no water supply.

She has put extra chlorine in the swimming pool (she doesn't really know why, since if there is a lot of rain the pool will overflow anyway) and she has asked Pete to bring in the patio furniture.

Robert has checked his MGB to make sure it has gas in case the gas pumps don't operate after the hurricane. They are going to church in Joan's car. "I'll drive," he says, holding out his hand for her keys, which she hands over without arguing. "It takes a *man* to hold a car on the road in all this wind."

It is indeed roaring in huge gusts. Dead palm fronds are dancing down their now- deserted street. She notices other neighbors have plywood on their windows, and wonders why Robert didn't think of that while she was doing everything else. Too late now.

"Now where are you going?" asks Robert. "If you go back in the house again, tell Susan to move her car. It's blocking the driveway and we can't get out."

Robert hates to have anything blocking his path. That's why he has demanded that Susan park in the driveway behind *Joan's* car, not his. Joan sees him frowning at an oil spot her car is leaking onto the concrete.

"I want to get Susan out of the house and make sure it's all locked up."

"Are you afraid of robbers, in this weather?"

Pete laughs at his father's question. "*Robbers!* That's funny, Dad."

At least Pete's over his pre-teen sulking, Joan thinks. All at once Susan, Excelsior heavy in her arms, dashes out and into her car. How does she *do* that? Joan wonders. She hangs around and hangs around and all at once she's ready. Joan wants to ask if Susan's got enough food for Excelsior, but the car roars off.

"Now where? JOAN– !"

"I have to be sure the trash cans are inside!" Before either male can ask more questions, she makes a tour of the house. Susan has indeed left a window ajar in the bathroom, and the front door unlocked. Joan takes care of these and runs outside, leaving the light on beside the front door in case they come back at night. And this way when they return they'll be able to tell instantly if the power is on or off! Joan congratulates herself for having thought of everything.

"The hurricane will *be* here before you're ready!" grumbles Robert. He does, however, drive them first to the ocean, where the waves are larger and grayer than they've ever seen them, and big airy chunks of foam like Florida tumbleweeds are blowing over the empty road.

Policemen are directing traffic over the causeway. "We're asking everyone to leave the beachside," shouts a policeman as wet and black as a seal in his raingear. "And once you leave, you won't be allowed back on. This is gonna be a bad one."

Pete slumps in the back seat. "Shoot!" he says. "I wanted to stay!"

But that last one, Benjamin last month when they *did* stay at home, spooked Joan enough to take this hurricane news seriously. The slamming of the wind and the unabated howling without Benjamin's wearing himself out, but instead seeming to build into more and more fury—and that was Category *One only*!– makes her glad they're leaving. And they'd be with their friends! Fran is lucky enough to have her own relatives on higher ground, way west on the mainland. Joan feels better, knowing she'll be all right. They join the steady line of cars going over the causeway, which seems to shake in the wind.

☆ ☆ ☆

There are no cars at St. Barnabus' when they pull up to the parish hall door. "I can't believe we're the first ones," Joan says.

Well, no matter. She directs the reluctant Robert and Pete to bring everything from the car into the hall. Robert, being a vestryman, has a key. She sets the sauce on the counter in the kitchen and finds a couple of big pots. She dumps the sauce in one and fills the other with water to boil for the linguine. "We'll have it all ready when the others arrive," she announces brightly.

No one else arrives. The water boils; she makes linguine; and the three eat in silence. Joan is quietly thankful that they do not accuse her of forcing them to come here. She does the dishes alone and puts the ample leftovers away for any stragglers. Pete finds some soft drinks in the refrigerator and opens one. She doesn't protest—these are unusual circumstances.

"Well, this is fun, anyway," she says just to break the silence. Robert has perched on one of the folding chairs, his long legs on another, to read his journal. Pete looks through the church's library collection in the corner. The wind is building up so steadily and rapidly that it soon keeps them from talking—they would have to shout otherwise.

The power quits about an hour later. Now they are in the dark. With the air conditioner off, the room begins to turn warm and muggy. Joan makes up sleeping bags and, taking turns with the church flashlight (she can't believe she forgot to bring a flashlight!) that Pete found while rummaging for more soda, they visit the bathrooms and get ready for their temporary beds.

They can hear the rain pounding the old tin roof next door on the hundred-year-old church. At one time there is a tremendous crash– "*Tree* fell down!" yells Pete, trying to see out a window into the darkened road.

✡ ✡ ✡

Joan sleeps fitfully, unused to the hard floor. Where are all the people Father Wolfe promised? Where is all the friendship, the jocularity, the good humor? She can hear Robert snore despite the unrestrained pounding of the storm.

In the morning she searches the kitchen for food and finds some cookies, pats of butter, orange drink (powdered, for the Sunday School kids), and some old cottage cheese. Since the power has been off all night she's reluctant to use these.

"The sun's out!" calls Pete. She hurries outside. Everything has become still. There is a light rain falling and the sky is a yellowy- gray, but the wind has thankfully stopped.

She listens; birds are twittering. They see now why the power went —a big old water oak branch had snapped and fallen against some power lines.

"Be careful of those wires!" Joan calls to Pete as he splashes in the street. A Florida Power and Light truck is already here and a man in a yellow slicker is tending to some downed lines.

"It's the *eye*!" he shouts. "We're in the eye! Tell your boy to stay inside—don't want anything to happen to him!"

Pete, disgusted that someone would call him a "boy", backs off a few feet.

Robert has eaten a cookie and has gone back to his journal. So far they have not said anything to each other all night. Joan stays outside to make sure Pete doesn't get electrocuted.

"You know what this eye means, don't you?" says Pete, his eyes shining. "It's coming *again,* only the wind will come the *other* way this time!"

Joan's heart sinks as she pictures another night here living like this in silence with no food.

"Hey!" Pete suddenly yells. Joan looks where he is pointing, and trudging up the street with an umbrella and wearing high black boots, is the Senior Warden, Paul Nichols.

"You been here all night?" he asks, a look of disbelief on his wet face. "I come to check on the church. Looks like she rode it out okay. The people who built this place built it like an upside-down ark. Water-tight and all. If you turned it upside down," he addresses this to Pete, "you could float away"

He then invites the Baldwins to his house. "Got a couple more parishioners staying with us. Gotta hurry. This here is a fast-movin' hurr-ee-cane and it'll pass through in no time. HOW COME– " he bellows to the FPL man– "you botherin' to fix things now? Why not wait 'til it's over?"

"It's my job," replies the repairman. Satisfied with that answer, the older man leads them down the street to his house, where Mrs. Nichols has just made coffee and brought out Danish pastries. She exclaims when she sees them, gets the report about the stormworthiness of the church from her husband, and finds everyone some dry towels.

Mr. and Mrs. Nichols are so chatty that they don't notice how quiet their trio of guests is. The silent Baldwins spend another night away from home, with Joan inwardly regretting it because their hosts are both chain smokers, with a tiny yappy dog that keeps licking their faces while they try to sleep on the carpeted floor which smells vaguely of urine. This would make a funny family story, Joan thinks, that she and Robert could laugh about later.

Although she has trouble summoning an image of Robert laughing about any of this.

The police re-open the causeway the next morning. Once more they drive to the ocean, where the surf has died down some, but the water is still dull gray and a few young skinny teenaged boys are battling the choppy waves with their surfboards. Pete wants to stay and watch them, but he's also torn, because he wants to see what damage has been done to their house, so he climbs back into the rear seat of the car and they drive through more downed palm fronds, both dead and green, and slalom past fallen tree limbs.

At home they find Susan and Excelsior. Susan's hair is now dyed iodine-red.

"How long have *you* been here?" Joan gapes. She stares at her kitchen, which now is a shambles. There are dirty dishes on every inch of the counters and in the sink. There is evidence of spaghetti sauce on the kitchen table and on the curtains, where Excelsior most likely wiped his hands after eating.

She shrugs. "I had a fight with my friend and decided to come back home. We've been here since about an hour after you all left."

"No *fair*!" protests Pete. He runs outside, slamming the front door, to jump in puddles and complain to his buddies.

"Power stayed on?" says Robert, calmly, as though he had been carrying on an uninterrupted conversation.

"Sure thing," says Susan. "Somebody turned off the AC, so I turned it back on. See all your friends at church? Oh, and who'd be crazy enough to stuff towels by the door? I could hardly get in."

Robert, without answering, walks into their bedroom. He closes the door behind him.

Joan empties her car of all the residue from their aborted hurricane camp party and she opens all the windows to get rid of the musty smell it now carries. She takes the wet towels and places them in the washing machine, first removing a mildewing load of Susan's and Excelsior's clothing and setting it in the dryer.

She then turns the refrigerator and freezer back to their normal settings. She stoops and picks up all the towels that have been bolstered against the doors . The towels are damp, so she adds them to the ones in the washing machine.

She brings Robert's overnight case into their bedroom. The bathroom door is closed and she can hear the shower running. She observes that he has removed his wet clothing and has heaped them on the bed (*Joan's* side of the bed), and she takes them up in her arms, walks out to the patio and to the pool.

The pool is flooded. To the brim. Joan tosses Robert's clothes in the pool. She removes her shoes and stomps with deliberation in some puddles on the concrete.

She notes that the fruit trees she planted have lost some leaves and the ground is now a brilliant eye-blinding, breath-catching shade of unusual green, with stripped leaves and pine needles its new cover. She inhales the fresh, clean, post-hurricane air, full of ozone. The sky stretches over her, a bright cloudless blue. Everything is as calm as a newly-painted fresco, as though all the frenzy of a storm had never happened.

Joan sets her shoes on the patio to dry. She walks barefoot back into the house and she opens the bathroom door. Robert has finished his shower and now sits naked on the toilet seat, a journal in his hands. He looks up, startled, for once defenseless, as Joan looks down at him and his manhood, shriveled from the hot water.

"Robert," she says—

No. NO.

"Robert," *I* say, surprised at this new calm tone in my voice, "By the way, I want a divorce."

WOMAN TARGETS LOBSTER DIVERS

An elderly woman, upset about who she believed
were lobster divers in the canal behind her home, opened fire
on them with a handgun. "That's my canal
and they have no business in there," Alice Mossman told
police officials. No one was injured and Mrs. Mossman was arrested,
protesting that she would "not take this lying down". Mrs. Mossman, 69,
when informed there are no spiny lobsters in Banana Bay's canals,
replied, "That's because the manatees eat them." When told that
manatees are vegetarians, Mrs. Mossman maintained the entire matter
was a plot against homesteaders.
A court date has not yet been announced.
—*Banana Bay Tribune, August 20, 1977*

Dear Father Wolfe,
You wanted me to write everything in this journal, and so I am. I would like to let you know that as soon as I announced I wanted a divorce, Robert agreed, saying that we had grown too far apart for this marriage to be mended.

I would like to say that we told the children hand in hand and we worked out a divorce settlement then and there, sitting comfortably across from each other at the kitchen table after brushing aside its crumbs, and drawing up what we each needed, on a piece of Robert's engineering paper.

I would like to tell you all that. However, I would be lying, because as soon as Robert was able to rise from his throne and yank on his bathing trunks, he hurtled himself after me, grabbed me in the kitchen, threw me over his shoulder, ran outside with me too surprised to say anything, and tossed me into the pool, where, swearing words I had never heard from him, even in high school, he pushed me under water every time I came up for air until he got tired.

I heaved myself, gasping and choking, onto the concrete. I could hear his MGB thundering down the street. And, Father Wolfe, my thoughts were not for me, but for *him*! I worried that his children might have seen him in this state and be scared of his rage, which they had never seen and I only seldom.

I worried that I had somehow brought this on myself and if anything happened to him, an accident, it would be my fault.

I needn't have been so concerned. And the kids didn't witness what had happened. I leaned against the shower walls, the water as hot as I could stand it, and shook until I calmed down. Then I phoned Fran, who cheered and insisted I call you for further help.

"– and I'll find you an attorney, and you're entitled to the house and– " I could listen to her no longer, I was so worn out. "And, Joan—don't say *anything* to him! Anything he wants to say, tell him you'll *only* talk to him in front of Father Wolfe or a lawyer. You got that? *Joan!*"

I nodded "yes" into the phone. I said "good-by," and lay down.

I must have fallen asleep, because I woke up to see Robert standing over me, our positions reversed from when I had made my declaration.

"So you think you're gonna get out of this just like that?" he breathed alcohol into my face. "Well, you just think again. I'm staying in this house that I have paid for, and I'm keeping Pete, and Susan's already told me she'll take over the housekeeping, and you'll be left with *nothing*! I've already retained the best lawyer in the area!" He scattered a few more curse words over me and went into the bathroom, locking the door behind him.

I got up and drove to Publix for food, although nothing looked appealing. When I came home the lock on the bedroom door had been changed and all my clothes had been stacked in the living room.

And so we came to see you, Father Wolfe, with me crying once more as I put my two hands in your one big one, and with Robert neat and pressed, looking as though he was the aggrieved party. I will recap, so that you can see my therapist's memory for conversations is intact:

ROBERT: "She's not getting *anything*. I've given her *everything* all these years."

YOU (FATHER WOLFE): "Well, now, Robert, that's not quite how it works– "

ROBERT: "It's going to hurt *you*, too! She won't be tithing to the church the way I do!"

YOU: "You won't have any say over where Joan's money goes, Robert."

ROBERT: "She *has* to tithe! It's *my* money!" (I think maybe he *does* have this bargain with God– "I did my part. Now You do Yours, and look the other way.") Robert looks as though he is Rumplestiltskin, jumping up and down in fury because someone has guessed his name.

YOU: "Well, now, as for tithing, and that's not actually one of the Ten Commandments, you could take that money and cut it down the middle. Then you could give your half to St. Barnabus'– "

ROBERT: "The *other* half is mine, too! What if—look at her just sitting there, not saying a word! What if she doesn't give her half to the church?" Robert is all but foaming at the mouth.

YOU (with a little smile, which makes me feel so much better): "Well, then—I guess she can go to hell."

I thank you for that bit of sense of humor in such arduous proceedings, Father Wolfe. You made me feel a little less guilty.

The lawyers' consultation did not go much better:

ROBERT'S LAWYER (pushing a piece of paper at my lawyer): "This is what my client is willing to offer."

MY LAWYER: "No. This is unacceptable." (pushing his piece of paper across the table in return).

I am sitting there, my hair mussed, my weight dropping, feeling as though I have unwittingly dropped an atom bomb on our home. Who imagined it could wreak such havoc?

ROBERT (grabbing my lawyer's offer paper and reading it and talking directly to me before his lawyer can stop him): "Are you *crazy*? Are you *nuts*? After all my years of hard work? While you've been sitting around on your fat ass– !"

BOTH LAWYERS (together): "This meeting is over."

Here's my encounter with my elder child:

I try taking Susan aside to sound her out. We walk through Banana Bay Park, Excelsior between us. He is holding our hands, running away, falling down, laughing, and coming back to grab a hand again. Susan 's hair is streaked in various shades of blue this week. I don't know whether to be envious that she feels such freedom from other people's opinions, or if I should tell her to put on a hat.

"I can take care of Daddy," she says with supreme confidence, "since obviously *you* could not."

I sense that she likes the idea of free room and board for her and Excelsior. "Daddy told me that you spy on him and you're paranoid." Oh, she has all the easy answers of a Hitler youth! And I'm not about to get down and dirty with Robert, pulling at Susan to get her on my side. *"Daddy* says you've been looking to get away from us and get your own place, so you can see *men* and nobody will know about it."

"Susan, men are—is— the last thing on my mind." Indeed, the idea of being with someone new clamps my stomach shut. I've been looking for self-preservation, not taking care of yet another man.

"Daddy says— "

"*Daddy* doesn't know a thing about me!" I snap. She shrugs the Baldwin shrug, takes a pine cone from Excelsior's mouth, squints a warning at him when he gives her that odd eyebrow frown, and gives him a swig of some carbonated drink she has brought along. He grabs the can from her and upends it into his mouth greedily. "*Daddy* says you're going through your change of life— "

So runneth our conversation. "Listen, Susan. Make sure you get Excelsior to a dentist twice a year. Not Doctor Griffin—he's got no understanding of children."

"That's *it,* Mother?" she wheels on me suddenly. "You're ruining all our *lives* and all you can think about is *dental* checkups?" She hoists Excelsior, who drops the can on the ground, and then walks away from me at a good clip, considering my grandson's weight. "Doan! Doan! Come! Come wid us!" he calls over her back.

I stoop over, pick up the discarded can, place it in a trash can in the shape of a pelican with wide-open bill. I know the two of them can't go far since I have the car key.

I don't have time to worry about Susan. Pete is in the Principal's office. I get the message when we arrive home. He has threatened Preston Mossman on school property. He is about to be suspended or expelled. Now this is serious; the Mossmans are a tribe who do not forgive and forget. Word has it their grandbaby cut his teeth on grandma's squirrel-hunting rifle.

I drop off Susan and Excelsior, the younger one chatty and the older one stony, and head for the Principal's office, where I am witness to a surreal story:

PRINCIPAL: "Mrs. Baldwin, I had to call you and Mr. Baldwin here to let you know that Peter stole carpeting from another boy's locker."

PETE: "I did not! He stole it from *me!*"

ME: "I *did* give Pete some small pieces of carpeting to take to school."

PETE: "Those were the ones, Mom! And Preston stole them! I showed him what I did to line my locker with them and he wanted to do the same thing, so he waited until my locker was open, and my back was turned, and he *stole* them!"

PRINCIPAL: "Even so, ah— "

PETE (who cannot be stopped at this point): " But I didn't know *who* did it. So I went down the line of lockers and I knocked on every one—bing, bing, bing, bing, plunk! That was Preston's locker and that was my carpeting!" Pete is near tears in the face of this injustice.

PRINCIPAL: "You threatened a classmate."

PETE: "I told him to give my carpet back or I'd knock his block off. Then he threatened me with his grandmother's handgun!"

PRINCIPAL: "Under the circumstances, Mrs. Baldwin, we cannot have this kind of disruption in our school. It's just one boy's word against the other."

ME: "I agree. Therefore I suggest you open Preston's locker and let me identify my carpeting."

Pete looks at me, his mouth ajar. He has never heard me talk so firmly. I stand my ground and wait for the Principal to respond. Eventually he does.

PRINCIPAL: "Well, that being the case—we will need to wait until Peter's father gets here."

ME: "That will not be necessary, since I am Pete's mother. And by the way– "

PETE AND I (together): "He's out of town." We look at each other and Pete *shrugs*! It is the Baldwin shrug and I love him more at this moment than I think I ever have. I shrug back at him. The Principal looks at us and I know I've done it. It's a very, very small battle, but that's how wars are won.

ME: "Oh, and another 'by the way'– I would suggest you search Preston's locker and clothing for any illegal weapons. It *is* illegal to bring knives, guns and the like onto school property, is it not?"

PRINCIPAL: "Well, oh yes, of course– "

ME: "– unlike carpeting, which is perfectly legal. Would you like me to describe the color and manufacturer? Better yet, would you care to come to our home and see our carpeting for yourself?"

PRINCIPAL (at a loss for words): "Ah—well– that won't be necessary."

ME: "And while I'm here with you—how come we don't have P.T.A. in junior high school, when we most need it? And how about some trained police dogs to sniff out all those lockers for drugs?"

I usher Pete from the Principal's office and we walk down the hall just before the bell rings.

We knock on the lockers. Sure enough, they go "bing, bing, bing, bing, bing, plunk."

"Preston's," we say together and nod.

☆ ☆ ☆

MAN ACCUSED OF USING PET GATOR AS WEAPON

A man is facing battery charges after police officials
say he swung a three-foot alligator at his girlfriend
during an argument. David Hasselbrenner, 43, was
scheduled for a bond hearing Saturday after being
held overnight on misdemeanor charges of battery
and possession of an alligator, Banana Bay Police
Chief Edwin "Big Ed" Carson announced.
"This will get Banana Bay in the national news
for sure," he said. The girlfriend's name was not released.
—*Banana Bay Tribune, August 25, 1977*

4 pm
Robert was mad enough to spit. He understood what "seeing red" meant:
it meant that your blood pressure was so high from getting angry that it
made tiny blood vessels burst in your eye.

Well, he was just going to have to calm down. He'd gone through too much
to have a heart attack right here, right on the beach. Not that he was going to have
a heart attack—that was just an expression.

That damned Annabella! This was partly her fault. He knew she'd try to make
it up to him tonight; that is, if she realized she'd done anything wrong. He knew
she was aware he was entitled to sex on a daily basis—he cursed Joan for having
put a crimp in *that* need!— and having confessed this to Annabella, she was now
teasing him with it, holding out, making him work too hard.

And it was harder work than ever. There she was, 21 years old to his 43. Hell,
that wasn't much of a difference, and he even had heard once from his father that
he had some Mormon blood in him— "You and me, son, we're too much for just

one woman", and look at all the wives *they* had!– not that Annabella was about to be his wife. He'd had enough of that to last him a long time, thank you very much.

But there was so much to be furious *at,* he thought as he leaned over in the sand, clutching his legs and panting with his head down. He counted his grievances, using the mental checklist he carried with him:

1. Excelsior, the kid with the stupid name, got into Robert's things one day when he forgot to lock his door, because he'd had Mexican food at a hole in the wall place Annabella liked, and it gave him the runs, and when he got out of the bathroom there was that brat standing on top of his desk with his papers trampled under the kid's feet, and a purple ballpoint pen in his mouth like a lollipop. And what was he holding but Joan's mother's jewelry, which he hadn't had time to take to Orlando and pawn! So he had grabbed it back and locked it away and that made the kid cry, so Robert had yelled for Susan and she finally appeared with a towel wrapped around her head, yelling right back at her own father!– and she quick as anything picked the kid up and washed out his mouth, even the purple tongue.

    Then she laughed and said, "Well, we know where he gets it," and took the towel off, and there she was with purple hair herself. Robert told her she needed to watch the kid better and she gave him some guff right back. Got her attitude from her mother!

2. Maybe part of that one should be Annabella because of that Mexican place—probably dirty and crawling with palmetto bugs—(Robert shuddered).

3. Then Annabella invited him to a gathering at the Banana Bay Community Theater Season Opener Party. "It'll be fun," she said. "We'll pretend we don't know each other and then we'll feel each other up when nobody's looking." Well, he'd gone, if only to get away from Susan and *her* stupid friends, who seemed to have taken over his house, talking, eating, listening to strange music. Talking—that was the theater gathering, all right. He disliked small talk, disliked standing around with a drippy little paper plate in one hand and an innocuous domestic wine in the other, having to pretend to listen to local people with nothing to say and no forbearance to shut up about it, and don't you know Annabella took the microphone and introduced him as her date for the evening! And who was there but *Joan,* Joan all dressed up and talking to all those people like they'd been her friends for years, and Annabella at the mike! It was more than he should have to tolerate

4. Joan—he thought he had one on her when he forced her to move out of their/his house and leave him with everything but the clothes on her back. But here Fran—Robert's lip curled at the memory of Fran's triumphant face, helping Joan—had found her this little rental apartment in a condo across the street from the beach and Pete got to stay with her on week ends (which was actually fine with Robert, who needed to sneak Annabella into the house, anyway, and it was easier without Pete around). And who was having to pay her rent while they settled the divorce agreement? *He* was, of course! One more example of the legal system screwing hard-working men.

And all this had come about just for making one simple error, taking Annabella for a boat ride after she begged and begged. "That first time was no fun," she had pouted. "You worried about your silly fire. Now I'm going to light you a *better* fire, Bobby." (He needed to get her to stop calling him that!)"I'll sneak aboard when nobody's looking," she had said, "and be ready for you when we get out to the open sea." That just proved to him that she had her idiot moments, like thinking they'd sail in the ocean!

5. He'd left off a *big* one: Annabella was no longer so easy to have sex with. Suddenly she was coming up with one excuse or another, making it very difficult for him to keep marking off his daily sex routine in his little book. *Joan* now—Joan was like the game of Musical Chairs he'd played at kids' birthday parties when he was young—the music stops, you try to have your hand on a chair so you're not left out. He disliked that game, too—so much noise and confusion and getting to be the last one because he wasn't as agile as the others. Anyway, for a quarter-century Joan had been his chair when the music stopped, his sure thing if there wasn't sex available anywhere else. And now that chair was gone!

Oh yeah. Robert added a sixth grievance. Here he and Annabella were on a secluded stretch of the beach, running together, when all of a sudden she'd looked back and laughed, and had pulled away from him so fast that there was no way he was going to catch up. He could hardly see her up the beach now. He thought maybe she was waving to him, but he couldn't be sure.

His medical doctor had told him, "You're ready for bifocals," and Robert had said, "I don't even wear glasses."

"True," was the answer. "But sometimes people go from no glasses straight to bifocals. I'll give you the name of a good eye doctor."

Well, he was going to put that off until he absolutely could not see any more. Joan didn't wear glasses, and he certainly was not going to if *she* didn't.

Well, there he went, competing with Joan again. He bet she'd had *lots* of boyfriends while he was out of town, that hypocritical—but he had trouble grasping the idea that she would do that when she had *him* all these years.

He started jogging again, trying to ignore the stitch in his side. He was only 43! He'd seen men his age, and they were losing their waists and their hair, and they patted their beer bellies like they were in love with their stupid stomachs. Well, he wasn't going to be that way ever.

When he caught up with Annabella it took him a few moments to be able to talk. She, however, glowing in the sun under her tan, wearing the smallest bathing suit he'd ever seen on a woman's body ("all for you," she'd whispered to him), was chatting with a young man Robert's height, with an equally bronzed look and muscles that made Robert think this man worked out all the time.

"Bobby, you remember Father Wolfe's son Jack," she casually introduced the two of them.

This was Tom Wolfe's lifeguard son Jack "The Jock"! No wonder he was in such good shape! "How are you, son?" Robert said, holding out his hand and hoping Annabella had caught the word "son". He'd have to get her to stop calling him "Bobby" in public, at least.

"Bella and I went to school together, sir," answered Jack .

Annabella laughed a little tinkly laugh he had never heard before. "Jack used to call me "The Bella The Ball," she explained.

Robert , however, only caught the word "sir". As if he was old enough to be called a word you used with old geezers! Jack was still talking– "I was in the same grade with your daughter Susan."

If Jack Wolfe had taken a sword and pierced his side, Robert could not have been more injured. So Jack was alluding to Robert's being old *and* dating a woman his daughter's age! It was more than he should have to put up with. Somehow this was all Joan's fault. An image of his wife laughing with glee, spending his money right and left, swam before his eyes.

"Well, guess I'll do a little more jogging," he said to Jack. "Nice to have met you."

"My pleasure, sir."

Robert tried to catch Annabella's eye. She, however, was glancing from one male to the other, a little smile playing on those full lips.

"Go ahead, Bobby. I want to catch up on the news with Jack. I'm a little tired, and he's offered to drive me home."

"I need to say hey to her folks before I go back to Tallahassee," added Jack. Robert noted how straight and white Jack's teeth were against his young skin.

"It's going to be his senior year at FSU," helped Annabella, now dazzling them both with her smile.

"Fine, fine," said Robert, caught. He turned and headed back down the beach where he knew his MGB sat baking in the sun and gathering salt spray. He hoped he could make it around the next curve before he passed out from the heat.

☆ ☆ ☆

2 pm

I, of course, am only interested in how to tell my client she cannot come and see me any more. She sits on the couch, a beach bag at her feet. For the first time she has not brought clean socks and she is keeping her manicured toes on the floor.

So we've made progress. I'll hate to see her go—a little of me, anyway. I'm still convinced she is borderline.

"Going to the beach?" I say, to get us started. Maybe she'll quit before I can fire her. I try not to stare at this younger, firmer body Robert has no doubt undressed. Well, that does it. I can't be sitting here, pretending I'm doing therapy, while all the while I'm picturing the two of them together.

She wiggles a little. "After my session I'm going to meet an old boyfriend of mine."

I stiffen. She continues, "Maybe you know him—Jack Wolfe. His football buddies call him "The Jock".

"Jack. I think so. He's in college, isn't he? Tallahassee?" Hm-m. Maybe I was wrong about Annabella, even though she introduced Robert at the Little Theater Party as her "date". He certainly looked disconcerted—and innocent. I'd like to do what I can to keep her as my client. I could certainly use the money.

Oh, what am I thinking? Fran had given me a pep talk to get through this. I need to keep Fran's words to use. "Annabella, we have to talk about a rumor I've heard."

"About me and Jack? Goodness. That was *so* long ago– "

"Actually– " this is harder than I thought it would be. "Actually, it's about my husband Robert."

There's a kind of dense look that Annabella can adopt when she doesn't want to listen or do some homework I've assigned her. "*Robert?* Robert Baldwin? Oh my gosh! That's your *husband?*"

"He's about to be an ex-husband. The rumor is that you and he– "

Oh, look at the eyes widen as she gives me the "I'm innocent" stare. "Ms. Baldwin, I just can't believe that you would think Bo—Mr. Baldwin and I would–" she hides her face with her hands. Then she takes them away and gives me a level look. "Ms. Baldwin, your husband must be my *father's age.*" She actually shudders. "I guess you're mad about that little lie I told, about him being my date and all– "

"Look, Annabella, if there is anything going on between my husband– "

"– soon to be ex– " she helps.

"Yes. If there is, I cannot in all good conscience counsel you; there would be such a conflict of interest."

"Well." I'm suddenly waiting for her to add, "La dee da," to her exclamation.

I've never witnessed this upright and rather haughty Annabella before. It's rather interesting. "If you think that of me, then certainly you *have* to let me go, no matter what good therapy you've done for me." I swear, she's going to do a Scarlett O'Hara impersonation, Southern accent and all– " If you're going to believe every rumor in this small town– "

I raise a hand for quiet so that I can think a moment. I *do* need the money. Robert is downright parsimonious about letting me have any cash before the divorce is final. Annabella's parents pay full fare, no discounts, and they pay every session. Their checks do not bounce.

It might just be my imagination. I know Robert was with someone, if it even *was* him on the boat. Maybe he *was* protecting another businessman. It would be totally unfair to accuse Annabella without proof–

"All right. Let's just continue as we have been," I say, and Annabella vaults from the sofa, puts her arms around my neck and, unexpectedly for me, kisses my cheek. "Good!" she says. "I have to go, to meet Jack. Thank you! You're terrific! Same time next week." And she is gone.

Well, I think. *That* seemed to be a good session. I think we're making progress.

Now I have to figure out some way to make this all sound solid to Fran.

5 pm

Robert sat in the backyard pool. The August sun had heated it to a temperature for boiling lobsters, but he was so worn out from walking, then dragging himself on the beach, then sitting down on an incredibly hot black leather car seat without remembering he had brought no towel to cover it with because that seemed like something an old fogey would do, that anything wet was a relief.

Then he'd had to spend time washing and drying his car. Damn that Pete! Where *was* he? This should be a boy's job, not a father's, who had better things to do with his time, he had grumbled under his breath as he'd run the water from the hose over his sun-sore body.

Several neighbors had driven by, calling hello to him, but he'd pretended not to hear them. He had an aversion to small talk, and maybe they were used to talking with Joan, but this was *his house* now and there would be new rules. They were probably dying to know where Joan was, and he didn't want to share any information he didn't have to.

His sunburned shoulders ached. He had envisioned Annabella and him spending an evening rubbing oil on each other aboard the SEE LEGS, and then— but she had made her own plans, and he wasn't part of them.

"What are you doing home? I thought you were eating out." Susan plopped herself down next to her father and tossed Excelsior idly into the pool, where he floated up to the surface laughing.

"Do it again!" he demanded and she did. The sight made Robert dizzy.

"I could use a drink– " he hinted.

"Plenty of stuff in the kitchen," Susan replied. "Wow, is that water warm." She looked at him, shading her eyes. "Daddy, you're red as a beet! Have you been in the pool all afternoon?"

"Been showing a prospective client around. He wanted to see the boat, and we were out longer than I wanted– " hell, this was more explanation than he'd ever given Joan, good old believe-anything Joan. Susan was a harder nut. "Then I took him to the beach."

"That's a lot of sun," Susan said mildly.

"Saw a school friend of yours. He said to say hello." Robert couldn't remember if Jack had actually said that, but best to cover all bases in case she met the boy and Jack mentioned him and Annabella in the same sentence.

"Oh, yeah? Who?" The sunlight bounced off Susan's purple hair as she leaned over to dip the screaming and over-excited Excelsior back into the water.

"Jack Wolfe. The Jock."

Robert was unprepared for Susan's high-pitched reaction: "*Jack's* in town?"

"Uh huh." He weighed his next words, but he did need to cover those bases. "He was with somebody else I think you know—Annabella Comstock– "

He blinked as Susan lurched herself up and screamed. "Jack! And Annabella! No *wonder* he's in town without letting me know! I'll *kill* him! I'll kill them *both!*"

She jumped up and ran into the house, crying. Excelsior grinned at his grandfather as the child paddled around the pool. "Don't you go in the deep end, now," said Robert to him.

Pete emerged from the house. "What time's dinner?" he asked. "Hi, Shaver." Pete made a running start and cannonballed into the water. He was still slim, but tall now, and the splash took Robert by surprise, drenching him. Pete emerged beside Excelsior.

"Shayvoo, Shayvoo," sang the little boy, paddling madly in circles.

"Look here," said Robert to his son, "do you know how to mix a vodka tonic?"

"Nope," answered Pete, diving under the water and cutting out Robert's voice.

"Well, time you learned. Listen to me, Pete. I'm talking to you."

Pete pushed himself up to the coping of the pool and rested his arms beside his father's reddened legs.

"Okay. Now here's the recipe— "

5:30 pm

Pete mixed vodka, tonic, and a squeeze of lime. He put the drink in a tall ice-filled plastic glass. He sipped it, reacted with a twisted-up face, and took it to his father. He told Excelsior, "Just five more minutes in the pool," and left the boy a towel.

He went into the house and removed his father's keyring from the kitchen counter. He could hear Susan crying loudly to someone, on the phone in her room. He picked up his father's keyring and opened his father's locked home office door. He shut it behind him and looked around. He rummaged quickly and carefully through his father's desk. He found a wad of bills. He extracted two twenties from its center and laid them on top of the desk beside the keyring.

Way back in one of the drawers he found a small velvet bag. He opened it to find a brooch, several rings, a pair of earrings and a wristwatch. "Shee-yit," he whistled quietly. He put the twenties in the bag and carried the money and the jewelry from the room. He locked the door and returned the keyring. Then he put the money in his shorts pocket and stuck the bag in the pocket of his rarely-worn Easter Sunday suit —the pocket closest to the dark closet wall in the bedroom he shared with Excelsior.

He walked out onto the patio. "How was that drink?" he asked his father.

"I could use another," Robert said, holding out the glass for Pete to take.

"You gotta get out now, Shaver," said Pete to Excelsior, who obediently climbed out and accepted the towel Pete offered him.

"I gotta go," he told his father. "Susan's in the house, probably getting ready to make dinner, and I told my friends I'd go to a movie with them."

"What're you going to see?" asked Robert without enthusiasm.

" 'Star Wars'. Some of my friends have seen it *six* times already. See, this guy Luke Skywalker, well, he— "

"Oh, yeah? Need any money?" said Robert. Pete nodded. "Take a five from my pants pocket," offered Robert in a rush of generosity brought on by the vodka. "And bring me another drink first."

"Sure thing," said Pete, fingering the forty dollars deep within his pocket. "Sure thing. And Dad,"he called back as he moved toward the kitchen, "May the force be with you."

"What's that supposed to mean?" thought Robert.

PERSONALS

"This is what you need to be doing." Fran taps the newspaper against my arm. We have been hanging curtains and are taking a break. She has brought homemade pastry. I pick one up and try it. It's delicious. "You just bop a can on the counter and they all pop out," she says.

"I have a job," I tell her, and I do. Besides my counseling of Annabella, I have my piano and am once again giving lessons. I have found, to my surprise, that no longer taking care of Excelsior has freed up my life considerably.

And here are two more surprises: I am sleeping better, by myself. The first night in this new place I was awake most of the night, talking to myself about how I was going to starve here all alone and nobody would know or care—the usual pity-me stuff; but as the weeks have gone by, sleep has come more and more easily. I am now used to the car sounds and one night late there was a drunk woman under my window calling, "Hey, caowboy! Hey, caowboy!", but the police came as soon as I called and then they *all* had a loud conversation under my window. I don't know if she ever found her cowboy.

Also, and this is *huge*! My agoraphobia is completely *gone*! My panic attacks have disappeared! Vanished!

"You have no idea how much anger you were having to stuff down over that man," says Fran when I tell her in a burst of joy. "I see it myself. You're the person I always knew you were."

But I'm damaged goods. I'm a divorcee. Robert has agreed to pay me lump sum alimony. He has done this, he says, by refinancing our home. He is mad as spit over this—I mean that expression, because when he told me what he was doing, his eyes narrowed and he foamed into my face with his spittle, he was so frustrated at having to lose his low interest rate to a much higher one.

"Shoot, he made out like crazy," Fran says. "Do you have any idea how much your property appreciated from 1963 to 1977?" I don't have to answer her. She knows how much in the dark I have been about Robert's dealings.

Anyway, my lawyer told me there was no way to find out where the half million that my mother had given Robert had gone. "He says he doesn't have any paperwork and we can't prove anything. He's a slippery one about money. He also denies having your mother's jewelry and there's no way to prove that, either. You're just going to have to let it go."

Robert has decided to give me half of what our house is appraised for. So I have just banked a check for $50,000. So— if I can live on $2,000 a year I can survive for the next 25 years. That's hardly a comforting thought. I have my piano and some pieces of furniture from the house, as well as some paintings (not worth anything except to me) and kitchenware. I keep pushing down my fear of being a bag lady.

Fran snorted when she heard what Robert had offered. "You were married for over 23 years. So that comes out to about $2,000 a year for being his personal slave."

Sometimes when Fran says something, even when it's true, it sounds a little harsh. And I am, despite myself, feeling sorry for Robert, who now has to learn to do things for himself.

Fran is pointing at the Personals ads in the Banana Bay Tribune. "Anyway, I don't want to date."

"Honeychile, this ad sounds like it was written just for you. Answer it! Meet him at the library. That's safe enough."

"Are you going to pester me until I do this?"

"You know it." We sit in friendly relaxation across the card table from each other and help ourselves to another pastry.

Maybe daylight wouldn't be bad. "Okay, how about this? I'll answer the ad. You come with me to the library to make sure this is no ax murderer. If I am okay about all this, I'll give you a signal and you can leave."

"Ma chere Hastings! At last you are ready to rejoin the world! I will be hiding in the mystery aisle!"

Oh. Besides the absence of my panic attacks, Doctor Freud is not talking to me anymore, either.

One week later. I have replaced the card table with a nice small round oak one. Who knew there were consignment shops for *furniture*? I have a pot of flowers on it, in case this Gentleman Caller comes back to my place—I realize I don't know any of the rules for this new game of meeting men. Should I even give him my real name? Tell him where I live? Give him my phone number? I haven't even memorized it myself, yet.

I'm driving to the library. Fran had forced me to sit down at that oak table and write out a personal ad myself. "College-educated Episcopalian" (I insisted on inserting 'Episcopalian', but Fran said that was too limiting. She wanted 'Christian'. I told her 'Christian' would make me sound like a Bible-thumping Salvation Army worker) "female desires to meet man in 40s for enjoyable conversations and movie-going. Must not smoke. Playing piano is extra credit."

"That's pretty limiting in this town," said Fran doubtfully. "But it's your ad."

We mail it together on our way to the library to meet my blind date. Fran coaches me: "Check yourself in the mirror ahead of time. You don't want to have lipstick on your teeth. Take a breath mint– "

"Do I need it?" I ask, breathing in her direction as she drives. "No," she says, "but be safe rather than not—do you have tissues? And a comb? And money, in case you have to call me from someplace? And definitely do not let him kiss you on a first date or he'll think you're easy– "

I have lost my nerve. The thought of kissing a strange man is almost disgusting. "Okay," I tell her.

The library is a perfect place to meet someone for a first date, I decide. That way, if he doesn't show up, I can still read a good book. And, remembering the therapist who discouraged couples from meeting in a dark smoky bar, this is ideal—I can see him, smell him, and if he speaks up in this setting, hear him.

I hear him all too soon. I am looking through a collection of hardbound piano books and wanting to know if they'd put this set out at their book sale and could I put my bid in early if so, when someone touches my shoulder. "Are you my confident, secure, healthy date?" a low voice asks. I turn around, smiling and nervous and stare. "Doctor Griffin!" I say so loudly that Fran comes running.

Doctor Griffin, our landlord, the dentist with the intrusive gossipy wife—my life is over right now. She will be on the phone as soon as she hears about this—"Doctor Griffin, you're *married!*" I hiss as the librarian puts a finger to her lips and raises her eyebrows.

Doctor Griffin is as surprised as we were. "You—you're my *date?*" he says to both of us.

Fran pushes me aside. "What are you doing out in the open, *cruising?*" she demands.

Doctor Griffin sighs. "I'm not really married. I mean—I'm married, but I'm not happy."

"Well, obviously, if you're going to put an *ad* in the newspaper– !"

Doctor Griffin turns away before I can tell him our date is off. "I'm sorry, ladies. I never did this before. I tried something and it didn't work– "

Fran clutches at his arm."Now wait just a minute! Joan got all dressed up for you– "

Doctor Griffin smiles at me. "You do look nice. And I got a haircut for the occasion."

"Then," says Fran decidedly, "we are going on a *date.*"

We sit all afternoon in the Zayre shopping center at a little coffee shop with handwritten poetry all over the walls – a nice quiet homosexual hangout, although nobody says that out loud. The place is mostly empty and the chairs are comfortable.

Several times I start, thinking I have to get Excelsior or meet Pete after school, and then realize I am on my own for the first time since I had been a – my goodness, a freshman in high school!

✵ ✵ ✵

I've decided you can't see any of this journal, Father Wolfe. Too many people are now involved. If I let you have this, you don't have a contract for privacy the way I do as a therapist; and that's why I understand now that I need to keep my writings to myself.

Anyway, during the course of the afternoon, what with the espressos and the sugary doughnuts and Fran and me doing free therapy for the dentist, Doctor Griffin comes to the conclusion that "I'm spinning my wheels with that woman!" He decides to lay his cards on the table with her and take that trip to Wyoming that he has always been wanting to take, to ride a horse and wear cowboy clothes, but "she'd always laughed at me when I talked about it".

"If she wants to go with me she can," says Doctor Griffin, "but I sure hope she won't. I don't want her making fun of me and coming home telling everyone here how many times I fell off a horse. I'm not very adept," he confesses to us. "Just with my hands."

He even tells us he had taken Mitzi– "Mitzi the Ditsy", he calls her because she never learned how to use the phone correctly, since when she took the gum from her mouth she would invariably stick it on the receiver—to see her relatives, who live in the same city as the dental seminar. "She got drunk on the plane *on* the way up and back," he shakes his head. "That's when I decided 'no bars' would be in my personal ad. Do you think it's a good ad?" We reassure him it is.

By the time we leave the coffeehouse Doctor Griffin is so impressed with our counseling abilities that he says he'll recommend us to all his patients. He also knocks our rent down a hundred dollars a month. Then he heads to the airport to make reservations for Wyoming. "Been carrying the brochures for this cowboy ranch in my car for years," he shows us, opening the trunk lid wide as though it were a patient's mouth. A patient with a very unkempt mouth.

"Well, *I'd* say that was a success as a first date," Fran says as we wave good-by. "Let's go back inside before we go home. My bladder is killing me and I didn't want to go into the ladies' room alone. They have Chinese symbols on the doors and I couldn't tell which was which."

"First date, hell!" I cry. "You and I just did an afternoon of *therapy* together. It was wonderful, didn't you notice? When I was interacting, you were sitting back and observing, and then adding something I hadn't seen, and then I got to sit back while you came forward and interacted with Doctor Griffin."

"Yeah– " says Fran tentatively.

"Yeah!" I tell her, hugging her. "I've been reading about co-therapists. It's the wave of the future. You and I could work together and clean up this town!"

"With not a neurotic left except Robert and Mrs. Griffin!" agrees Fran. "So okay. Bathroom first, business second!"

✻ ✻ ✻

GUNMAN BREAKS IN, WANTS TO TALK

Brenda Mitchell said she was awakened by her alarm clock
to find a stranger with a gun sitting in the chair next to her bed
in the Banana Bay Mobile Community.
And for three hours all he did was talk to her about his marital problems.
"Apparently what this guy wanted was someone to talk to,"
said Police officer Lt. Frank Gooding.
He made no threats, Gooding said, and Mitchell, 21,
was unable to give more than a sketchy description of him.
If caught, the intruder would face charges of armed burglary
and false imprisonment. Mitchell, who describes herself as a
"clean freak", washed the glass he had used for a drink
of water before the police arrived, erasing all fingerprints.
—*Banana Bay Tribune, Sept. 23, 1977*

W hile we were having a good time counseling a dentist, Excelsior was drowning.

That's a bit over-dramatic. Here's how Pete tells the story:

"Susan is gone for the day and she's left Excelsior with Dad and me. Dad is mad. He wants to watch something on TV—not football. Dad can't stand sports on TV—so he says, 'Would you and the kid like to go to the beach?'

"Well, Excelsior is jumping up and down and kind of knocking me over, he's so excited, so we get in Dad's car and he warns us not to bring any sand home when we're done, and I know what he means is not get any in his car or I'll have to clean it out. Then he takes us to the beach and says he'll pick us up in an hour.

"Well, I see we're only a block from your apartment, Mom, and I think if we get thirsty we can come to your place for a drink– "

"I wasn't home!" I cry. What a bad mother I am, out carousing around at the library while my only grandchild is drowning– !

"Don't interrupt," says Fran. Pete looks at her gratefully. I hold onto Pete, my baby, my son, wrapped in a blanket and no longer shivering, by my side and he is *not trying to get away*. Fran is holding Excelsior in her lap. Their rescuer stands in my doorway.

"Then," says Pete," we're walking on the beach and all the snowbirds haven't come yet, so the beach is kinda empty. See, I forgot to bring a pail for the Shaver– "

"Pay-o!" says Excelsior. He and Pete are no longer blue with cold, I am relieved to see, having been plunged into hot baths at my apartment.

"Yeah. Anyway, I think I could look in the trash cans for something to use for a pail, 'cause the Shaver here is picking up shells and stuffing them in his mouth."

"My mouf," says Excelsior, pointing.

"Yeah. Well, I had to hurry so he wouldn't choke on a shell, and I turn around and I see the Shaver thrashing around in the water! Shi– ! Shoot, I didn't know he could move that fast! So I run down to the water and I don't even take my sneaks off and I grab him by the hair and that's all."

(That's *not* all, thinks Pete. I was mad at *him* and mad at Dad and mad at Susan and mostly mad at Mom for leaving me with all this crap. Now I gotta wash Dad's precious shitty car *every week* and then he doesn't pay me, but he always tells me what I did wrong and I gotta do it *again* and he makes *me* cook shitty stuff that I don't know how to cook and he tells me to "just shut up and do it", and then I gotta do the dishes *and* my homework and he doesn't tell me when he's going out of town and he doesn't tell me *where* he's going to be.

Then he keeps sticking me with this little shitty brat when I want to be with my friends, so when I see Excelsior in the water, going in and out with the waves, and he can't stand up, a piece of me says Good. *Good.* Like I'm *hypnotized.*

Then I like *wake up!* And I run like shit for the Shaver and all of a sudden I'm in the water, grabbing for his hair, and he hangs onto me and we're both under the waves and they're so *big* near the shoreline. Oh hell there's an under-tow! and coquina rocks and I'm sucked under and I'm tumbling around, trying to get to the surface and get a breath, and the waves keep knocking me into the jagged coquina which I can feel is razor *sharp,* and now I'm scared I'm bloody and sharks will come, but the waves keep crashing on us, over our heads, and I'm trying to hold the Shaver up to keep his head above water, but he's weigh-ing me down and pulling me under and I want to call "Mom!" as loud as I can, but I keep swallowing salt water and I'm pushing the Shaver toward the shore as hard as I can, but I've never been so *tired* in my life! My clothes are heavy. They're so *heavy*! And my arms aren't doing what I want them to do. Everything's black.

But then thank you God there's this *hand* pulling me out on the beach and the Shaver, too, and we're both coughing up water and puking and everything and I think I'll just lie here on the beach and die, and I hear the Shaver crying—or maybe it's me, I'm not sure—and this man is kneeling over us, asking us what our names are and if we're okay.

And my teeth are chattering so I can't even talk! I want to see if I'm bleeding, but I don't have the strength to lift my head and check. And the Shaver keeps crying, or maybe it's *me*.

And so help me *God* I can't think of my own phone number, but I know Mom is near here and I try to tell the man where she lives and so this guy carries us one at a time to his truck, and he doesn't seem to care that we're all wet and sandy and pukey, and I tell him how to get to Mom's, and I still can't believe we just went through all this! I wanted my *Mom* and it didn't matter any more that I was mad at her. That didn't matter one bit! And I wanted the Shaver to leave me alone, but *that* didn't even matter when he needed me! And I never can tell anybody what I'm thinking because then they'll know how bad I am and how it's my fault, it's gotta be my fault somehow that my Mom and Dad are getting divorced.)

"Your son is a hero," says a pleasant calm voice. We all look up. We have neglected this rescuer in our need to make sure family members are safe. " I was going fishing. I'd just gotten to the beach and parked, and that's when I saw this young man race into the water. Then I saw he was trying to save someone and I ran, myself."

(I'm not a hero, thinks Pete. I almost let the Shaver go.)

The man looks at Pete. "You became a *man* today, Peter," he says. Then he smiles at me.

I am trying to take in the man's words. There are miles and miles of beach! Dear God, what if he'd parked in a different place– ? His smile rests on me. "Just call me Max," he says.

☆ ☆ ☆

Later on Fran and I help pile the exhausted boys into Max's truck. "No sense getting your car sandy, too, and mine cleans up easy", and he drives us to my former house. I ring the doorbell—that's a first for me!– and finally Robert, yawning, wearing a bathrobe, comes to the door. The garage door is closed and I am suspicious that some woman's car is inside. As well as some woman.

We all start to talk at once. Pete wins. I am unprepared for his maddened fury. "You *left* us, Dad!" he yells, pounding on Robert with not much effect, since he is so tired and he has to make sure the blanket he is wearing does not slip off, and Robert's robe is thick. "You *left* us and you didn't come *back* for us!"

Fran pushes past Robert without a word and takes Excelsior into the house. Pete is still pummeling Robert one-handed, Robert who is trying to look like the paterfamilias, even while his robe blows open and Max stands there. I don't make a move to stop Pete until he sways, worn out, and bursts into tears, and staggers down the hall to his room. I try to go to him, even though I know I'm not allowed in my own house any more, and Robert, looking for someone more calm to confront, steps into my path.

Max squeezes my arm. "The boy can't use any more Mama right now," he says, and follows Pete down the hall without a glance at Robert.

Robert, alone outside with me, closes the front door—a little late after all these people have just pushed their way in—and regards me. His hair seems thinner, and the bathrobe makes his middle seem fat. "You always have to make scenes about nothing, don't you?" he lectures me. "Always stirring up trouble."

I stare. Is this the man I was bedded with for almost a quarter of a century? Does this man know me at *all*? I sit down beside the door on the bench that I stained (centuries ago, it seems now) while Robert continues to lecture me. I've heard all these words from him before, I think. Why did they used to affect me then, and they don't now?

The door opens before I can say anything and Max and Fran emerge. "Nice meeting you," says Max, without shaking Robert's hand.

"You son of a bitch," adds Fran pleasantly. "They're okay," she says to me. "Both sleeping."

"Peter said he'd call you later," Max tells me. "He's done in. And he's pretty embarrassed that he got so emotional. I know what I was like at that age. What is he, fifteen, sixteen?"

"Just twelve."

"That makes him even more of a hero," Max says. Robert is still standing by the door, his hand on the doorknob, an ungracious host to all these intruders.

"Invite him back to your place for dinner," Fran whispers to me as we return to Max's car. "After Doctor Griffin, this one looks like he could stay on a horse."

Glancing at Max's profile and his strong hands (hands which saved my son and grandson!) on the steering wheel, I am changing my mind about dating.

And he's not even wearing a camel's hair coat.

At dinner I found out that Max is a writer for the Banana Bay Tribune.

The article Max wrote is in the paper the following week. I have cut it out and pasted it in my journal as a memento. Susan, to my utter surprise, even framed a copy for Pete's room.

BOY PULLS NEPHEW FROM HEAVY SURF

Peter Baldwin, twelve-year-old son of Robert Baldwin
and Joan Baldwin, became a hero last Saturday when he
rescued, despite an ankle gashed by coquina rocks,
his five-year-old nephew Excelsior, son of Ms. Vronsky Baldwin
from the heavy undertow off Banana Bay Beach.
He will be honored by his school and presented with a medal
by the mayor of this community, "for showing exemplary behavior
in the face of extreme difficulties".
Peter is a seventh grade student at John F. Kennedy
Junior High School and plays outfield for the
Roosters Little League Team. Excelsior attends
the Special School at Banana Bay Beach Elementary School.
Both are fully recovered.
—*Banana Bay Tribune, September 26, 1977*

"Now that I see my new name in the paper, I'm not sure I like it any more," says Susan. "How old was that guy who pulled them both out? I don't see any mention of his name—Max?"

"He wrote the article," I say. "He works for the Banana Bay Tribune."

I do not mention to her that Max has asked me out on a date. He has also presented me with my personal ad and my uncashed check made out to the Tribune—"I saw your name on your check and wanted to meet you—never dreamed it would be *this* way!– before I posted it in the paper. I know that's against all rules and ethics, but I was being selfish, and I wanted first dibs," Max said. "I can still place it if you like. I work the ads department as well. You know what a small paper we are. Old-timers call us the "Mullet Wrapper".

He takes a moment before going on. "You don't remember me, do you?"

"I've met you?" I ask him, astonished. "St. Barnabus', Publix, the post office– ?"

"Tony's," he replies. "I used to come in for lunch and watch you work like a whirlwind around those tables, never making a mistake, always cheerful. I wanted to meet you then, but I could see by your ring hand that you were married, and I was going through a pretty bad divorce– "

"Honestly," I answer, wondering at this view of me when I had no idea anyone had noticed me, except for wanting extra helpings of Tony's garlic bread, "I never had the time to see who I was serving."

"I wanted to take you somewhere so you could sit down and let somebody serve *you*."

I am touched. What an easy man Max is to talk with.

✫ ✫ ✫

"Jerk had no manners," Susan tells me her father said about Max when she showed her father the framed newspaper article. "Entered my house without even being asked."

So Susan has brought me the hand-framed article to get my approval instead. I am humbled that we can meet, equal to equal. Susan is growing up, too. Or maybe she was grown all along, and was also in Robert's shadow, as I had been.

Susan's hair this week is a cobalt blue. Where *does* she find these colors? I wonder.

"Mom– " she begins, taking a cookie from the plate I have set on the table, "I'm having a—little trouble living with Dad."

No kidding, I think. "Really?" I say. "There's so much room in that house to stay away from each other– "

"It's just not *fair*!" she bursts out. "I have to take care of him *and* Pete *and* Excelsior *and*—it's just not *fair*!"

"I agree. What taking care of Pete do you do?"

"That's right, jump straight to problem-solving! Aren't you supposed to listen to my *feelings* first?"

"If that's what you want, sure." So this is to be a counseling session. I pour more hot tea into my cup and hold the pot up. She waves the tea away.

"I know I kind of dumped Excelsior on you for a little while– "

"For about three years," I correct her. "With no prior warning."

"Jeeze, *okay*! I had my reasons!"

"But you didn't give me a chance to say yes or no to you."

"Could you just hang *on*? Is this how you treat your *clients*?" Susan angrily brushes cookie crumbs onto the floor, waiting to see if I will jump up for a broom. I ignore the crumbs.

"No, you're right. One issue at a time. I forget I'm a counselor and instead I turn into a mother."

"Yeah, well– " Susan doesn't like winning this easily. The mother-cleans-the-crumbs-instead-of-listening-to-me game hasn't worked. I watch her assess her mental processes for her next strategy.

She looks at me, her eyes narrowed, and apparently decides to trust me. "Okay. I have a job."

"That's terrific!" I say. I picture Susan at the Seven-Eleven handing out Slurpees to acned teenagers. "I'm working at LoRayne's Beauty Salon."

Sweeping up hair! I change my mental image to Susan, and now *she* has the broom in her hands.

"I'm a *hairdresser*! I have my license and everything!"

"Okay, wait. You took me by surprise. So when did all this happen?"

Damn. I see her eyes hood over as a wall impervious as steel comes up between us. I am not to be given the gift of being in on this part of Susan's life. "Let me just say that when I left Excelsior with you, I went to school. It took a *long* time! I had to work while I was learning hairdressing and some of the jobs were scummy!"– oh, Susan, I realize I don't *want* to know that part of your life or my heart would break– "and it took me two years to do it, but I *did!* And LoRayne thinks my hairpieces are *outstanding!*"

"I know how hard it is to go to school when you've got children and obligations," I say mildly, holding back this overwhelming impulse to take my daughter in my arms and comfort her, keep her from the hurts of life, seeing not the angry adult but the tender little toddler she was.

"Yeah, well, anyway. *Anyway!* Dad is getting on my nerves, so I thought I'd move in with you." She looks away and takes a sip of tea.

I glance around the apartment which is becoming home to me. The wall colors are those I have picked out myself and applied, as well as the draperies and bedspread pattern. I have throw pillows which Excelsior, if they move in, will spend much time throwing. I will have handprints on the curtains. There will be music at odd hours. I will be asked to carpool. There will be noise and confusion, Susan's friends coming and going.

Oh, Lord help me, I am getting old. I finally have my own space. I want to hoard it, even from people I love.

"You've *got* two bedrooms– " pleads Susan. "I'm used to sharing one with Excelsior. I can do that again."

"I keep that for Pete when he visits on week ends," I say. But she is my daughter! I think.

"Susan," I venture carefully, noting that she does not correct me with her Russian name Vronsky, "ask me for a kidney, a quart of blood, I'm right there for you. But I need to be by myself."

"Yeah, that's what Dad told me *he* needed, too. But he's *never* alone."

Oh boy. I mean, I had my suspicions, but– "What do you mean?"

"He's with some woman or other every night. It's like he's a—sexaholic or something."

There's that word again. But I must not react. "Are you kids in jeopardy?"

"Nah. He's in his end of the house, we're in ours. But it's *tacky* and I don't want Excelsior exposed to that kind of thing. I think Dad sneaks somebody in at night when he thinks we're all asleep, and then he sneaks her out early in the morning. He thinks he's getting away with something. But you can tell if a woman's been here—he's stupid about leaving wine glasses around with lipstick on them."

I know those wine glasses. They were a wedding gift from my college roommates. Images of the three of us as schoolgirls give me an adrenalin surge. Why didn't I take those glasses with me in the rush of packing and moving out? Why doesn't he just smash them and pierce some shards through my heart?

"I'm sorry, Susan—Vronsky– "

"I'm dropping that name. LoRayne says it's too hard to pronounce, anyway. She thinks I *look* like a 'Susan'—more classy."

"Look, Susan. This is hard for me. I want more than anything to say yes to you, yes you can move in, but I don't want to build up any resentment toward you and I know me better now and I know I *would* be resentful and I'm afraid you're going to hold it against me if I don't give in. But that wouldn't be honest for either of us."

This is the strongest, longest, most honest statement I have ever made to my daughter. She sits back in her chair and assesses me. Then:

"Mom, when we moved down here I was just starting kindergarten. You put me in a church school—why?"

"There were no public kindergartens here in 1963. There was also segregation, which made me so mad, coming from the north—you went to public first grade the next year."

"Yeah. I remember when our school was first integrated. We had no idea what was going on, all those school buses coming to our school, all those kids different from our white bread Banana Beach friends—but in school that first day we kids all stared at each other and then we stood in a circle and patted each others' hair. *Hair*!– maybe that's why I wanted to be a hairdresser! Touching hair, all kinds, was so keen! "

I remembered that first day, too: those small scared black faces staring out of the school bus windows, so far from home. I'd wanted to hug them and tell them, "It's going to be all right," as though I had all the answers. There were supposedly no segregated beaches in those days, but white people and black people knew without talking about it, which ones were off-limits–

"Anyway, you took me to kindergarten and I was the first one in the class, so you stayed with me."

"I didn't want you to be alone," I said.

"Well, you sat there with me and you all of a sudden said, 'That's not right.' and you went to the blackboard, where my teacher had written, 'This is a new month. February is it's name'. And you erased the apostrophe!"

"*I* did that?" I say, amazed at my certainty back then, a young mother with panic attacks.

"Then after the other kids came in you left, and the teacher came in and she got mad. She said, 'Who touched my board?' and nobody, especially me, said anything. We were all shaking, she was so mad! Then she went to the board and put the apostrophe back in."

"I'm touched that you remember that. I do, now that you remind me."

"Yeah. Tell me why you didn't stand up to Dad that way years ago. You were so wimpy, you'd lie down and let him roll right over you."

"Well—that's what women *did* in those days. Women who worked outside the home were looked upon as having something wrong with them, and those who stayed inside the home were kind of revered as saints. It's hard to make independent choices when society insists on calling you a saint."

I stop and think. The things we've had to do, the roles over time we women have had to play– Victorian corsets so tight some women had ribs removed to have waists a man could span with his hands; women drinking *arsenic* so they would have colorless complexions, since the ruddy faces came from common laboring women out in the fields, and a pale fainting woman was a man's evidence that he earned enough money so that his wife, thank God, did not have to work; and then the strong fearless women of World War II who had stepped into jobs and pinned up their hair and put on slacks to help out while their husbands were off fighting and getting killed! What had become of *those* women?

I already knew. After the war ended those same women had been urged to go home to a washer and dryer in each of their homes, or there wouldn't have been enough jobs for the returning men. And the men were given jobs manufacturing those washers and dryers. What a circle we all got caught up in: the fancy hats, the white gloves, the childishness of Lucy Ricardo begging Ricky for a job, of Gracie Allen telling George Burns she felt depressed, so had gone downtown to buy a new hat to cheer herself up—

I blink at Susan, coming back to her. "Good thing life is reversed now."

"Well, that's good for *me*. If I can get away from Dad. He's driving me crazy. You babied him, Mother. He never took care of you in return. I know he hated that you're so strong."

"Me, strong?" I am stunned once again. "I always believed if I were dying, someone *else's* life would flash before my eyes."

"Nope." Susan gets up. "Gotta pick up Excelsior from school. And that's another thing that's making Dad so angry. Excelsior tested below average in intelligence and emotional maturity and I made the mistake of telling Dad, who can't stand that he doesn't have a genius grandson. "

"So how are his special classes going? " I had of course noticed the slowness in Excelsior myself, but his loving nature made up for any shortcomings he might have.

"I've got plans. I've always got plans. We Baldwin— *Gibson* women are known for being resourceful." She looked around. "I'd like to get a place like this. Our house isn't home anymore. "

I appreciate her using my maiden name. Maybe I'll go back to it. "I'm proud of you." I give her a fervent hug. I dare to ask, "Want to cut my hair at LoRayne's?"

"Can't. LoRayne is starting me out on really old ladies. They seem to prefer blue hair and LoRayne says I'm a natural at coloring."

"You always were creative with Easter eggs,"

She widens her eyes as if thinking of a new hair style. I laugh, and surprisingly, she laughs with me.

☆ ☆ ☆

We have a new client! Actually, it's Mrs. Griffin. She doesn't pay, but wants us to see her and we won't have to pay rent for six months!

She is depressed and angry. Years ago she put her life on hold to help her husband get through dental school, and she wants to know now how to get on with that life while he's out west falling off horses. She has fired Mitzi and come back to work, but this is not what she wants to continue doing.

Then she asks if some friends can come with her and suddenly we have a group of women sitting in our office, talking about their lives, grousing, bitching, crying, and then looking for solutions. Fran and I have moved them to the waiting room, where there are more chairs. We make tea and someone brings cookies or something else that's fattening, but we don't care, and I realize we are doing something that we didn't learn in our psych books and it's working out great!

One of the women suggests we say a prayer before and after we talk, and that's surely not in the psych books, either. Also they are mostly Methodists, but then I find out they use a lot of prayers from our Episcopal Book of Common Prayer. Fran and I are making up the rules as we go along.

✿ ✿ ✿

What in hell has happened to women since he was in high school? Robert wonders. He had lines he could use on them and they'd drop like a row of dominoes. Now he says things meant to make them follow him anywhere, and they look at him like he's developed leprosy. Telling women his name is "James Bonde with an e" used to make them stare longingly into his eyes and ask for another drink. Now they pay for their own drinks and then slide away from him without a good-by, right off the barstool, their firm behinds swaying over to some loud younger group, which they join and then glance back at him with a small smile, all of them bursting into laughter—at him? Could it be at him?

Well, he sure as hell can't go out with women his age—they look like *grandmothers*.

Right now he can't go out with anyone. His MGB is stuck in a sand dune, the result of letting Annabella drive. He curses at her for the first time in their relationship. She doesn't blink.

"Well. If you're gonna be in a pissy mood, I'll just go get us some help." And she's over the sand dune and down to the beach on the other side while he shoves driftwood under the wheels, which just digs them deeper into the soft sand. Damn that Annabella! Robert thinks she did it on purpose. She's been saying stuff like, "You must hate me," and maybe he does. At this moment he sure as hell does!

He is wiping the perspiration from his eyes onto his expensive shirt, purchased to impress out-of-town women, when he hears some voices and over the sand dune appear a half dozen youthful Adonises—at least that's what they look like to his eyes salt-stained with sweat.

"Hey," one of them shouts. "Bella says her Pop's stuck in the sand."

"Nice little car," another one says. "This'll be easy."

Annabella appears, laughing, behind them. Why is she wearing that skimpy swimsuit today? What has happened to women's sense of modesty in public? One of the young men slaps her playfully with his towel and she pushes him playfully herself, glancing at Robert while she does so.

"Don't you worry, Pop– " says a fourth young man who looks like the "after" in an old Charles Atlas ad, the body he coveted for himself when he was ten.

"I'm not her father– " corrects Robert. But he is interrupted by Annabella, who calls, "He's also a *Grampa*!"

"Well, Gramps, just you stand back now. Don't want you doing any heavy lifting at your age. You could get a hernia or a prostrate." They all laugh. One of them offers Robert a beer, which he declines, and Annabella accepts, guzzling it so some beer runs down her slim neck and they all stop working so they can jump to her side and wipe it off while she laughs in this breathy kind of laugh Robert is sure she has been practicing at home by herself.

"Damn! We're gonna need my truck with the winch and some rope," one of the men says.

"We can go in my truck to get it," says another.

"I'll go with you!" sings Annabella. They pile into an old pickup truck standing on the packed sand away from the dune. The driver calls out to Robert: "Let's go! Hey, Gramps, you stay out of the sun now. Anybody got some water for Gramps?"

And that is how he sits nursing a half-cooled Coke in his hands while he waits, impotent, for them all to return.

That damned Annabella. He'll show her he's no old grandfather. Later.

If she comes back.

☆ ☆ ☆

PET PIG BOBBY A HOUSE GUEST

Loretta Willis of West Banana Bay has asked permission
of the City council to keep a Vietnamese potbellied pig
in her home as a pet. She sought relief from the city's
requirement of 2 ½ acres of land for livestock.
"Bobby is like a member of my family," she told local officials.
Council members asked Willis to find out what other cities
are doing about the unusual pigs and report back to them.
—*Banana Bay Tribune, November 14, 1977*

I never dreamed that a dead cat would bring Robert back to me. He had an
aversion to cats and dogs even before a Schnauzer ran in front of his two-wheeled
Schwinn and he refused to veer. Fortunately the dog had better acceleration
than the teenaged bicyclist and escaped injury, although the Schnauzer's owner
chased Robert down the street with her garden rake.

Annabella had a cat named Pretty Baby. I heard all this later from Margaret
Wolfe, who, allergy-prone, had spent two nights at the Comstock home during
Hurricane Clancy and used up their entire supply of Kleenex: Pretty Baby was a
longhair with a pushed-in face and nose, crossed eyes and a mean temper that only
an overweight feline with claws who is guarding its dinner dish can muster.

During the month before our divorce, Robert, unbeknown to me, was "dating" Annabella, who had sworn to me that nothing of the kind was going on. Then
right after our divorce proceedings Pretty Baby fell ill and died at the Comstock
home.

"She never liked that cat," confided Margaret to me while we set up tables for
the church rummage sale (more about that later, and I am now *so* glad I made the
decision not to give these pages to Father Wolfe!)

Anyway, Pretty Baby died, and although Annabella had never professed any love for the animal, she went into her "drama queen" act of grief and mourning.

Robert cannot abide anyone grieving. He refuses to go to funerals. When his parents died he would not let me go north with him to the burials; I think it was so nobody who knew him would see him cry. It must have pained him, trying to put up with Annabella's histrionics.

And yet there she was, pouring out her woe in front of him and then continuing it full throttle in my office, while I gave her my full attention, thinking all the while, "it's a *cat.*"

I was balancing my meager checkbook one evening (Fran had taught me how) and enjoying the coolish autumn evening breeze through my open windows when there was a knock on my apartment door. I opened it and there stood *Robert,* of all people. Pushing past me to make sure I was alone, he announced, "We have to talk."

I knew this meant he had to talk and I had to listen. I could smell that he had been drinking and I foresaw a nasty time of it if I tried to remove him from my place in front of my new next-door neighbors.

"What is it, Robert?"

"What's there to drink? Fix me something." I made him iced tea, which he let sit, grumbling, "I meant something *strong,*" on my coffee table (a bargain for $5.50 at Goodwill!) while I got a coaster and dried the table of its ring.

"Joan," he said, "we go back a long way."

"Can't argue with that," I said, sipping my tea.

"I will come right to the point. Bottom line, I am of the decision that we need to be back together, grow old—er together, have our 50th anniversary together."

Well. This was a new Robert with a sense of familial history. And I have to admit I missed him. Actually I would wake up some nights in a sweat, my heart pounding, tormented by the fear of not being able to support myself, haunted by the idea that I had just spent Pete's college tuition by causing Robert to have the house refinanced.

I can't tell you why I missed him, except for that doggoned family history. And I *did* yearn to have a 50th anniversary. We had a 25th coming up in just two years! Or would have, if I hadn't blown everything. Right at this moment I couldn't remember why. I was still feeling guilty about not letting Susan move in, and I guess it crossed a part of my mind that we could all be back together again, happy Cleavers.

"Joan," Robert said, "I still love you *so* much. I never realized how much until we were apart. We can work things out again. I know we can. We've both been through so much and I have come to understand for the first time how much you mean to me. You've had your fling at independence. Now you can come home."

It would have been easier to listen to him if he hadn't been unzipping my bathrobe, so that I stood naked in front of him and wondered only briefly if people across the road could see anything.

Oh, I had missed his hands, his smell, his eyes! He led me unprotesting into my bedroom, his old familiar touch all over me. "Damn, I've missed you!" he said. And then he carefully, slowly, deliberately folded back my bedspread.

And he folded back my bedspread.

And he folded back my bedspread!

All at once my entire remembered life with him came crashing onto me, so that I sat down hard, my nude rear end on the secondhand mattress I had bought and dragged inside to my apartment—me! Joan!— and my legs collapsed out from beneath me like a cheap card table.

Robert was still concentrating on his folds. "This is *much* better," he was saying. But now, now as never before, I was hearing his voice as an annoying buzzing in my ear, like that mosquito in the dark after you go to bed, and you swat at it and even turn on the lights, but can't find it until you turn out the lights again and it's right back there in your ear, waiting to draw blood.

Gritting my teeth, I stood up. "Robert," I said, going to the living room and putting on my bathrobe, "go away." The shorter the speech the better, I guessed. I went to the front door, opened it and stepped out into the common outside hallway. A refreshing Florida breeze brushed my face.

"Go *away*!" I said again, louder, so that my next-door neighbors, the elderly Mr. and Mrs. Magruder opened their front door and poked their heads out.

Robert stood in the short hall that led to my living room. "What?" he said.

The Magruders, looking like a matched short and chubby set of salt and pepper shakers, joined me outside. "She said *go away*!" they said in tandem. Apparently there wasn't much on TV tonight to distract them. I was oddly grateful for their presence. They took my hands, one on each side of me as my own Tweedle-dee and Tweedle-dum, while Robert sidled past us with all the dignity he could maintain.

"My goodness, you must have *really* wanted her," marveled Mr. Magruder, looking boldly at Robert's still-swollen silhouette.

"I don't *care* if I don't have a 50th anniversary with you!" I called after him. I could hear the roar of his MGB as he threw it angrily into gear. It seemed to have some new scraping sounds to it.

"My, that was fun!" said Mrs. Magruder. *"We've* only been married three years ourselves. We're counting like dog years—seven to one. Should have our 25th in 1984."

I listened to the sound of Robert's car die away. The first thing I'll do, I decided, is crumple up that damned bedspread and throw it on the floor.

Mrs. Magruder had turned into a hostess. "Want to come in for a snort of booze?"

"You know, honey," said Mr. Magruder to his wife, "all that action has, uh, kinda worn me out. Think I might want to go to bed early." And he actually winked at his wife.

"I'll take you up some other time on that snort," I thanked them.

"Any time," waved Mrs. Magruder.

"Call first," added her husband. "We might be—well, you know."

STOCK CLERK ADMITS PUTTING KEN IN
BARBIE'S CLOTHING

A stock clerk at a Banana Bay toy store was fired after
he acknowledged he redressed the doll one night while
goofing off. "We always did crazy things like that,"
Ron Zero told reporters. "We'd put Barbie in her doll house
with Ken spanking Barbie. Nobody noticed."
Mrs. Teresa White gave the doll to her daughter, only
to find that she had actually bought a Ken doll outfitted
in a purple tank-top with lace-covered purple and turquoise skirt.
Customers who have bought Barbie dolls at the Doll House
in the Banana Bay Shopping Center are urged to check the dolls
to make sure they are the owners of Barbie and not Ken.
Manager Warren Spofford apologizes for any confusion and
guarantees a full refund. Ron Zero ("yes, that's my real name")
has taken a new job as billboard paster.
—*Banana Bay Tribune, November 15, 1977*

Fran and I have our first couple for counseling and we are overjoyed! We are
seeing Mr. and Mrs. Comstock, and their presenting problem is that they
are sick of Mexican motifs, but are afraid their daughter Annabella will run
away from home if they go to English Tudor.

When they told her what they planned to do Annabella threw a fit and told
them they didn't love her any more and how could they do this right after her cat
died.

Mr. Comstock explained that he never knew he was allergic to cacti until he
buried Pretty Baby under a yucca plant, got stuck by thorns, and his arm swelled

to twice its diameter. He still has the thorn marks, he says, rolling up his shirt sleeve and pointing out the little red evidence. Mrs. Comstock sighs beside him on our couch, where just a day before Annabella had shoved her new white socks under the cushions.

"I can get them to do anything I want and they'll never kick me out," she had bragged to me.

"Have you thought of alternative living arrangements for your daughter, so that you can redo your home the way you two want?" Fran asks.

Mrs. Comstock brightens. "There's this man who wants to marry her," she says. "Annabella won't tell us who he is and never tells us anything about him and hasn't invited him to our house to meet us, but– "

"I just want to give Annabella a beautiful wedding in an English Tudor setting," Mr. Comstock adds. "I don't want anyone coming to a wedding reception at our house and getting stuck by *thorns*."

Is Annabella going to marry Robert? Our divorce is not yet final. Robert won't let Pete live with me—my husband has actually stuck his face into mine and threatened to take me to court, prove that I am an unfit mother and mentally unbalanced and should not even be a *therapist*.

Fran has laughed at all this but still I am reluctant to test the courts and so have allowed Pete to stay home. And since Pete hardly talks anymore, I don't know how he's doing with his father and Susan.

"Robert's terrified to be *alone*, don't you see?" says Fran. "He *can't* be alone."

I find this hard to believe, Robert who traveled so often and surely was alone most of the time, except for meetings. I have become used to being by myself and while refusing to have a formal out-in-the-open date with Max, have cooked dinner for him a half dozen times.

Max, such a strong man just a little older than me ("My father was a butcher and taught me how to haul sides of beef across my shoulders. ") is a relief after Robert. Max doesn't even own a library card and he has an apartment full of deer heads—he says in mock bafflement his ex-wife didn't want them– and I can't see anything long-term ever coming of this; but oh, he is a good listener and he enjoys my cooking.

I enjoy the cuddling too and in case this journal falls into the wrong hands, will swear that nothing out of the ordinary has taken place in my bedroom.

His bedroom has a wild Florida boar's head over the bed. A nasty-looking animal which doesn't seem to get in the way of our pleasure.

Anyway, I wonder about Robert and Annabella. She would make such a mediocre stepmother for Pete.

But Annabella keeps her private life under wraps and as long as I don't ask and she doesn't confess, I can keep taking two separate checks a week from the Comstocks.

✫ ✫ ✫

Robert and Annabella turned out to be not a problem after the Cocoa Beach Holiday Inn incident. You might have seen it on the local CBS (out of Orlando) evening news:

"A man calling himself 'James Bond' was embarrassed to find himself on camera when vacating a room at the Banana Bay Holiday Inn earlier today. An alert front desk clerk"– and here the camera cut to a shot of Mitzi, Doctor Griffin's gum-chewing former employee, snapping her wad and pretending to write something on a piece of paper while staring big-eyed into the lens– "caught the name 'James Bond' on the guest register, realized she had a famous movie star staying here, and called our studio.

"But the joke was on us, as this was no Sean Connery"– and here the TV camera held a shot of Robert, of all people, trying to duck his head away from the camera while saying over and over, "It's Bonde with an e, Bonde with an e!" while beside him, dressed in a white dress and light blond wig and looking devastatingly gorgeous as a Marilyn Monroe wannabe, Annabella mugged for the TV camera.

The newsbite was used as a "teaser" locally, mostly due to the toothsome Annabella, and shown every hour, and was also picked up nationally since it had been a slow news day. Thankfully for Robert *his* appearance was clipped so short that no one recognized him, except for the several dozen women who recognized his voice, picked up on his fake name and sent him hate mail inside James Fleming paperbacks. Susan told me she was red-faced every time a new one showed up at the front door in the hands of a beaming Mr. Whitney the mailman, although everyone knew he was not ordinarily one to get out of his truck and walk.

"Got his own pen pal club, Mr. Baldwin does," joshed Mr. Whitney

And Annabella!– Annabella was asked to come to New York to audition for a "Name This Celebrity" show, which aired for three months before she and the show were canceled.

However, she remained in New York, auditioning at every off-off-Broadway theater that was reviving "Bus Stop". Since she couldn't afford an apartment by herself, she sent for her best friend and confidant, Mitzi. Rumor has it that they're both waitresses in the Big Apple.

You may have seen Annabella in a Marilyn Monroe commercial for snow tires. Yes, that is Banana Bay Beach's own actress. Her chosen stage name is Bella D. Balle. With an e.

The Comstocks, indirectly due to Robert, now have their English Tudor house, complete with Huck Finn dressed as a Palace Guard on the bridge. There are dark timbers crisscrossing the cypress garage door. They had to have their garage door opener changed as a result of the heavier construction.

✮ ✮ ✮

I am at St. Barnabus' Church, picking through rummage to set on tables for our annual rummage sale.

The women who volunteer to help at this event do so thinking they will get first choice of the merchandise, but Margaret Wolfe, Father Wolfe's wife, has made herself the head of the sale and will let nothing be sold before the doors open on Saturday morning.

I think the rule is too stringent and a good way to discourage volunteers, but as I have not found anything I want to buy, I'm willing not to challenge Margaret this year.

"I have prayed long and hard not to hate you," Margaret says to me in a low voice as we throw out babies' bibs too spat-up on to even give away.

Hate *me*– I can't believe what I am hearing!– and in the parish hall where we stayed with all that spaghetti!– and by a *priest's* wife! I am stunned into speechlessness. I didn't know they were allowed to hate.

"You have ruined my son's life." she goes on, glancing around to make sure no one else is listening. "Absolutely *ruined* it."

My face, I am sure, is flushing. Is the woman crazy? She looks hard at me. "You do know, do you?"

"Well, if it's about Robert being on TV– "

"It's about *my* son and *your* daughter. The way you raised her has *ruined* his life and I pray for you every day—what kind of mother lets her daughter run away from home, sneak into a men's dormitory and *live* there while he tries to study and she gets her hairdressing license and abandons their child?"

She squints at me. "It's well known that football players are discouraged from having– " she drops her voice– "sex– the night before a game. It hurts their—masculinity, so they don't play as well– "

"Because they're too tired?" I finish her euphemistic sentence. "Margaret, I assure you this comes as a shock to me." I sit down on a metal folding chair, perhaps the very one Robert sat on during the hurricane. "Wait a minute—Excelsior is *Jack's* son?"

"Of course he is! Haven't you ever seen my son do that eyebrow frown thing that Excelsior does? How can you be so dense?" And here she bursts into tears. "It breaks my heart!" she wails.

Immediately the other women look up from their pricing and come to Margaret's aide, offering her old tee shirts to wipe her eyes on. They are fussing over her when Father Wolfe comes into the room and I see by his face that he understands all too well what his wife has just told me.

"Come,come," he orders, taking his wife firmly by the arms and moving her toward his office. "You too, Joan." I follow in their wake. "She's all right," he calls back to the volunteers before they can come to their own conclusions. "Just tired."

Since I just used that same word, the image of Margaret and the good Father making love stops me a moment in my tracks.

I spare myself writing dialogue that comes pouring out, the crying and accusing from Margaret, the bafflement from me, with the old Joan-guilt—yes, I should have followed Susan to Tallahassee and forcibly pulled my daughter off their strapping son Jack, who was possessed by the demon Sex.

"Wait a minute!" I say again, so that Margaret pauses in her harangue and Father Wolfe stops patting her hand. "You've known all this time and didn't tell me? Why not?"

Well, —it seems they are in love. Have been for years. Since way back in junior high school. And they want to be married as soon as Jack graduates. At St. Barnabus'. With Excelsior as their best man. They are set to announce it on Sunday, while Jack is home.

"He comes home so often," wails Margaret "I always thought it was to see *me*. But no—" ah, that old demon Sex.

"And I had total care of that baby—" I say. "And I was so jealous of you for having him," adds Margaret, to my mounting surprise.

"We helped all we could," Father Wolfe states. "I paid Susan's way through hairdressing school out of my discretionary fund."

While I have been tearing my life apart and rebuilding it, all this has been going on— "I have a confession to make to you both," Father Wolfe says. "Once after church I sneaked away into the nursery and—I christened Excelsior. I named him Jack Thomas Wolfe."

His wife gapes at him. "I christened him *myself* one Sunday when he was the only baby in the nursery. I named him Jack Fulton— after my own father— Wolfe."

They wait. "Okay," I say. "I christened him, too. Excelsior Robert. But it was with tea, so I don't know if that counts."

"We have," says Father Wolfe, "a pickle." We all sit quietly now. Margaret's storm has passed and we are all working together, united in a common goal—to keep the child from going through life with the name Excelsior. "It's a pickle because Susan and Jack have asked that I christen the child this Sunday."

"What name?" We two women ask in tandem.

"They haven't decided yet. Now, I don't know about you two grandmothers"– I choke up and Margaret and I stare at each other—we are!– we are united in having a grandchild in common!– "but I think we need to forget this entire conversation. God knows– " he stops and grins– "yes, that's it. God knows."

And that's how I end up having lunch with the Wolfes that day, and how Father Wolfe asks me to fill out an unexpired term as the first, the very *first vestrywoman* at St. Barnabus', to replace Robert, who has just sent (the envelope inspected first by Mr. Whitney, who delights in thinking it's a love letter to Margaret) the church his letter of resignation.

As I accept I wonder if Robert signed his letter "James Bonde"– with an e. "Oh Lord," prays Father Wolfe before we eat lunch, as though he has read my mind, "please don't let the child be named 'James'. With an e," he adds, crushing my hand in his huge one.

"Amen," Margaret and I respond, nodding at each other.

And miracle of miracles, I talk over dessert with Margaret about the rummage sale volunteers getting first crack at the tables before the regular buyers stampede it, and she agrees!

I am the first Vestrywoman in the history of St. Barnabus' Episcopal Church, Banana Bay, Florida. All those old traditionalists resting out back can just turn over in their ashes—how *far* we females have come!

And I *won't* be the one to take secretary's notes or make the coffee, no sir. Oh, I need to phone *Fran*!

✡ ✡ ✡

Joan Baldwin Forster
2011

POLICE SEIZE ALLIGATOR FROM CONNECTICUT HOME

A reptile taken from a home in Middlebury has been identified
as a 12-inch-long American alligator.
Police tell the *Hartford Courant* they found the alligator
over the week end in an aquarium while on an unrelated
call to the house.
The owner, Ken Johnson, told authorities he got the reptile
from a man in Waterbury and thought it was a lizard.
It is illegal to own an alligator in Connecticut, though
there is no penalty associated with breaking that law.
The gator remains in state custody, pending confirmation
of its identification.
—*The Associated Press*

The old Joan was the one who loved collecting newspaper articles, but I thought this one a tribute to my mother, who believed she was so safe at home in New England.

There is no truly safe place in life. We just try to make our places as much a sanctuary as possible and lie to ourselves that this is where moth and rust can surely not corrupt, or thieves break in and destroy.

What sweetness and light there was in 1977, compared to our post-2001 malaise. Every problem back then could be solved in less than thirty minutes with time for commercial breaks. Black was black and white was white and there were no shades of gray.

Except that is not how life spooled out. Sweet-natured Excelsior survived the Atlantic Ocean, only to lose his life at age nine in the Indian River. I need to talk about it, since other lives went with it:

Father Tom Wolfe and Excelsior formed quite an attachment. One of the passions they shared was fishing, and I had found in a thrift shop an old pair of black rubber boots that fit the youngster as long as something was stuffed in the toes. Eventually he grew into them and needed no more wadded-up socks.

His grandfather had black wading boots, the hip-high ones with suspenders. *Now* there is a sign where they drowned stating WARNING! WATCH OUT FOR DEEP HOLES! YOU COULD LOSE YOUR LIFE! Mosquito County shut the barn door too late for our family.

A terrified motorist who saw the flailing couple in the water not ten feet out in the shallow lagoon stopped and tried to help. Apparently Father Wolfe had stepped into a hole and his boots had filled immediately with dark silty water. He found to his horror he could not stand up and as he fell he tried to yell to Excelsior to stay on shore; but the child thought his grandfather was playing and splashed out to join in the fun.

Excelsior's death had a dramatic effect on Pete: he decided to go to veterinary school. Now he saves lives—the lives of owners' beloved pets. His patients, human and animal, adore him.

I had drowning nightmares for several years. In them I was always trying to save someone who was dragging me down to the darkness.

Margaret Wolfe was never the same. She moved from the area as soon after the double funeral as she could and later joined her son Jack in Atlanta, where he had a new job.

When Excelsior died Susan and Jack grew far apart, their haunted eyes accusing each other of neglect.

They divorced. Susan tells me Jack is remarried. After the accident, my depressed daughter stopped yelling at me and sometimes for a while I wondered if I didn't want the old Susan back again.

I stayed unmarried and Max came around from time to time until he met a woman at a line dancing bar.

He apologized to me about it, but I could see we had no serious future together.

For one thing he had a smelly dog named Bones, possibly part German Shepherd and part Alsatian. One day Max and I went for a ride in his pickup truck. Max had given his beloved dog some worm medicine that morning. The untethered dog, riding on Max's silver metal tool chest just back of the rear window, had an attack of diarrhea and as Max rounded a curve, slid off his now-slippery perch right into the woods.

Max tried to be calm about it, but I had been the one peering out the back window anxiously, since I had never seen a dog who could ride like this before, with no leash to hold him, and the *one* time I looked away (because Max shouted, "Did you see that *deer?*"), Bones was gone.

Max tramped the woods yelling,"Bones! Bones! Come on, boy! Come on, you damned dog!" and when he returned with no dog, he asked me rather brusquely why I hadn't cleaned off the truck. The fact that I had no hose, water, cloths or soap didn't seem to register with him.

We ate sandwiches passively, upwind of the truck and when Bones appeared, smiling the way a dog does, with his tongue hanging out, Max had him sit between us on the silent ride home.

☆ ☆ ☆

Oh, Max. He wanted so much for the two of us to stay together, but he had let his library card lapse years before and he hadn't even bothered to update it; and I grew tired of get-togethers where the women sat in the kitchen and complained about their husbands while their men hunkered down on black faux-leather sofa sets in front of the warmth of an oversized TV set to watch wrestling. Since I'd read many books about personality types, I could see that neither of us was about to change much, and after spending one wet week end in Max's place with the odiferous Bones, I looked forward to my own apartment as though it was an old friend.

But being alone also got tedious. After I'd read all the Updike books I could find, I was sensitive to some old-fashioned courting. And Quentin, who would sit at my kitchen counter while I cooked and read to me in a soothing voice while not mispronouncing words, seemed to fill the bill.

And so we were married. And then he started reading me proctology articles in that same soothing voice.

He asked me to come work for him in his office, and so I cut back my own client load to help him.

I take total responsibility for doing this. And I liked his patients and I never pulled rank with his staff. Rear ends proved a satisfactory change from mental problems for a few years.

But then he forgot I ended my day when I came home from his office, and he grew to expect the same kind of attention he'd gotten used to. I had told him when I went to work for him that I would never ever get angry with him in front of anyone while we were working, and I kept to that promise; but I did hum a lot under my breath.

He no longer read to me while I cooked. Instead he napped and woke up when I called him to dinner.

He liked music while we ate, especially Mantovani. I took to reading a book at the table while he flipped the newspaper in front of his face and those damned maple-sugar-sweet orchestral sounds made my eyes water.

So— what if we hadn't built a house together? Would things still be all right? As it was, I got to see another side of Quentin, the perfectionistic man who argued with the contractor for an hour one time, both of them drawing diagrams on the new white wallboard, while they pencil-fought with one another about which way the stairs should ascend to the second floor.

And ignored *my* ideas.

That was when I quit working for my buttocks husband and went back to working with heads.

✳ ✳ ✳

"You don't deserve a new toaster oven!"

I cannot believe I yelled those ugly words at Quentin, who withstood them meekly and headed upstairs to do whatever private things he did in his bathroom in the morning before going to his office.

Nineteen years married to this man, and this is the stupid fight I get into!

I state my case: we have a nice shiny toaster oven. Quentin likes to put buttered bread in it. He also puts cheese pizza slices on the wire rack—stuff that oozes down onto the crumb tray. Then he doesn't notice the mess. Apparently the medical-perfectionistic tendencies stop at our front door.

I wrap aluminum foil around the tray until after a couple of weeks it is coated with oily crumbs and smells rancid. Then I shake the crumbs out of the upside-down toaster oven and I scour the wire racks with a brush.

I put it back all nice and clean and new-aluminum foil-wrapped, plug it in and Quentin's gunking process begins anew.

So, I think. I am so smart! I will buy my *own* toaster oven. And then we'll have Quentin's dirty one and my nice clean one. What a grand idea! And then I'll have no reason to nag at my husband.

Except. Except. He does not have a good sense of boundaries and he is likely to forget and then use mine and it will get like his and I will have *two* toaster ovens in the same room to clean. Shades of "The Sorcerer's Apprentice" fill my mind as multitudes of small appliances dance in my kitchen

It is at that moment, as I sit in my car, fresh from a trip to Macy's, an unused brand-new toaster oven fresh from the factory, wrapped carefully and sitting in its box, ready for me, Joan, that I realize I don't *want* two of these in one kitchen; I want mine in *my* kitchen. Alone. I am suddenly, wearily fed up with cleaning up after another person.

I dash home, grab the classified pages and circle some rentals I think I can afford. Is this me? Is this *me*, making such a life-altering decision? Didn't I get married nineteen years ago in order to share my life with another? What is the matter with me?

✻ ✻ ✻

"What are all those boxes doing in the foyer?" Quentin asks, looking up from a proctology newsletter.

"Quentin, I told you a month ago. I am moving out. I found a rental house and I have taken a six-month lease on it. The movers are coming tomorrow. These boxes are full of my books and piano music. I need to write a book that I began thirty years ago and I need a quiet place to think in."

"Are you taking your piano?"

"Yes, I am."

"Well— don't expect me to move. I like it here."

"I understand. Now I've left you a dozen frozen meals that I made in advance. All you have to do is pop them into the microwave or the oven— "

"You haven't packed the remote, by any chance?"

"I can see it from here. It's on top of the TV."

"Where?"

I come across the room and hand him the remote. Oh Lord, this man is helpless without me. How will he survive? I know he survived without me before we met. That thought keeps me going.

"Quentin. I will be *three* miles away. I'll probably see more of you than when we were living together.

Now, I have notes for the pool and what time in the week the trash people come and you'll have to get the newspaper yourself from the driveway and also the mail when it comes— "

But Quentin has aimed the remote at the TV and is now channel-surfing, oblivious. I will not miss this. I am taking the small TV from the den. I had learned to record every show I wanted to watch, so I could put my finger on the Pause button, because as soon as I settled down to watch a movie while Quentin was busy in the living room with a football game, he would be popping into the den— "I need another stamp. What're you watching? Hm-m-m. Looks boring,"— and then pop out again.

Wow. I will be able to watch a movie from beginning to end, interrupted only by bathroom breaks!

☆ ☆ ☆

When I was a young girl in Plainview, Connecticut, my life consisted of a parallelogram of places I enjoyed going— from home through a neighbor's back yard to the corner grocery store; then up the street and past the post office, fire station, five and ten and the other stores in the center of town to the library; then reversing my walk and up another street past the bus depot and movie theater to the Episcopal Church; then down one block to the elementary school, and then turn left again to go home.

In the center of town across from the Strand Theater was a bar. The odors coming from it were sickly sweet and strong and smoky, no matter what time of day. There was a side door that read LADIES ENTRANCE and I wondered why men and women couldn't go through the same door out front.

There were old grizzled unshaven men hanging around this area, but no old women. I wondered about this too, and then decided it had to be because women knew how to cook and do housework. So as long as there were people and houses, there would be jobs for old women. I was so relieved I was female!

Now I am old and I don't want to believe that any more. My six-month lease is about to be up in this 55+ community of 180 homes, all with identical green roofs (Oak Glen joke: "How do I find your house?" "Just look for the one with the green roof.") and I am going to renew it. Quentin keeps going to his office and I am sure he is gooping up the toaster oven and possibly will burn our house down; but oh, I love being alone again!

Of course I am still traveling that huge distance of three miles to go back to our old house and do a little cleaning while Quentin is out. I have finally despaired of this Herculean task and quit doing it. I like my new house with the green roof, that I can tidy in a half-hour every morning, and then on to water aerobics with a dozen other cheerful women all my age. We all wear the marks of our lives—wrinkles, gray hair, bifocals—and the wonderful surprise is that nobody notices or cares.

And I have been busy going through old boxes still in our garage and rediscovering my old journals. I'm finding more and more notes for my book. Most of them are unreadable now. Part of it is my handwriting and part is that palmetto bugs have chewed the paper. "Eating one's words" makes a lot of sense in Florida.

I have changed my phone number twice already. I don't know how Derreck finds them out; he has been sending me obscene messages. He sends them from different phones so when I see a strange number on my phone I do not pick up. Most of the time they are messages from my great new neighbors, but every now and then. . . .

And I'm in a gated community,but it's easy enough to get in by waiting beside the gate until an Oaker shows up in a Prius and opens the gate with a remote button.

The residents are wondering about me, since it is only *my* trash cans that are knocked over on trash days. I have been forced to leave my smelly black plastic bags in the garage until I hear the garbage truck, and then run outside, my bathrobe flapping around me while I chase after it with my refuse.

Well, in for a penny, in for a pound, my Dad used to say. I can't go this far in my story and not tell the rest.

Here's where Emily came from: I have no idea. Susan arrived at my apartment one day, not long after she and Jack had divorced, and announced, "I'm pregnant."

"Yes?" I said in my professional therapist's stall-while-you-recover-your-composure voice.

"I'm pregnant and I want this child and I will never tell you who the father is, so never ask, or I'll just make up a name."

I didn't think she did so well at making up names. "O-kay." So it probably wasn't Jack's. I tried mentally counting on my fingers—

"Oh, *Mom*," and to my surprise she flung herself against me for a moment. "I screwed up so with Excelsior and I'm not going to do it again!" She sniffled and I gave her a paper napkin. It was all I had nearby.

"You certainly did not screw up. And of course you're not going to do that again because you didn't the first time."

"Anyway, I just wanted you to know."

"I'm glad. Are you going to be okay?"

"Yeah. I've got money saved, so I can take time off from work when the baby comes." She had gone back to LoRayne's after the divorce. "

"I'll help all I can." And I did. I couldn't do enough for my granddaughter Emily. When that lovely little girl was five years old she was the flower girl at our wedding—Quentin's and mine. I still catch my breath when I look at that group photo, she looks so serious. And I know she's my granddaughter because when she started up the aisle to throw rose petals from her basket, she halted and announced in a loud voice, "No, I won't *do* this. It's too *messy*."

Susan had to throw some first to get Emily to comply.

Where did we go? Where did Quentin and I go? When I look back, I think it was because he simply would not *engage*. Whatever from his childhood had caused him to guard his emotions, I had no magic key to open that heavily defended door. I thought about proctology and how he didn't even have to look his patient in the face. Maybe if I could just have bent over and dropped my drawers while I talked, we could have had some genuine conversations.

This is what our talks are like metaphorically, Quentin—we are on opposite sides of a tennis net. I lob a ball over the net and you stand there and don't even raise your racquet. So I send another ball your way and the same thing happens. Soon you're standing there with dozens of balls at your feet and you are smiling in your nice amiable way, but we're *not* playing an active game.

Actually I could have had a better game if I'd just bounced tennis balls against a wall. I remember the play "Shirley Valentine" and the actress talking to to her kitchen wall– "Wall," she would say, and oh, how I would identify!

My toaster oven after six months looks like new. I could take it back to the store and nobody would ever know I had used it. Obsessive-compulsive workaholic, I have become. A neat freak.

When Emily comes by with Derreck, he has been pleasant to me lately. So pleasant that I was taken by surprise when I walked out in my slippers one morning to get my newspaper and there was a dead bird on my sidewalk.

It could have been an accident. Sometimes birds flew into windows or sliding glass doors and killed themselves. Except I don't have any glass near where that unfortunate Mourning Dove lay.

Accidents—I think suddenly of Robert and his plane. Years ago we were flying to Connecticut, he on business (and, I discovered later, a quick trip to visit an old high school girlfriend) and I to see my parents. I was a reluctant flyer and was sitting by his side reading and trying to calm my panicky need to open the door and get out, when apparently the plane read my mind and ran out of gas.

Note: it's extremely quiet up there when the engine quits and turns into a heavy glider.

Now in an accident you always want to have a workaholic like Robert in charge, because workaholics are able to compartmentalize and pay attention to the situation at hand, while I sat busy praying that we would survive, that we wouldn't hit anyone on the road below, that the kids would remember us as good people, that Fran would take them in—and we were *down!,* across highway 301 and lurching to a stop in the woods, where an outwardly calm Robert half-turned to me and said, "Well—get out of the plane, stupid," and I figured he was talking to me, not himself, so I climbed out and stood uselessly aside while dozens of excited passersby came running up to help and Robert picked up papers which had fluttered from his briefcase.

The plane was totaled. Someone gave us a ride to the airport Robert had been aiming for, and I found myself in the ladies' room not a half hour since we had been airborne.

"Lordy, what happened to *you?*" exclaimed a woman who was combing her hair. "You are white as a sheet, honey!" I stared at my reflection. All the bones in my face seemed to be standing out in relief from my skin.

"Hurry up," said Robert, steering me to an entrance with his hand on my elbow. "They're holding the plane for us."

"The– the plane?" I repeated stupidly.

"I have to get to my meeting. Come on!"

I buckled my seat belt automatically and tried to make sense of the words the stewardess was saying. As we took off Robert turned to me. My teeth were chattering.

"Is anything *wrong?*" he said. I'm not making any of this up.

And the time we went skiing at Aspen! It was the end of the day, when people are so tired that they have accidents. Robert wanted one more run. "I'll find you a nice beginner's slope, Joan," he said when I protested. "Come on!"

We were the last ones on the chairlift. I heard the motor stop after we got out. "Remember, you said a beginner's slope," I reminded him as we wiped thick snowflakes from our goggles.

The slope turned out to be an intermediate one– full of moguls. It had now started to snow more heavily. As I headed down exhaustion washed over me. I was so tired I couldn't keep control of my skis and I kept picking up speed despite my efforts to brake. I was too worn out to yell.

Then all at once Robert came flying from my left side and, skiing over my own skis, brought me to a quivering sudden halt. I looked ahead of me through the falling snow and not ten feet from the tips of my skis loomed a deep rocky crevasse.

I sat down heavily; undid my skis with shaking fingers full of adrenalin.

"I'm *walking* down," I announced, "and when I get to the bottom I am going to kill you." I must have been terrified, to speak so to him, the man who had again saved my life while first putting it in jeopardy.

I must give him credit for skiing more slowly while I fought my way down the mountainside with my now-cumbersome skis as the visibility dropped to nothing.

We doubtless had sex that night. As I have reported, Robert's workaholism gave him the benefit of being able to compartmentalize, while I kept picturing black unending rocks.

Joan Baldwin Forster
2011

Susan has been lecturing me: "Why the hell are you meddling in Emily's life, Mother?"

"I didn't know I was meddling."

"Well, I saw Emily last evening and she said she and Derreck had had a big argument and your name came up."

"Hard to believe."

"Derreck thinks you don't like him. In fact, he thinks you *hate* him."

"Ridiculous. I don't hate anyone." But still, I am bothered that Emily is bothered. And I see that the clever Derreck is getting us women to fight among ourselves.

"You hated Daddy."

"Sorry. That is untrue. And anyway, why bring past stuff up now?"

"I just don't want you driving *Derreck* away. Emily loves him. Now are you going to butt out or not?

Oh, I wish I could level with her! But I've seen her look at me with a calculating gaze of, "When can I put you in a nursing home?" and I realize that my wrinkles have her convinced I am much older than I actually am. Susan has a misguided belief that she is the center of the universe and I am a way-far-removed constellation, too cold and distant to support any life.

Witness: we took a trip once in Susan's car when Emily was still a toddler, to visit Pete in Columbia, South Carolina, where he was working at the time.

I had packed a few DVDs and that was a good thing, I thought, since she had left hers at home. We seemed to have a pleasant visit and Pete had been a kind and funny-joke-telling host. We were on our way home when Susan started snorting through her nose—a sure indication that fireworks were to follow.

I fell right into it: "Is anything wrong, Susan?"

"You should know."

"But I don't."

She hunched over the steering wheel and refused to glance at me. "Well, *guess*."

"I'm not a very good guesser."

"I *never* get my way, do you know that? It's always got to be *your* way!"

"I don't think so– "

"You coddled Pete, you coddled Excelsior, you're coddling Emily" (who slept peacefully through all this in her carseat) "and you left *me* to take care of Daddy."

"I thought that's what the two of you wanted."

"No! And I never get my way. *Ever*!"

"I still don't know what this is all about– "

"Okay—how about having to watch stupid movies just because *you* like them! Dumb foreign films so you have to jerk your head down to read the titles and then up again to see what's going on, over and over again!"

Probably "Au Revoir Les Enfants" and "Wings of Desire" would have been good choices for me to watch at home alone, but– "

"You are giving me a heart attack!" Susan screamed.

I looked at her, startled. "Do you want me to drive?" I asked. "Are you unwell?"

"Just sit there and shut up. Just don't say another word. I should have come alone with just Emily."

So I sat there and shut up. All my mothering skills, all my therapist's skills were worthless until she calmed down. In the meantime she appeared to be driving carefully enough, although her snorting continued.

On I-95 outside of Savannah I told her I needed a bathroom break and coffee. Without a word she swerved off the interstate and up to a Burger King. She sat there, still not looking at me, the engine running as I got out of the car. "Can I get you anything?" I asked. Her face was now a dull purplish-red. Emily slept on.

"Okay, Susan, I'll meet you out here in five minutes."

The restaurant's cold air blasted my face as I walked in. I used the restroom and ordered a bottle of water—thirst was what was getting to me, not caffeine withdrawal; and I needed to dilute the bile buildup in my innards, that old familiar pain Susan raised in me at times like these—and I bought a bottle of water for Susan too, and headed outside.

I walked all around the parking area. There was no sign of Susan's car. I walked around again, this time the other way. Still no sign of her. A young boy on an old bike too big for him careened up to me. He said, "Are you Joan?"

"Ye-s?" I said, distracted, still trying to make sense of this surreal situation.

"Lady left you a note. Said you'd give me five dollars."

I fortunately had a five dollar bill in my wallet. The boy beamed at the money, mounted the bike and wobbled off.

The note, written on a blank page torn from, I guessed, the library book I had been reading in the car, stated (in Susan's spelling) "YOU ARE GIVING ME A HEART ATTAK!! FIND YOUR OWN WAY HOME!!!!"

I studied the missive as though deciphering a foreign language and then walked carefully back inside Burger King, still gripping the two bottles of water. The note was now crumpled and wet from the moisture on the bottles and my hands. The girl at the counter smiled at me.

"How—how far to the bus station?"

" 'bout ten miles. But you're only a mile from the airport. Would that do?"

"Uh-yes. I guess maybe—yes, okay."

"Ralph!" she called to a young man with curly red hair. "You going back to the airport?"

"Soon's I finish my lunch."

"Take this lady with you?" He nodded yes, his mouth around a hamburger.

"Ralph's a good guy," she said to me. When she smiled she had a space between her two upper front teeth. Right now she was my beautiful guardian angel. "Ma'am, you maybe oughta sit down 'til Ralph's ready. Is there anything I can get you?"

Oh, the kindness of strangers! "No, thank you," I said, my throat rebelling at the idea of solid food at this moment. "I think I will use the ladies room, however, if you will be so kind as to ask Ralph to wait." How proud Mother would have been of my good manners!

The formalities over, I went into the handicap booth in the women's room and jumped up and down, muttering, "Shit! Shit! *Shit!*" without even considering that some innocent female in the next stall might think I was ordering a reluctant colon to perform.

Then I phoned Fran. "She dumped me off!" I sobbed. "My own daughter! In *Savannah!*"

"Savannah's a pretty place," said Fran.

"Not when you're stuck at a Burger King!" I wailed. "Your kids would never do this to *you!*"

"Honey, Susan's never done anything with subtlety. Now, do you have enough money to get home?"

"I have credit cards and– " I searched through my purse and broke into tears again as I found a toy of Emily's.

"Okay. Now weren't you smart to take your wallet with you and not leave it with Susan? So– rent a car or get a plane ticket and I'll meet you in town when you get here and give you a hug and a drink."

"Okay," I snuffled. "Oh, gotta go—Ralph's finished his lunch." Fran is such a good friend that she didn't ask me who Ralph was.

The young Ralph, smelling like gasoline and onions, dropped me at the entrance to the airport and refused to take any money from his passenger. I found the car rental counter and in a choking voice told the uniformed young woman with a soft Georgia accent that I needed a car one-way to Banana Bay, Florida.

"One way's going to cost you a lot more than if you bring it back here," she explained politely.

Now I began to cry. "There's been—a death in the family," I choked. (That's sure what it felt like.) She looked at me with real concern. "I'll see what I can do," and within the hour I was on the road in a rented Chevrolet that needed to go back to Orlando anyway, so I was given a monetary break.

I watched the roadside on I-95 all the way through Jacksonville, Daytona Beach, Titusville, hoping I would not see Susan's car abandoned there because an ambulance had taken her to the nearest hospital with a massive heart attack brought on by her *own mother*. I ached for Emily.

I also looked (until it got too dark) for my luggage, tossed out of Susan's car in a thundering rage and strewn all over the highway.

I needn't have worried. When I pulled up to Susan's place (my old house!) all the lights were out save for the flickering blue of the TV set. My suitcases were stacked haphazardly beside the front door. She did not answer when I knocked and called, although I could hear Emily crying and Susan shushing her.

So was I now going to butt out? You betcha.

After a restless heartburn-filled night of wondering what the hell I had actually done wrong I decide to take the high road. I will bake my famous Key Lime pie and take it to Derreck and Emily as a peace offering. They will be so pleased! And we will sit around their kitchen counter in their apartment. Oh, I can picture us eating pie, laughing and planning the wedding together—surely that cannot be considered "butting in"! and if Susan shows up I will act as if there is nothing wrong, that her sticks and stones can't get to me, that she has not again broken my heart, because I am not only a mother, but also a well-thought-of *mental health counselor*!

Also as a lifelong Episcopalian I am primed to forgive.

✡ ✡ ✡

Now, heating the oven and getting the ingredients together, my plan seems more and more foolproof. Anyone deserves a second chance, I decide, and there must be a side of Derreck I have not yet seen, since both Emily and Susan are so ecstatic about him. Of course! He really doesn't know *me*, either. And wouldn't I look like a damned fool, making something out of nothing. The knife in the dishwater was an accident. The slipping into the St. John's—another accident. Nobody *else* is getting alarmed; I won't, either. I quiet the little paranoid voice in my head that whispers, "But how about– ? And how about– ?"

And don't I know, from years of counseling others (as well as playing for countless weddings and suffering through interminable wedding rehearsals) how *weird* women can get and how irrational when they demand their own way. Well, I will not be one of those women! I am no neurotic fussbudget, looking for problems where none exist.

Oh, and I will need to be a calming influence for Emily while Susan goes through her periodic histrionics. Periodic– maybe for her it's menopause. Or maybe she's finally given up smoking.

Just to be on the safe side, I phone my Jiminy Cricket. "Fran?" I say.

"Hey, Joan, how are you doing?" Fran's voice sounds as though she's next door, although I know she and her husband have rented a travel trailer and are visiting their extended family out west.

"Listen, I wanted to check something out with you– " I start.

"Hang on—Evan!" I hear her yell. "Don't stand so close to the edge! Where's your grandfather?"

"Where are you?" I ask.

"Grand Canyon. The kids are trying to spit in it. I need a dozen hands right about –Evan! Quit scaring your sister!"

"Maybe you'd better go," I suggest.

"It's Ken's fault, feeding them Mountain Dew," Fran tells me. "Hold on!—no, it's okay. What did you call about?"

"Oh—nothing that can't wait. You have a good time. I'll see you when you get back."

"*Next* year," Fran promises, "I am taking them to someplace that's on flat ground. 'Bye!"

I feel better having made contact with my old friend. It's almost as though she gave me the go-ahead to do what I am going to do. I admire the pie, carry it carefully to my car, then head for Emily and Derreck's apartment across town, first having read my horoscope: "This is indeed an auspicious day for you." I don't know if Episcopalians are supposed to follow signs, but I figure it can't hurt. Weren't the Three Wise Men astrologers?

I am in luck—both Emily's and Derreck's cars are parked in front of their apartment when I drive up. I remove the pie from the cardboard box I packed it in to keep it from moving around. It looks delicious. Smiling in anticipation, I step up to their door and knock.

The door, oddly, is ajar. I push it open a little at a time. "Hello?" I call politely, walking into the dining/kitchen area. There is a sound from the far end of the hallway. "Hello?" I say again.

Derreck emerges from the bedroom. He is wearing only briefs and is barefoot. I note how strong and well-muscled he is at the same moment I wonder with embarrassment if I have interrupted Emily and him at lovemaking. But then why would their front door be open? Expecting the pizza man?, I think wildly.

"About time!" he snarls. "Where the hell have you *been*– ?" he stops when he sees me.

"What the *hell* are you doing here?" His grim face is not the least bit welcoming.

"I—I brought you a pie," I say brightly, holding it out in front of me. "I thought you and Emily—I saw her car– "

"She's at work."

"Oh. But her car– "

"Battery died. Friend gave her a ride."

"Oh," I say, placing the pie on the counter near him and backing off again. He glances at it and moves across the kitchen to the refrigerator, where he gets himself a beer. He leaves the door ajar and opening the bottle, downs it, raising it first in a mocking salute to me. I shuffle first one foot and then the other. I'd like to get past him and shut the refrigerator door before everything spoils, but I sense he's daring me so he can play "It's my place and I can do what I want" with me if I try. There is an uncomfortable silence.

"So– I guess I'll be going– "

"How 'bout you just stop where you are." The tone is quiet and menacing. I *do* stop and turn to look at him. "Why do you keep coming around us, spying and meddling where you don't belong?"

Oh Lord, more "meddling". Will it be the only word on my gravestone?

Upon saying the word "grave" to myself, I notice how hard my heart is pounding. I see now this was such a mistake!– and I need to leave. I clutch at my shoulder purse for reassurance.

"You got Charleen's cell phone in there." He is staring at me, his eyes black.

I need to *pray*– I feel as though I am staring into the depths of hell as I look back at Derreck. This has been a terrible mistake, my coming here. I call up all the courage I have, knowing I am alone with this man. And now a spurt of terror raises the hairs on my arms: *nobody knows where I am.* And then a worse thought: could he have done something bad to Emily and does he have her hidden in their bedroom?

"I—I know all about Charleen," I stammer. "She told me everything and I wrote it all down and it's on a tape recorder with her cell phone—uh, in a bank vault– and if anything happens to me Emily takes it to the police– "

"Nope. Emily'd never do that. 'Cause I wouldn't let her." Oh, good Lord, he *did* do something! "So," he stares harder, if that is possible. "You *lied* to me." He takes the beer bottle and with a lazy motion smashes its neck off on the edge of the counter.

Why had I told him that? I take a step backward. I pray the door is still open. Or was I so careful that I had stupidly shut it behind me? I have to get help! I have to help Emily!

"You—you should be careful," I stammer. "You could cut your feet."

"Or your face," he answers. We look at each other and then he suddenly tosses the broken bottle backwards into the sink, where it gives an empty rocking clatter. Oh Lord, he can *see* how scared I am!

"So. You wanna know what you can do with your goddamned pie?" I stand, uncertain of my next move. He moves closer. His eyes are so dark I feel like shuddering. Drugs? I wonder. His face has taken on the most evil grimace I have ever seen. I can smell the beer on his breath, and something even more foul.

Without warning he moves as fast as a snake darts, picks up the pie in his left hand, shoves the right one into its center, and pitches a huge glob of lime and whipped cream into my face. I gasp at the cold stinging sensation and wipe the sour/sweet mess from my eyes. I hear, more than see, him hurl the pie and pan onto the floor. Half-blind, helpless and suddenly knowing this man is going to *kill* me!– so I must scream, must scream, but my throat seems to have closed tight and only a little rasp of breath comes out. I step back a few feet to the door and feel for the knob. Had I locked it automatically when I came in? I pray this is not so.

To my horror the door is shut and my slippery hands cannot move the knob.

I hear him growl, a deep animal noise, and he moves to me, his hands out to—choke me!

Then all at once I sense him through my blurry sight (and this feels as though it is happening in slow motion), *skid* on the remains of my pie and as he slides, his eyes now looking baffled, yet slow-reacting, – and to me the entire action must be taking *hours* to play out– the back of his head slams hard into the sharp corner of the counter with full force. The sound is sickening. There is a sharp intake of his breath as he clutches at the air and then with another sickening sound he hits the back of his head a second time as he smashes it and his body onto the slippery tiled floor.

I stare. (There is a high-pitched noise in my ears. But I must not faint! I must help Derreck somehow!) His eyes have a fixed look, not moving. I am more scared of him now than ever before. The white whipped cream and key lime green mix with red blood like some bizarre flag. I bend down, fearing to get close and touch him. What if he's faking and when I lean over he grabs me? But there is no sound of breathing. I feel carefully for a pulse. There is none.

But I have to do *something*! I abandoned that poor innocent squirrel; I cannot leave him.

And so I do the only thing I know in my shocked state to do: I dip some of the sticky liquid from the floor onto my finger and I watch myself make the sign of the cross on his forehead. Then I say in a whispery thin croak, "Derreck, if you have not already been baptized, I baptize you in the name of the Father, the Son, and the Holy Spirit. Amen." I don't know why I have started to cry.

I somehow get out of the apartment, using a corner of my shirt to manage turning the knob. I am shaking violently. I find my car. There is no one around. I wipe my face with the shirt, unbuttoning it and pulling it up so that my bra is exposed. There is key lime pie in my hair. My hands are sticky and I'm afraid to look at them to find out why. It takes me several tries before I can fit the key into the ignition, my body trembles so.

And the refrigerator door is open! The food will rot! But I can't go back inside and take care of it.

I can't.

Emily—I have to call her and make sure she's actually at her office. Oh Lord—please don't let her be in the apartment. But I can't –I can't—go back in there again. What is her cell phone number? I mean, I know it by heart, but my brain isn't cooperating with me.

My cell phone rings and I gasp. The police?, I think irrationally.

It is, serendipitously, Emily! "Can't talk long, Grandma—I'm at work," she says "Can you come for dinner tonight? It'll just be pickup stuff, but we can talk about the wedding. And Mom says she'll come—she's afraid you and I will gang up against her," she laughs.

I agree to dinner—what else can I do? At least now I'm sure she is safe. I drive slowly, close to some bushes around the corner from Emily's apartment before stopping and being sick in the oleanders. I know in a part of my mind that oleanders are poisonous and I wonder dazedly if I have maybe found a way to neutralize them by throwing up on them.

I am out of the parking lot before a young woman comes to the address Derreck had given her, puts her own hand on the same doorknob I had just touched, walks inside and then screams and *screams*! until every dog in the complex is howling and an old irritated man who had moved to Florida for the quiet, not all this confounded commotion waking him up during his mid-afternoon nap yet, dials 911 without even looking from his window.

✵ ✵ ✵

NEWS ITEM: Derreck Thompson, A.K.A. Darryl Thompson, Donny Tompkins, Rick Toms, and Dick (The Dog) Timpkins, age 33, was found dead at his home late yesterday afternoon by a female named Kiki Holloway, age 21, who said she had just "dropped by" to see an old friend, although police searching her discovered she was wearing nothing under her raincoat. One officer told this reporter he was suspicious because rain had not been predicted.

The victim had apparently dropped a pie and then slipped, causing a head injury and instant death. He was alleged to have ties to an organization so secret the C.I.A. does not know of its existence.

(The C.I.A. disavows the above assertion.)

Mr. Thompson was also the primary suspect in an ongoing investigation into the disappearance of Miss Charleen Walters, with whom he was last seen.

It is thought that a rival mob may have been responsible, since there was a crude cross-marked sign on the victim's forehead. Again, the C.I.A. Will neither confirm nor deny.

Funeral arrangements have not been announced, pending a state-ordered autopsy, since drugs were suspected to be the cause of the accident. Authorities have not been able to locate any relatives.

Banana Bay Tribune, July 31, 2011

✵ ✵ ✵

"How were you able to keep our names out of the paper?" asks Emily. Her eyes are red-rimmed.

She reads my look. "I haven't been crying much. I've forgotten, now that I'm back living with Mom, how allergic I am to cigarette smoke."

Susan scowls and doesn't react to this mild criticism as she reads the article, snapping the newspaper pages viciously.

"Remember Max, my friend from years ago, who worked on the Bulletin? He still knows people who know people and he was glad to do this for Excelsior's mother and sister."

"I had to change *all* my plans for visiting Dad and his wife in Connecticut," Susan interjects.

"How is Robert?" I ask. I wonder how all this drama has affected him.

"Bald. Old. Bushy beard—looks Amish.. Whenever I'm up there he lectures me like he's been memorizing religious tracts. He's saving dried food in case there's a holocaust. His wife's mad because if there *isn't* one she's going to have to use all that dried stuff and she doesn't have any recipes for it."

Emily interrupts: "I couldn't move out fast enough! Even though the place was already cleaned up. The worst part was that my car battery was still d-dead– " she stops and her eyes grow large. "Grandma– ," I nod. "They said there was a *pie* there. But there was no pie when I left for work– "

"You know, I'll just bet– ," I say, and God forgive me, and you too, Emily, but one evening when you were a baby and I took care of you, I christened you the same way I had Excelsior, only I had a glass of wine in my hand, but since Jesus turned water into wine, I guess this one *really* took—and I never told anyone and I am not about to tell you, because your mother refused to have you christened and I can smile, knowing you are one of God's own and there's no way Satan can get to you. However, if she finds out, she'll try to have you *un*-done, and she'll call me a meddling woman.

(Dad, there's a time for lying. People who are truthful all the time get steamrollered by the manipulative ones in this world, like Derreck. But Dad, about this you *were* right: *never lie to yourself.*)

And I am. By God I *am* a meddling woman. And (in my mind I am standing in Tara's field with a gnawed parsnip and raising my hand in defiance to heaven) I will keep on interfering for my family and the good Lord until I die!

There were no relatives who came to claim Derreck's body, so I arranged a service at our church for him. Our new priest, a tall Jamaican woman with a musical accent, officiated. Susan, Emily and I then scattered his ashes quietly into the same river area where he'd shoved me in. I swear I saw alligator heads surface when the ashes hit the water. Anyway, there were enough low grunting sounds from the St. John's that we didn't hang around after we said a few short prayers. We three women wept, talking about Derreck's ultimately being so alone except for us.

"Grandma– "

"Well, Emily, I'll bet he went out and bought you that pie, so he'd have something special for you when you came home. He was that way, wasn't he?"

"I guess," she says doubtfully. "Am I wrong if I say I didn't really love him? It's just that *Mom* was so sure—". Susan snorts. "Anyway, I'm so excited about going back to school so I can become a lawyer. Derreck never wanted me to, and now I can– " and again Emily seems torn between rejoicing at her freedom and mourning a man she never really knew.

As if reading my mind, she says, "So many different names! Aliases! It's like he wasn't the person I thought he was. And if he actually did away with poor Charleen Walters– " she shudders.

"I saw through him from the *start,*"asserts Susan . She has left the alcoholic Timmy. A woman I have yet to meet (Emily likes her a lot) has moved in with her. Susan is showing a softer edge without men around, although I'm probably the only one who can tell. Could she be a lesbian? Not that it matters.

"And you're finding your own place as soon as possible, young lady," Susan reminds Emily. "We—*I* need my privacy."

I know enough to leave that one alone. Sometimes it's better not to pry.

"Grandma, Mom says that back in the sixties and seventies when you were rais-ing her and Pete, women didn't work outside the home." Emily states this fact as though saying, "Didn't you used to wear a hoop skirt and drink Lydia Pinkham's?"

"Funny story for you, Em—when packaged cake mixes first came out, all a woman had to do was add water. Well, women couldn't stand that. They knew a cake consisted of more than flour and water, so they began adding extra ingredi-ents. But then the cakes wouldn't come out right. So the cake manufacturers got wise to the idea that housewives needed to feel involved, so the directions now called for adding eggs, which satisfied the housewives and their egos. I said funny, but it's kind of sad, too."

Emily frowns, then says, "I can't even *picture* those days."

And I say, "Good."

I think about the one time I went to a singles dance. I was asked to dance quite a bit by various older men—probably because I was like the new girl in town—and I couldn't relax while dancing, because I had to figure out instantly the different moves each male dancer made, and follow. Sometimes I couldn't pick it up fast enough and my partner would frown at me and not ask me again.

Easy for them—they developed their own way of dancing and the woman had to fit in. Luckily, women have this adapting mechanism in their brains. It gets stronger with motherhood.

We've had to fight so for our freedoms: women jailed for wanting the right to vote. And why was poor Hester Prynne made to wear that "A" when her lover got off, in those days when women were denounced as witches and stoned?

Emily breaks into my thoughts: "I'm glad I live now."

"Me too."

Susan gets up and stretches. "I'm going home. Emily, why don't you stay with Grandma for dinner? She'd love to have you." She scowls narrow-eyed at me so Emily can't see. "All evening. Right?"

"Right," I say. You owe me one, I think.

✳ ✳ ✳

Pete shrugs and scratches in his best suit. Susan, of all people, has insisted he dress up for church this Sunday. Excelsior is bouncing all around the house, getting in his way. Maybe they are going to point Pete out as the kid who saved the Shaver's life. He hopes not. "I already got a medal," he says aloud to himself.

"Medo, medo. *I* want a medo," says Excelsior. Yeah, the little guy deserves a medal or something for all he went through. And while Pete had needed stitches after he got sliced by a coquina rock, Excelsior didn't even come down with a cold! "You're some tough kid," he says now, fluffing the Shaver's hair with one hand and sticking the other hand into something lumpy in his pocket. What had he put in here? He feels around. Oh, yeah–

His Dad is taking a new job. In Connecticut. Pete has listened in and heard his Dad talking to an old high school girlfriend back there. His Dad is fighting with Pete's Mom about how Pete needs to move up there with him. He doesn't care *what* Pete wants!

His Dad is going to rent their house to Susan, who is going to get a commission when she sells it. Pete doesn't want to stay in the house, though. He wants to move in with his Mom.

"You will *not* stay anywhere near your mother," Robert had told him. "You are moving with me and that's final." He held up a hand like a cop. "And don't argue with me."

His Mom had looked stunned when Pete told her he had to move. "Oh, Pete, he told you," she said in a dejected voice that matched Pete's. "I guess maybe it's a good opportunity– "

"I don't want an opportunity," he had shouted. "I want to stay here with my *friends*!" I love Florida, he thinks now to himself. I was born here. I'm a *native*. There aren't all that many native Floridians. I want to stay *here.*

✳ ✳ ✳

"We'll get a plan together," Max has told Pete and me. "We'll keep you where you want to be, Pete."

I watch Pete's face . "You don't know my Dad," he says. We are all having dinner at Max's place. We are not alone. When Max gets his barbecue grill going and the smell of hickory chips fills the air, his neighbors come with more food and we sit and talk and laugh, and then the kids start bouncing a basketball on the driveway and someone brings out a guitar and we sing until the mosquitoes, who for a while were deterred by the smoke, return and drive us onto our screened porches lit with candles and in the comforting dark we watch the car headlights over the causeway from Max's apartment on the Banana Bay mainland.

That's a long sentence, but it is all of a piece to me and I'm glad to know Max, who may just turn out to be a friend and nothing more, but who is relaxing to have around.

He's in "Streetcar Named Desire" at the little theater and I am in charge of props. They have even given *me* a part—one line at the end. I have already memorized it. It's in Spanish: "Flores. Flores para los muertos." I carry flowers for the dead and the director likes the way I say "muertos" like a dirge.

Max is one of the card players. Although in real life he's not supposed to have anything to do with cards, being a true Southern Baptist.

He tells Pete and me a joke and says it's true: the Baptists and the Episcopalians in Banana Bay wanted to start a bowling league. "But the Bab-tists wouldn't go to a bowlin' alley that served liquor and the 'Piscopals wouldn't go to one that *didn't*, and they never did form the league."

So far we *don't* have a plan and I am concerned. Robert has closed off that forbidding custard face and I don't have the money to fight him in the court system. Pete is a year too young legally to make his own decision about which parent to live with. Robert has demanded, "Boys stay with their fathers and girls with their mothers. That's the way it is. We don't want you growing up to be a sissy." He has hired a very expensive, very aggressive attorney. Mine seems like Jell-o by comparison.

"So we'll pray about it. You can use some good old Bab-tist prayers. Mix 'em up with th' 'Piscopal ones. Good combination." Then Max leads Pete and me in prayer and he prays 'em powerful, so we say "Ay-men!" at the end, as well as "Ah-men", the Episcopalian way.

I can't help feeling a little intimidated though. There's all that *tithing* money Robert has spent to buy the Lord over to his side!

ORGANIST FOILS WOULD-BE PURSE SNATCHER

Mrs. Amanda Griffin, organist at St. Luke's Methodist
Church in Banana Bay, proved herself a worthy opponent
when a young man (name withheld because of age) rode
his bicycle past her and grabbed her purse. Mrs. Griffin,
wife of local dentist Doctor Edwing Griffin, held on tight
and brought the purse-snatcher to the ground when she
knocked him off his bike with a hard-bound
hymnal in a homemade heavy canvas satchel she
was carrying. Next Sunday will be designated
"Amanda Griffin" Sunday at St. Luke's after the
10 am service. All food donations will be welcome.
—*Banana Bay Tribune, November 30, 1977*

"You can only divide a prime number by itself or one," I explain to Excelsior, who is not listening and who sits bouncing beside me at St. Barnabus'. I can sit in the congregation because for this special day Mrs. Griffin has once more offered to play. The stops she chooses are, to be kind, original, but no matter. I can sit down here today with my family and friends.

Prime numbers. There's something sturdy, I think, about a number refusing to allow itself to come out even. "There's Pete," I say to Excelsior, to distract him.

Yes, look at Pete wearing his suit. He looks so grown up dressed that way. His arms have grown longer, right out of the suit. I'll set it aside for Excelsior after today. It should fit this youngster in a few years. Wait. Are those choir girls ogling my son? They're his age and they're wearing *lipstick*!

Max sits next to me. "Never been in a church where they bowed to candles," he tells me. He's having trouble knowing when to sit, when to stand, when to kneel, and which book to use, but he follows my lead in his good-natured way.

Robert sits by himself. He seems to have shrunken some in the past few months. The custard face has a few wrinkles now and if I were to go up into the choir loft I am sure I would be able to look down and view the new bare skin showing on the top of his head. He glowers across the aisle at me as I am thinking this.

I've shown some of my writing to Max, and he thinks I should write some short pieces for the newspaper. "They might print them, Joan. Local color." He adds carefully that he could help me, if I want, learn how to remove many of the "that"s and the "and"s.

I tell him that's how I talk.

Excelsior is still squirming. "I'll take him out to the bathroom," Pete whispers to me. Excelsior still has accidents and we are all somewhat uneasy, as though we have brought a live bomb to church

I turn around. Susan is at the back in the church entryway with Jack. Her hair is her natural auburn and she looks conservative and beautiful, Jack mature and attentive to her.

Fran sits behind me next to her husband Ken. She leans forward: "Amanda Griffin is so happy about that newspaper article," she whispers.

"Thank Max," I say. "He wrote it."

"Thanks, Max. She really loves it because you spelled her name right and her husband's wrong."

"I did it on purpose," Max answers. We'll never know if he did. Fran and I were so delighted to find that Amanda Griffin played organ. We persuaded her to let her pastor know. Churches are always looking for substitute organists and suddenly she found herself quite popular.

Father Wolfe is finishing with the usual announcements, and although we could read them in the bulletin, they have much more impact coming from him.

"Mrs. Wolfe and I are delighted this morning that our son Jack is here. He'd like to say a few words."

Jack comes forward with Susan, clasping her hand and walking her up the aisle as if they were rehearsing for their wedding. "Uh—hi," he says to the now wide-awake churchgoers. "You all know Susan Baldwin. That's her Dad over there, and her Mom over there– " he points us out as we sit on opposite sides of the aisle like the Hatfields and McCoys. "Where's the kid who's going to be my brother-in-law?" He points to the back of the church. "Hey, Pete. The one with him is my son and we're going to christen him today. And we're inviting you all to our wedding on New Year's Eve Day."

Well, Lord love Episcopalians. It takes a lot for them to show their amazement. Even so, there is a ripple of a reaction.

"Medo!" suddenly shouts Excelsior, the way Bambi did the day he was allowed out in the open. "I got *medo*!"

And as everyone watches Excelsior dances up to Susan, proudly wearing—I gasp, tears filling my eyes—my mother's brooch, wristwatch, pearls and earrings!

I wipe my eyes. Then I notice Pete. He is standing still, looking his father full and straight in the face, so deliberately that Robert is the first to turn away and I sense that Pete has won some kind of victory.

The stone font is carried to the center of the church. Father Wolfe holds Excelsior in his large arms. My mother's earrings drop from the child's earlobes into the blessed water as Father Wolfe takes us through the baptismal service, then commands, "Name this child!"

Susan and Jack answer together as Excelsior laughs at the water dipped over his head. "Jack Peter Wolfe, I christen you in the name of the Father, the Son and the Holy Spirit." He holds his grandson high in the air and we all applaud. "Welcome your new brother in Christ—Jack Peter Wolfe!" Susan is beaming. Susan and I are wearing the identical kind of wobbly grin mothers have at the sight of their newborn children.

☆ ☆ ☆

Peter comes to my side as we join Mrs. Griffin in a loud and overfast version of "I sing a song of the saints of God".

"I don't have to move away with Dad," he whispers. "He'll let me stay here."

"I'm so glad!" I whisper back. I don't understand what just happened between Pete and Robert, and when I look over at my ex-husband and point to our son, he nods his head ruefully. "Now you can come live with *me*. Hey— remember to fish for those earrings after the service."

"If I dip my hands in holy water," he says, more to himself than me. "maybe that would help my batting."

"Wherever did Excelsior— Jack— find my mother's jewelry?" I ask. I can hear Max singing beside me, stumbling over the timing of "and the saints of God are just folk like me". He has a nice rumbly deep voice.

I look at Pete. His face is a mixture of child and grownup. He's holding onto at least two secrets. Maybe someday I'll get an answer.

"The Peace of the Lord be always with you," roars Father Wolfe.

"And also with you," we answer, and then everyone moves into the aisle for handshakes and hugs. Max looks surprised at the sudden pandemonium. The noise level rises. I put my hand out to shake one woman's hand—Lord forgive me, but if she hugs me, her cloying perfume stays on me all day.

"When I was saving—Jack— ," Pete says, "I was so close to the shore and I couldn't get there. The beach looked so *safe* there, only a few feet away from me and I couldn't get to it. I was so scared I'd drown! and I was so *close* to being safe."

"You struggled," I tell him. "You struggled because you had to. You're made that way. We all struggle for what's precious to us." Our very lives, I realized.

"Huh." he says thoughtfully. Then, "I guess I don't mind so much that they used my name for a middle name," he says. "But I'm still gonna call him The Shaver."

✵ ✵ ✵

Joan Gibson 2011

That's my maiden name, the one I owned for the first two decades of my life. I like it. I'll take it back when I am divorced. I think of all the hassle: Social Security, driver's license, credit cards, those lovely address labels from the Paralyzed Veterans of America. I almost waver. But as Emily says, "It's only a bit of trouble one time." She's right.

Susan, Pete and Emily have taken small notice of my separation from Quentin. I realize they are occupied with their own lives and to them I am an old silly woman who might as well be allowed to do what she wants, because what else does she have in her life?

I have decided to *buy* this little house in Oak Glen. It suits me. I have found a Siamese cat mix at the local shelter. When Kitty (the only name she answers to) is not following me around and yowling for my attention, she is ignoring me completely. I find this endearing. When I buy a cat litter she does not like, she poops *outside* her litter box until I exchange the grit for something that she approves of. I find this almost endearing.

I have joined the water aerobics group: sixteen women, flailing around in the Oak Glen pool in the morning, the skin under our arms shaking like turkey wattles, laughing and telling jokes while our instructor tries in vain to make us pay attention.

I ride my thrift store (some things never change in my life) bicycle in the evening with other neighbors. Sometimes I join another small group to walk and chat instead. We exchange information about our car insurance and electric bills. I am considering giving piano lessons or forming a musical chorus.

I visit Quentin. I get depressed going to our old house any more. I tried cleaning there once a week for a while after I moved out (did I already say that? I must be getting old), but, unlike Hercules in the stable, gave it up. Doesn't the man know what a *wastebasket* is for?

Quentin sits on the sofa surrounded by magazines, stacks of them. The dining table has its own mounds of unopened mail, bills, receipts, flyers, expired offers, lottery tickets—his one foray into thrill-seeking. He will never acknowledge his paper hoarding. Since I'm not there, he doesn't have to.

I find a place to sit at the other end of the sofa. I try to put my feet on the coffee table, but he has now moved it to adjust to his long legs and I can't reach it even if I slide down so that my backbone is curved uncomfortably. His cell phone, home phone and TV clickers are placed on the end table beside him, at the ready. His man-cave appears complete.

It also looked like this when I lived here.

I have brought dinner for the two of us. I am frankly scared to use anything in his refrigerator. Even if a container from it smells all right, I can't be sure he didn't leave it on the counter overnight "to cool", he is fond of saying.

I am convinced his stomach is cast iron and impervious to ptomaine.

"So," he yawns, talking to me, but with his eyes drawn to the nature program on the TV screen, "when are you coming home?"

I look around, remembering Kitty waiting for me. I think of the blue and white color scheme in my house with the green roof, of the book I want to write and all the things I want to do, like learning to line dance and take a trip on a paddle wheel boat on the Mississippi, in these final two decades of my life. Why, just last evening I cleared $10 playing Bunco at the club house!

An e.e. cummings line sings in my head: "Listen, next door there's a hell of a universe out there."

Will Quentin understand that I need to take care of *me*? I don't want, on the point of death, to have my *husband's* life flash before my eyes, instead of my own. I want to fill my life to overflowing while I still can. I want—I want to eat *cereal* for supper if I choose!

I stand up and pull my car keys from my jeans pocket.

"Quentin," I say kindly yet without hesitation, "I *am* home."

We make plans to go next week to a cremation talk which has a lunch included afterward, at the Red Lobster.

"There's no such thing as a free lunch," Robert used to say, not following his own rule.

Yes, there is, Robert. I'm going to be cremated and I'll leave strict instructions that Emily is not to make a locket from some of my ashes and wear it around her neck. I won't have an open casket, because I don't want Susan messing with me, turning my hair some weird color. I am going to pick out my own music and I may even write my own obituary ahead of time. "Ahead of time"– of course!

So am I meddling and controlling? "No!" I say out loud to the car in front of me. I've just spent my life looking for some kind of *community*, of belonging.

I can hear Kitty yowling as I enter my garage. At the same time my cell phone rings. It is Pete, I am delighted to see.

"Mom— I'm coming to Orlando for a seminar and thought I'd spend a couple of days with you. Okay?"

"*More* than okay!" I laugh. " Wait a minute. I'm just going into the kitchen to check my calendar."

There it is on the wall my new revised life: water aerobics, Bunco, get-together breakfasts, choir rehearsals, lunch dates with friends, watching a taped Merchant Ivory movie, reading my latest library books to get them back before their due date, an eye appointment, a bake sale, a volunteer morning at the Banana Bay Elementary School Rolling Readers, a funeral, a wedding to play for, a garage sale, a trip to the zoo, a movie....

"Tell me the days you'll be here," I say to Pete. "and let's see what we can do."

The End

The author has five children, eight grandchildren and six great-grandchildren. She is a retired licensed mental health counselor in Florida. She is a church organist and an award-winning playwright.

Many, many thanks to family and friends who read this first chapter some thirty years ago and asked, "When are you going to write the next chapter? " Three decades later here it is.

Many thanks to TraMi Willey for her proofreading and to the ladies in the pool who were so delighted for me when I announced, "I finished my book!"

This is, of course, a work of fiction. The truest part is that my middle name is Joan.

✻ ✻ ✻

Made in the USA
Lexington, KY
13 November 2012